Certificate of Cloud Security Knowledge CCSK v5

Master The Certificate of Cloud Security Knowledge And Elevate Your Career In Cloud Security

John Meah

Book Cover by John Meah

Illustrations by John Meah

First edition 2025

Contents

Preface

Welcome to the world of cloud security, where safeguarding critical information holds paramount importance in today's technology landscape. The Certificate of Cloud Security Knowledge (CCSK v5) is essential to enhance your resume and highlight your expertise.

The CCSK certification is a comprehensive program meticulously designed to equip professionals with the knowledge and skills to protect cloud data and systems. With the escalating adoption of cloud computing by organizations across diverse industries, the need for proficient individuals capable of mitigating cloud security risks has never been more critical.

Embark on a journey through cloud architecture, data security, identity and access management, encryption, and incident response with the CCSK certification. Empowering you to confidently confront the constantly evolving challenges of securing cloud environments, this certification propels you toward becoming a cloud security superhero in your field.

Unlock a realm of opportunities within cloud security by embarking on this path today, bearing in mind that achieving the CCSK certification is just the beginning of your cloud security expedition. Continued learning and adaptability are imperative to staying abreast of industry advancements.

One of the most significant advantages of the CCSK certification lies in its vendor independence, ensuring that the knowledge and skills you acquire are universally applicable across various cloud platforms. While familiarity with leading cloud platforms such as Azure, Amazon Web Services (AWS), and Google Cloud Platform (GCP) is beneficial, the CCSK certification enhances your mastery of cloud security fundamentals, irrespective of the provider.

If you operate in the technology sector or for a managed service provider (MSP), acquiring cloud and cloud security terminologies is pivotal. Commencing the CCSK certification is an exceptional pathway to gain comprehensive knowledge in this domain.

Distinguished as a recognized standard for cloud security proficiency, the CCSK certification gives you the insights necessary to safeguard cloud data, regardless of your chosen cloud vendor. This certificate lays a solid foundation for pursuing other specialized credentials tailored to specific vendors or job roles within cloud computing.

Upon obtaining the CCSK certification, you can design inclusive cloud security programs aligned with worldwide standards. This encompasses implementing best practices in identity and access management, cloud incident response, application security, data encryption, harnessing Security as a Service (SECaaS), and safeguarding emerging technologies.

Regardless of your expertise level in the tech field, management team, or cloud sales department, the CCSK certification is tailored to suit professionals across various industries. Bridging the gap between securing cloud services effectively and addressing cloud security concerns with confidence is made possible with the CCSK certification. By emphasizing crucial areas like identity and access management (IAM), cloud incident response, application security, data encryption, and protecting emerging technologies, the CCSK ensures you are well-prepared to overcome the challenges of safeguarding cloud environments.

Whether you aspire to specialize in cloud security or enhance your knowledge, the CCSK v5 certification opens many opportunities within the rapidly expanding cloud computing domain.

Chapter One

What Are the Benefits of Earning the CCSK v5

Career Growth Opportunities

The CCSK certification is recognized worldwide as a benchmark for cloud security expertise. Holding this credential can unlock new job prospects, promotions, and leadership roles. Employers value professionals with proven knowledge in cloud security, making this certification a strong asset for advancing your career.

Preparedness for Emerging Challenges

As technology continues to advance, so do cybersecurity threats. The CCSK covers critical topics like Artificial Intelligence (AI), Generative AI (GenAI), and Zero Trust principles. These areas are increasingly relevant in addressing modern security risks. By mastering these concepts, you'll be better equipped to protect organizations from current vulnerabilities while staying ready for future challenges.

Showcase Verified Expertise

Earning the CCSK allows you to display an official digital badge and certificate on platforms like LinkedIn or within your resume. This visible proof of your skills enhances your professional credibility and helps you stand out in competitive job markets. Employers can quickly verify your qualifications, giving them confidence in your abilities.

By earning the CCSK, you're not just gaining technical knowledge—you're building a foundation for long-term success in cloud security. Whether you're looking to grow professionally or stay ahead of industry trends, this certification positions you as a trusted expert in one of today's most critical fields.

Chapter Two

Overview of the CCSK v5 Certification Exam

The CCSK v5 exam is structured to assess a candidate's proficiency in various key topics crucial to cloud service management. This includes understanding cloud security principles, governance, compliance, risk management, and the practical application of these principles in real-world scenarios. The exam dives deep into service models and deployment models, enabling you to demonstrate your knowledge in not just theoretical concepts but also their implementations. You'll also encounter questions that evaluate how well you grasp the essential frameworks and tools necessary for effective cloud management. Being well-versed in these topics isn't just beneficial for passing the exam; it's fundamental for your career and efficacy as an IT professional in today's technology-driven environment. The main purpose of the CCSK v5 exam is to validate an individual's knowledge and skills in cloud security, ensuring they have a solid understanding of the principles and best practices for securing cloud environments.

Exam Name	CCSK v4	CCSK v5
Exam Duration	90 Minutes	120 Minutes
Number of Questions	60 Questions	
Exam Format	Multiple choice questions	
Passing Score	80% Minimum passing score	
Exam Language	English, Japanese, Spanish	

CCSK v5 Exam Structure

The format of the CCSK v5 certification exam is primarily multiple-choice, which means you'll be asked to select the best answer or answers from a set of options. This can include scenario-based questions, where your problem-solving skills and expertise in cloud services are tested. The types of questions you may encounter range from straightforward queries to more complex scenarios that require critical thinking and the application of knowledge. Understanding the logical flow of such questions will be tremendously valuable in preparing for the exam and enhancing your professional acumen.

Coverage of the Exam Syllabus

Cloud security is a fundamental aspect of cloud computing, and it involves implementing measures to protect data and applications stored in the cloud. This includes protecting against unauthorized access, data breaches, and other security threats. Understanding cloud security principles and best practices is crucial for individuals who want to secure cloud environments effectively. Data protection is another critical aspect of cloud security, as it involves safeguarding data from unauthorized access, loss, or corruption.

This includes implementing encryption techniques, data backup and recovery processes, and ensuring data is stored and transmitted securely. The CCSK v5 exam covers various topics for understanding and implementing cloud security measures. By successfully passing this exam, individuals can demonstrate their expertise in cloud security and enhance their credibility in cloud computing. These areas are critical for individuals who work in or plan to work in cloud computing, as they are essential for protecting sensitive data and mitigating risks. Format and Structure of the Exam The CCSK v5 exam follows a specific format and structure to assess an individual's understanding of cloud security knowledge. As mentioned, the exam last for 120 minutes and consists of 60 multiple-choice questions that test the candidate's knowledge and application of cloud security concepts. The exam is divided into several sections, each focusing on different aspects of cloud security.

As you gear up to tackle the CCSK v5 exam, consider integrating practical study methods alongside traditional learning. Simulation exercises that mimic real-world scenarios can be particularly helpful. They prepare you for the exam format and develop your skills in a way that translates effectively into your daily work. Online study groups and forums can also provide different perspectives that might clarify challenging topics. This holistic approach will not just make studying more enjoyable, but it will also empower you with a deeper understanding of cloud service management.

Chapter Three

CCSK v5 Security Domains

Chapter Four

Domain 1: Cloud Computing Concepts and Architectures

Introduction

Domain 1 explains the significance of cloud computing in modern IT environments. It highlights how cloud computing has transformed the way organizations utilize technology by enabling scalable, flexible, and efficient resource management. This introduction sets the stage for participants to understand the foundational concepts, terminology, and architectural models that underpin cloud services, preparing them for deeper exploration of these topics throughout the domain.

Learning Objectives

The **Learning Objectives** for Domain 1: **Cloud Computing Concepts & Architectures** are designed to equip participants with foundational knowledge and skills related to cloud computing. Here are the key learning objectives explained:

1. **Understanding Cloud Computing Definitions**: Participants should be able to define what cloud computing is, including its essential characteristics, and differentiate it from traditional computing models. This foundational knowledge is crucial for grasping the broader concepts in cloud security.

2. **Recognizing Cloud Service Models**: Learners will identify and describe different cloud service models, including:

- **Infrastructure as a Service (IaaS):** Describes the provision of virtualized computing resources over the internet.

- **Platform as a Service (PaaS):** Focuses on platforms that provide a framework for developers to build applications without dealing with the underlying infrastructure.
- **Software as a Service (SaaS):** Understanding these models allows participants to comprehend how services are delivered in the cloud and the implications for security management.

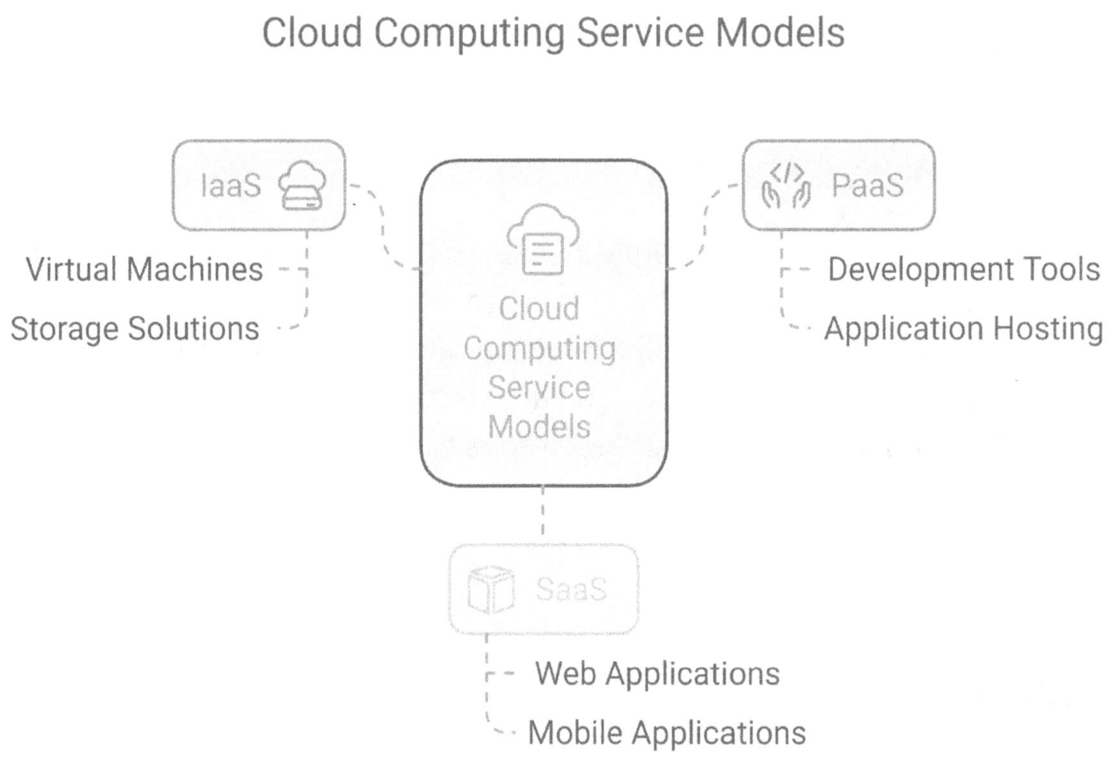

3.Exploring Cloud Deployment Models: Participants will examine the various deployment models of cloud computing, such as public, private, and hybrid clouds. Understanding these models is fundamental for implementing security measures tailored to specific deployment scenarios.

4. Comprehending the Shared Security Responsibility Model: One of the critical objectives is for learners to grasp the shared responsibility model, which delineates the security roles of cloud service providers and customers. This understanding is essential for managing and enforcing security practices in cloud environments effectively.

5. Identifying Cloud Security Scope and Responsibilities: Participants will learn about the broader scope of cloud security, including the responsibilities associated with different components and services in the cloud ecosystem. This knowledge is vital for developing comprehensive security strategies that align with organizational needs.

Overall, these learning objectives collectively prepare participants to understand the foundational aspects of cloud computing that are essential for effectively managing security in cloud environments.

1.1 Cloud Definition

The cloud is a network of remote servers accessed via the internet that provides on-demand computing resources (like storage, processing power, and services) without requiring local physical infrastructure.

This definition captures the key aspects:

- Remote access via internet
- On-demand availability
- Shared computing resources
- Elimination of local hardware needs

Cloud computing offers an innovative way to access and utilize technology resources over the internet, eliminating the need to rely solely on local servers or personal devices. One of its most notable features is on-demand availability. Users can instantly access storage, processing power, or applications without dealing with complex installations or setups. It's akin to having a fully stocked toolbox always ready to deliver exactly what's needed at the right moment.

Another significant advantage of cloud computing is its scalability. For instance, when a project experiences a sudden spike in traffic, resources can be scaled up effortlessly to meet demand and then scaled down once activity normalizes. This flexibility resembles a rubber band that stretches as far as necessary without breaking. With cloud solutions, there's no longer any concern about whether infrastructure can handle fluctuations; adjustments are made seamlessly, either automatically or with just a few clicks.

Transitioning from traditional IT models to cloud-based systems may seem like a major shift, but it's one that delivers substantial benefits. Historically, managing physical servers and on-premises systems was both time-consuming and costly. By adopting cloud technology, organizations can streamline operations, reduce expenses, and eliminate the burdens associated with hardware maintenance. As businesses delve deeper into this transformation, they often uncover new efficiencies and opportunities for growth as technology continues to advance.

For those considering exploring cloud computing, starting small is highly recommended. Many providers offer free tiers or trial options that allow users to experiment with various tools and services firsthand. This approach not only builds confidence but also helps individuals and businesses determine how these solutions align with their specific needs. Over time, it becomes clear why so many organizations are making the move to the cloud—it's an investment in agility, efficiency, and future-proofing operations.

1.1.1 Abstraction & Orchestration

Abstraction in Cloud Computing

Abstraction hides the complexity of underlying hardware and software. It provides users with simplified interfaces to interact with cloud resources without worrying about infrastructure details. For example, instead of managing physical servers or storage devices directly, you work with virtual machines (VMs), containers, or APIs that represent those resources.

Key benefits:

- Simplifies resource management by focusing on functionality rather than technical specifics.
- Enables scalability since users can provision resources dynamically without dealing with hardware constraints.
- Promotes flexibility as developers focus on applications while leaving backend complexities to the cloud provider.

Example: A developer deploys an application using a Platform-as-a-Service (PaaS) like AWS Elastic Beanstalk. They don't manage server configurations; they just upload their code for deployment.

Orchestration in Cloud Computing

Orchestration automates tasks across multiple systems and services within your cloud environment. It ensures different components—like VMs, networks, databases—work together seamlessly based on predefined workflows or policies.

Key functions:

1. Automating deployments (e.g., launching instances).
2. Managing dependencies between components.
3. Scaling up/down workloads automatically based on demand.
4. Ensuring consistency during updates/patches across environments.

Example tools include Kubernetes for container orchestration and Terraform for infrastructure automation at scale.

Together: **Abstraction simplifies interaction**, while **orchestration coordinates actions**, ensuring efficient use of complex cloud infrastructures effortlessly from end-to-end operations perspective.

1.2 Cloud Computing Models

Cloud Computing Models provide a foundational understanding of cloud computing by establishing essential terminology and concepts. It explores the various service models available within cloud computing, including Infrastructure as a Service (IaaS), Platform as a Service (PaaS), and Software as a Service (SaaS). The domain outlines the characteristics that define cloud services, the deployment models available, and the importance of the shared security responsibility model, which delineates the security obligations of both cloud service providers and customers. This comprehensive overview equips participants with the knowledge to navigate and leverage different cloud computing frameworks effectively.

1.2.1 Essential Characteristics

Cloud computing refers to delivering computing resources, like servers, storage, databases, and software, over the internet. This allows organizations to access and utilize these resources without investing in infrastructure or maintenance. The cloud provides a flexible and scalable environment that can adapt to businesses' changing needs, offering numerous advantages. Therefore, understanding the five key characteristics of a genuine cloud service is essential, as not all services may meet the necessary criteria outlined by NIST SP800-145. Ensure your cloud service has these five essential characteristics for optimal efficiency and performance.

The 5 Cloud Characteristics at a Glance:

1. **Resource Pooling** is a key feature of cloud computing, where providers efficiently allocate computing resources to meet client demand. This consolidation optimizes resource

utilization, ensuring scalability and cost-effectiveness. It enhances cloud services' efficiency and flexibility, benefiting providers and clients.

2. **Broad Network Access** in cloud computing refers to delivering computing resources over the internet. This includes servers, storage, databases, networking, software, and analytics. It allows users to access these resources from anywhere, anytime, using various devices such as laptops, tablets, and smartphones. This level of accessibility is what makes the cloud so powerful and versatile.

3. **Rapid elasticity** is a pivotal characteristic of the cloud, enabling quick upscaling and downscaling to meet varying demands. Unlike traditional computing environments, where scaling resources for a sudden increase in demand is cumbersome and expensive, the cloud lets companies seamlessly allocate more server resources, ensuring optimal performance and cost-efficiency. For example, a retail website experiencing a traffic surge during a flash sale can effectively handle the increased load by automatically provisioning additional server resources.

4. **Measured services** denote the significance of tracking and evaluating the performance and usage of cloud resources. Cloud usage transparency, typically determined by metrics like storage, processing power, and network bandwidth, aids organizations in understanding their resource consumption, facilitating informed decisions concerning resource allocation optimization. Consequently, a software development firm can analyze its cloud-based development environment's usage across different teams, refining resource allocation to ensure efficient usage.

5. **On-demand self-service**, an integral cloud characteristic, offers the convenience and speed of obtaining resources without manual intervention. Users can provision and access cloud resources, enabling organizations to be responsive and agile in adapting to their evolving requirements. For instance, a startup can quickly spin up virtual servers and storage resources in the cloud, supporting its product development without facing the protracted procurement process.

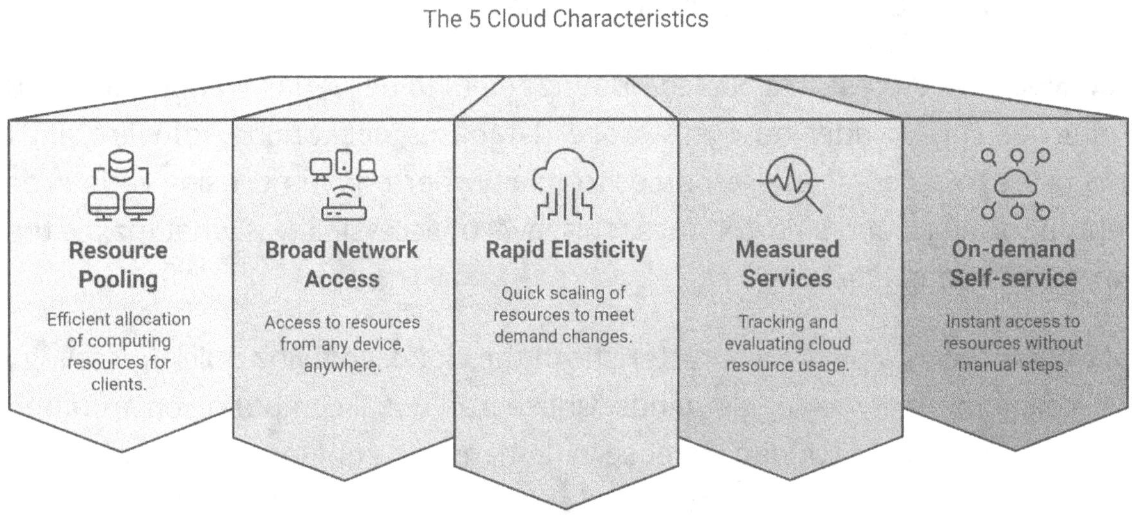
The 5 Cloud Characteristics
Resource Pooling
Efficient allocation of computing resources for clients.
Broad Network Access
Access to resources from any device, anywhere.
Rapid Elasticity
Quick scaling of resources to meet demand changes.
Measured Services
Tracking and evaluating cloud resource usage.
On-demand Self-service
Instant access to resources without manual steps.

1.2.2 Cloud Service Models

Cloud service models shape how businesses access technology. The three main types—Infrastructure as a Service (IaaS), Platform as a Service (PaaS), and Software as a Service (SaaS)—offer different levels of control and flexibility. IaaS provides raw computing power, PaaS simplifies development, and SaaS delivers ready-to-use applications. Choosing the right model depends on specific needs, whether managing infrastructure, building applications, or using software without maintenance hassles.

1.2.2.1 Infrastructure as a Service (IaaS)

Infrastructure as a Service (IaaS) is the most fundamental cloud service model. It delivers virtualized computing resources such as virtual machines, storage, and networks via the Internet. With IaaS, customers enjoy unparalleled control over the underlying infrastructure while assuming responsibility for managing operating systems, runtimes, and applications.

(See diagram on next page)

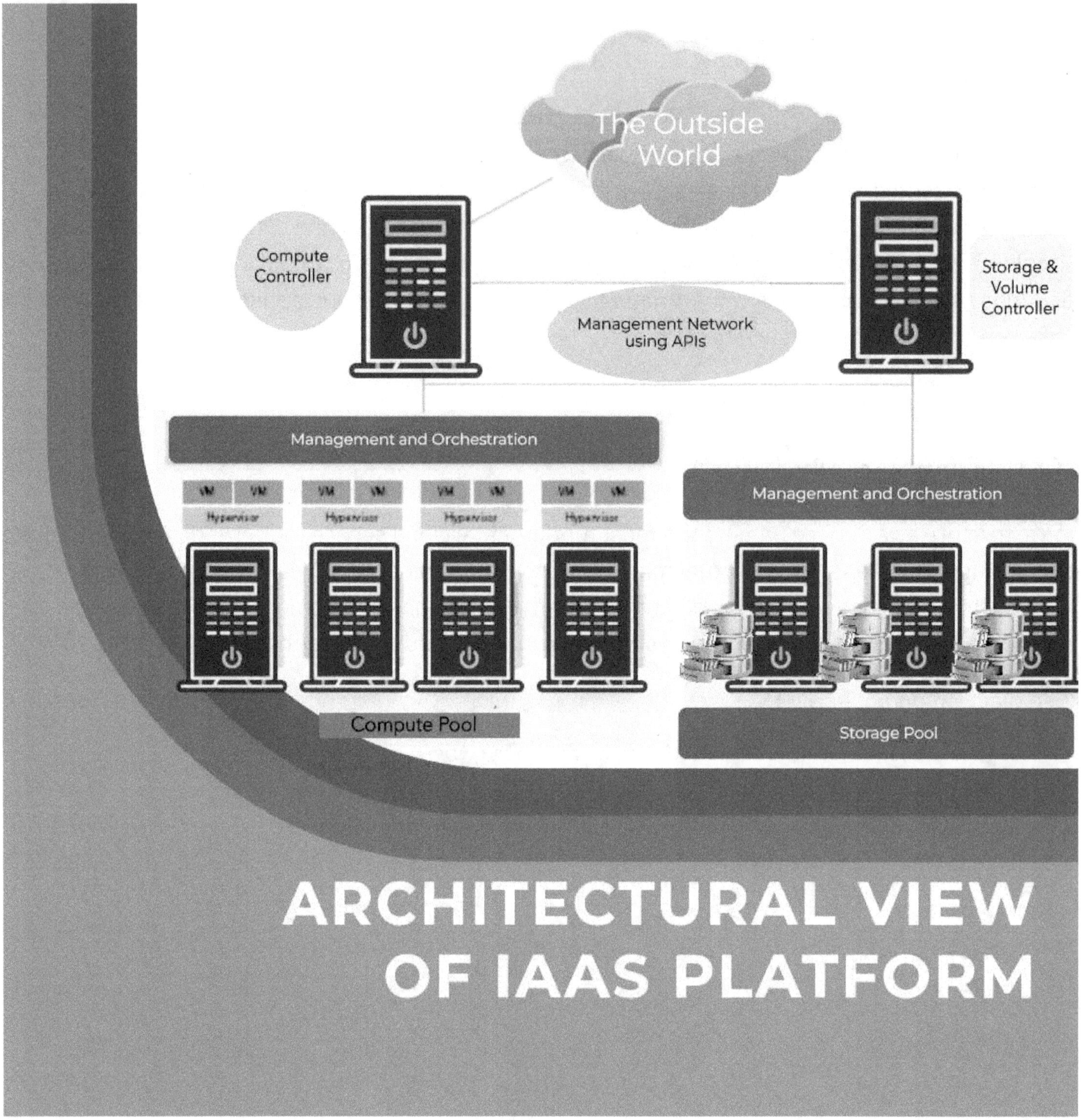
The Outside World
Compute Controller
Storage & Volume Controller
Management Network using APIs
Management and Orchestration
Management and Orchestration
Compute Pool
Storage Pool
ARCHITECTURAL VIEW OF IAAS PLATFORM

IaaS

1.2.2.2 Platform as a Service (PaaS)

Building upon the IaaS model, Platform as a Service (PaaS) provides a higher level of abstraction. PaaS offers a platform where customers can develop, run, and manage their applications without needing to concern themselves with the underlying infrastructure. PaaS providers care for operating systems, runtime environments, and infrastructure maintenance, allowing customers to focus solely on application development and deployment.

(See diagram on next page)

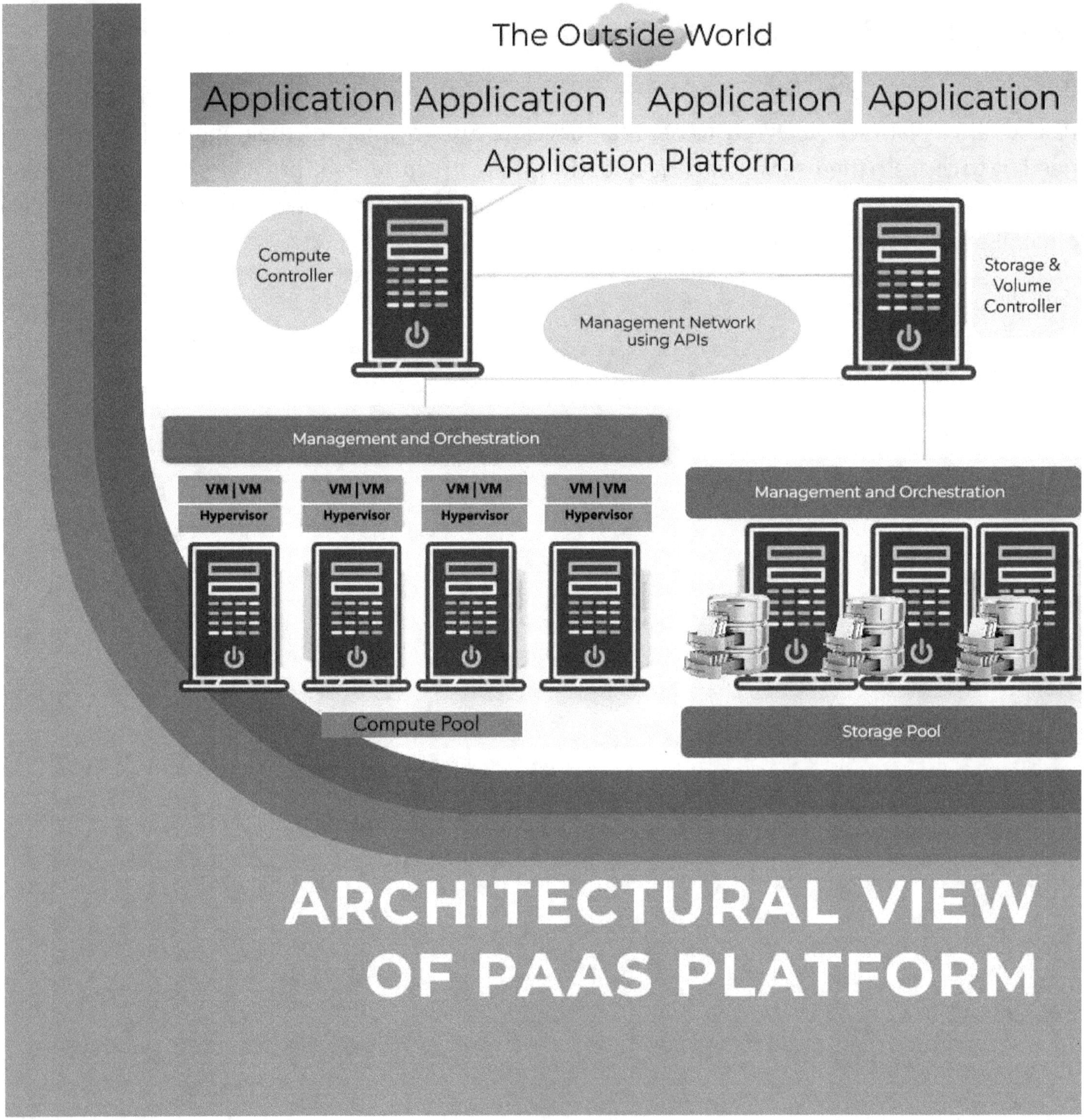
The Outside World
Application
Application
Application
Application
Application Platform
Compute Controller
Management Network using APIs
Storage & Volume Controller
Management and Orchestration
VM | VM
Hypervisor
VM | VM
Hypervisor
VM | VM
Hypervisor
VM | VM
Hypervisor
Management and Orchestration
Compute Pool
Storage Pool
ARCHITECTURAL VIEW OF PAAS PLATFORM

PaaS

1.2.2.3 Software as a Service (SaaS)

Software as a Service (SaaS) is the most advanced cloud service model. SaaS delivers applications over the internet on a subscription basis. Customers can access and use software applications without local installation or maintenance. SaaS providers assume responsibility for all underlying infrastructure components, including servers, storage, and networking.

(See diagram on next page)

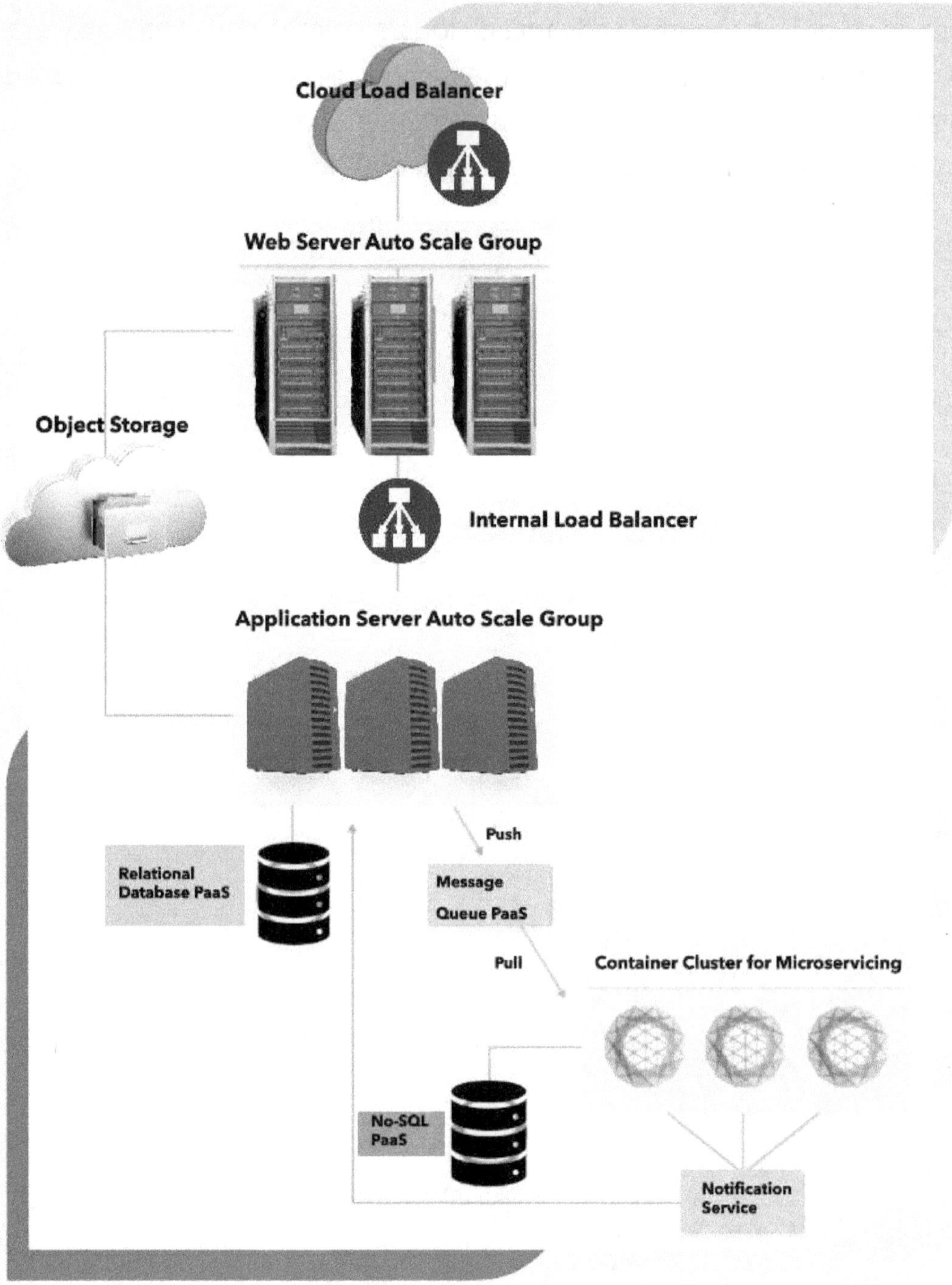
Cloud Load Balancer
Web Server Auto Scale Group
Object Storage
Internal Load Balancer
Application Server Auto Scale Group
Push
Relational Database PaaS
Message Queue PaaS
Pull
Container Cluster for Microservicing
No-SQL PaaS
Notification Service

SaaS

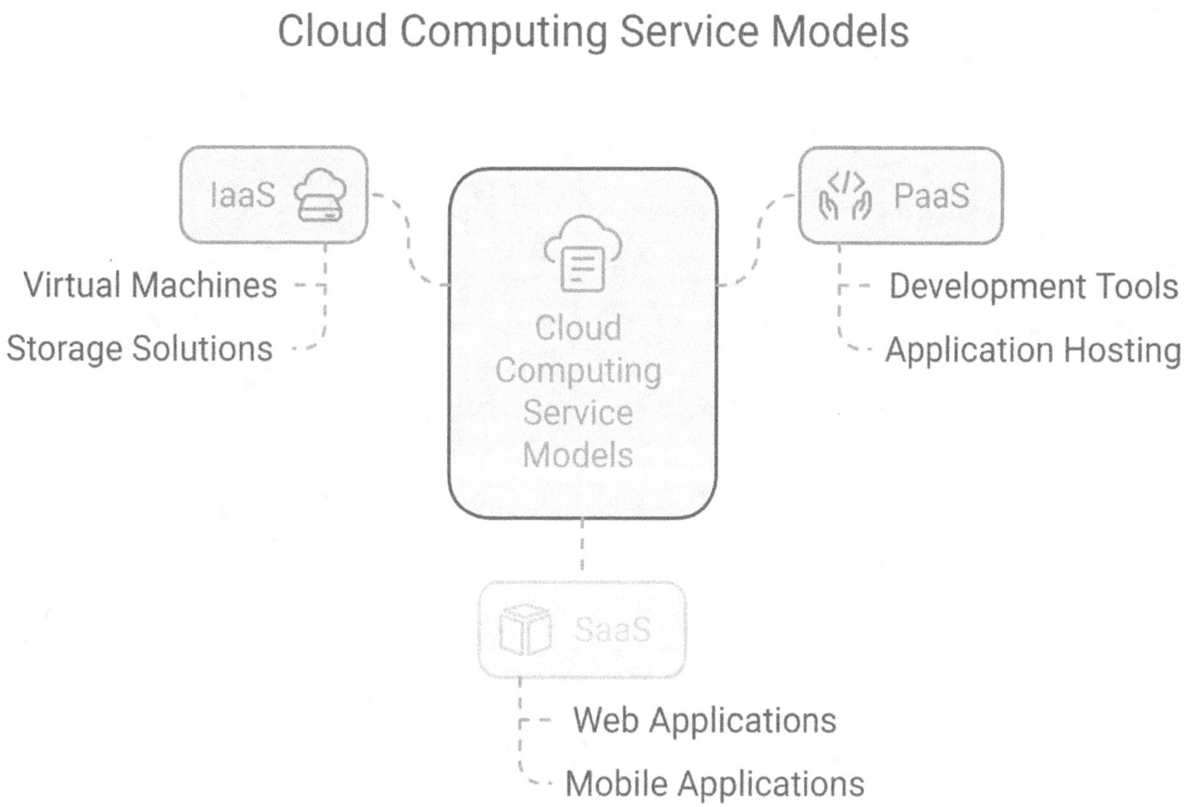

Tip: The above are also referenced as the SPI tiers.

Various iterations have emerged from the fundamental idea of 'as a service' offerings, catering to specific requirements and needs. These diverse variations span different forms and functions. Unsurprisingly, the array of choices provides businesses with tailored options. This dynamic evolution ensures enterprises have access to the perfect technology enhancement solution designed to meet their unique demands. Variation is the key to unlocking bespoke support and innovation in today's landscape.

This is, by no means, an exhaustive list:

- aPaaS (application-as-a-service
- DaaS (data-as-a-service)
- FaaS (function-as-a-service)

- SecaaS (security-as-a-service)
- AIaaS (AI-as-a-service)

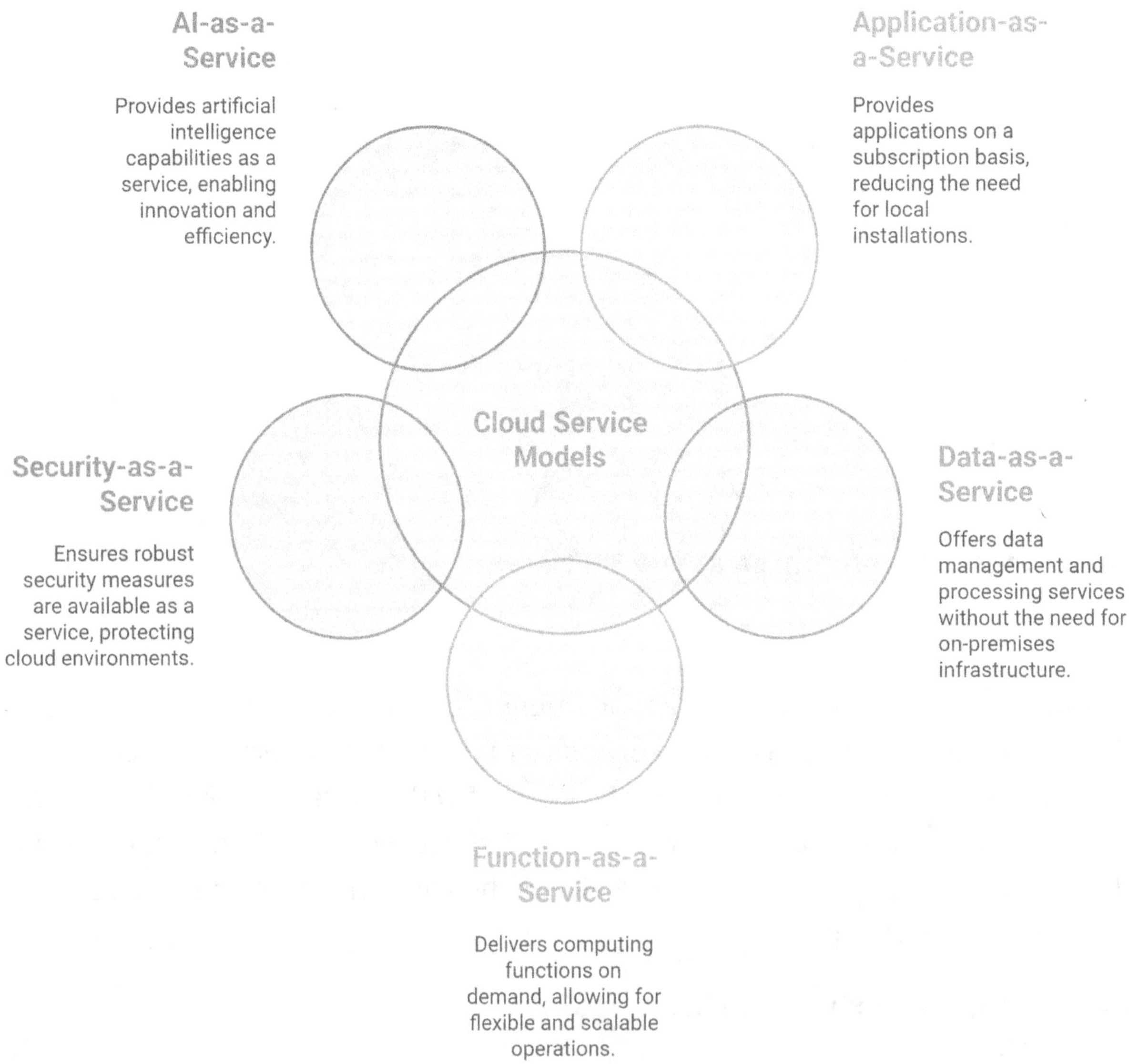

1.2.3 Cloud Deployment Models

Cloud deployment models determine how cloud services are operationalized and managed. There are four main cloud deployment models:

1. Public Cloud: Public cloud deployments make cloud services available to the general public via the Internet. Cloud service providers own and manage the underlying infrastructure, which multiple customers share. Public clouds are renowned for their scalability, flexibility, and cost-effectiveness. However, organizations must consider data privacy and security concerns with public cloud deployments.

2. Private Cloud: Private cloud deployments are dedicated solely to a single organization. These can be hosted on-premises or managed by a trusted third-party provider. Private clouds give organizations complete full control over the infrastructure, ensuring higher levels of compliance and security. Private clouds suit organizations with stringent regulatory requirements and sensitivity concerns.

3. Hybrid Cloud: Hybrid cloud deployments combine the benefits of both public and private clouds. Organizations leverage public clouds' scalability and cost-saving advantages while maintaining sensitive data and critical applications in a private cloud. Hybrid clouds offer flexibility and enable seamless workload portability between various environments.

4. Community Cloud: Community cloud deployments are designed for a specific group of organizations with shared interests, such as government agencies or healthcare providers. Community cloud deployments allow these organizations to share infrastructure and resources while maintaining control over their data and applications. This model promotes collaboration and cost-sharing among the community members while addressing their unique security and compliance requirements. Community clouds balance public and private clouds, providing a tailored solution to a specific group of organizations.

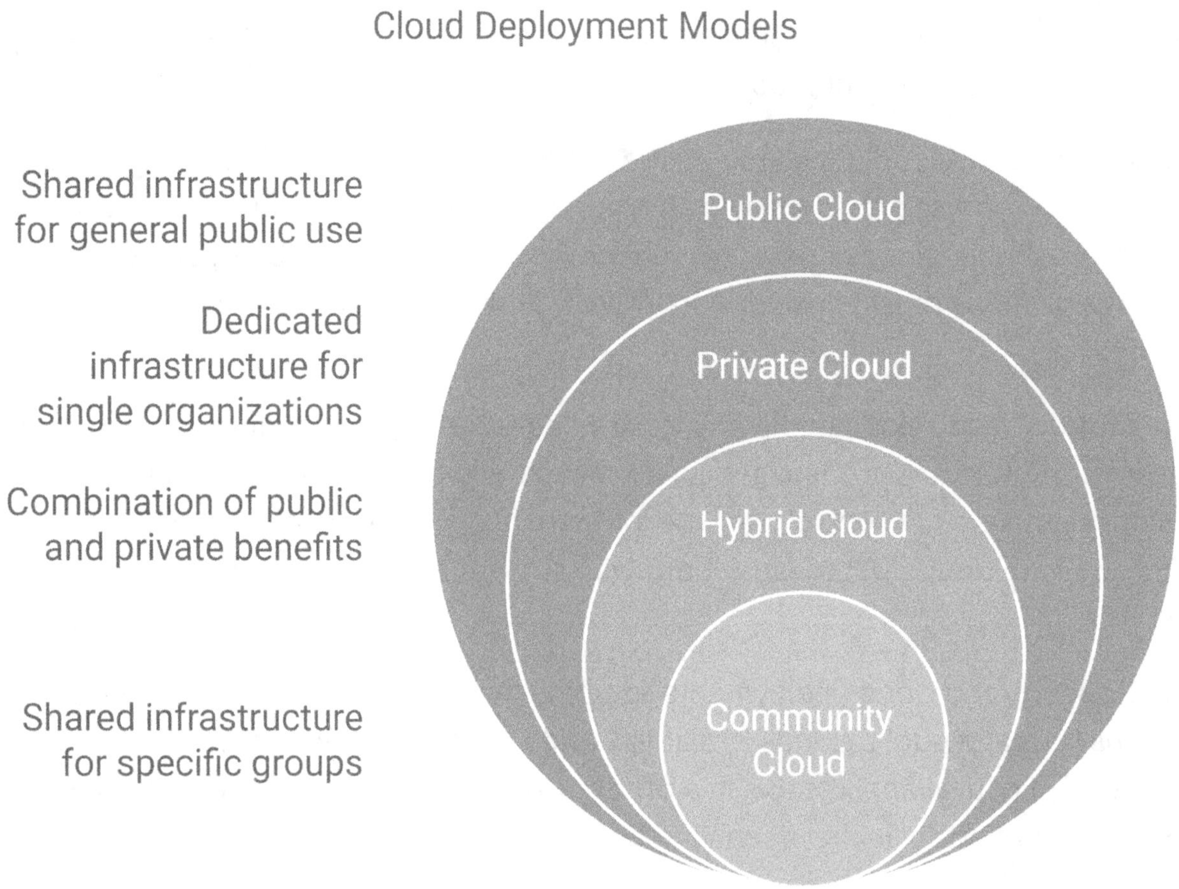

1.2.4 CSA Enterprise Architecture Model

The Cloud Security Alliance (CSA) Enterprise Architecture Model provides a framework for securing cloud environments. It helps organizations understand how to design and implement secure systems in the cloud by focusing on key components, relationships, and security controls.

Key Layers of the CSA Enterprise Architecture Model:

1. **Business Operations:**
    - Represents organizational goals, processes, and services supported by the cloud.
    - Focuses on aligning IT resources with business objectives while maintaining compliance.
    - Example: Ensuring customer data privacy aligns with GDPR regulations when using SaaS

platforms.

2. **Information Layer:**
   - Involves managing sensitive data stored or processed in the cloud.
   - Emphasizes encryption, access control policies, classification schemes (e.g., public vs confidential), and secure storage mechanisms.
   - Example: Encrypting databases hosted on AWS RDS to protect financial records from unauthorized access.
3. **Application Layer:**
   - Covers software running within your environment—whether custom-built apps or third-party solutions like Salesforce or Office 365.
   - Addresses vulnerabilities such as insecure APIs or misconfigured permissions that attackers could exploit at this layer.
4. **Technology/Infrastructure Layer:**
   Includes physical servers managed through virtualization layers beneath compute/storage/network interfaces forming backbone infrastructure supporting workloads securely provisioned inside multi-cloud ecosystems connected globally via SDN/MPLS links ensuring resilience backed-up DR plans operationalized seamlessly

Overview of CSA Enterprise Architecture Model

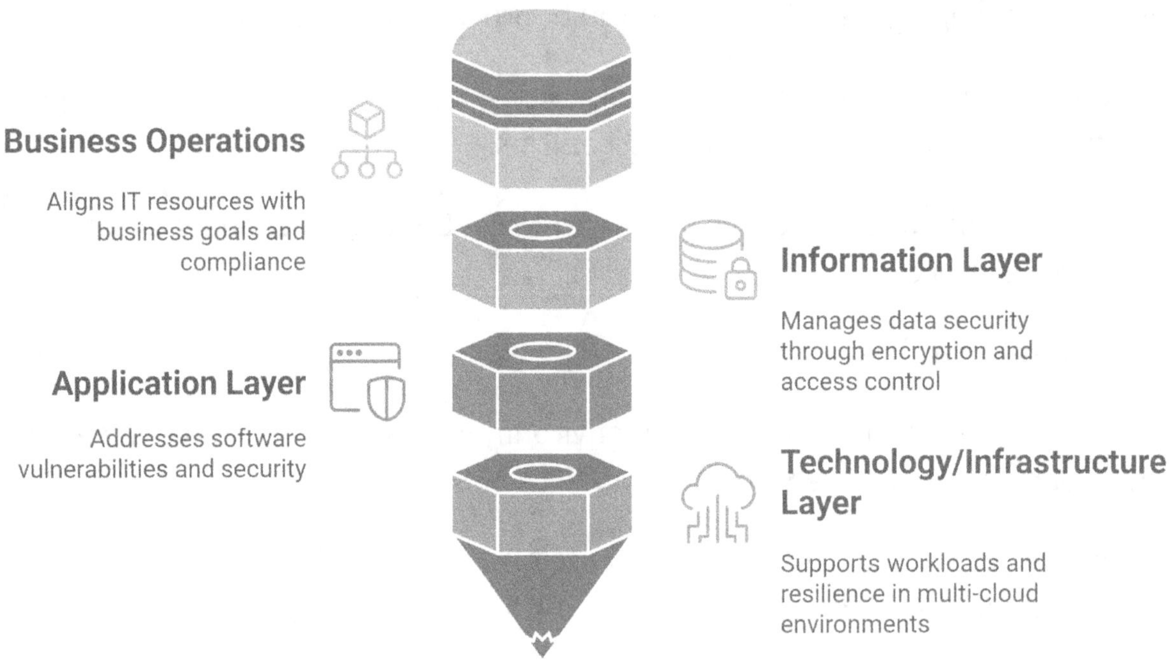

Cloud Architecture Components

Cloud architecture components are the essential building blocks that unify a cloud computing environment. These components guarantee the scalability, availability, and security of cloud services. The primary cloud architecture components include:

1. Virtualization

Virtualization is the cornerstone of cloud computing. It provides the capability to create virtual resources like virtual machines, virtual networks, and virtual storage from physical hardware. Virtualization facilitates efficient resource utilization, isolation, and flexibility in deploying and managing applications.

2. Networking:

Networking ensures connectivity and communication throughout various cloud architecture components and services. It involves configuring and managing critical aspects such as virtual networks, load balancing, firewalls, and virtual private networks (VPNs). Networking safeguards secure, reliable connectivity within the cloud environment.

3. Storage:

Cloud storage furnishes a scalable and reliable platform for storing and accessing data efficiently. It offers diverse storage options, including object, block, and file storage. Cloud storage facilitates seamless data replication, backup, and recovery, ultimately ensuring data durability and availability.

4. Security:

Cloud security is a pivotal component that fortifies any cloud architecture. It encompasses an array of measures and practices to protect data, applications, and infrastructure from unauthorized access, data breaches, and other security threats. Critical elements of cloud security include identity and access management, encryption, threat detection mechanisms, and efficient incident response frameworks.

5. Management:

Cloud management comprises the administration and control of cloud resources and services. It encompasses critical tasks such as resource provisioning, monitoring, capacity planning, and cost optimization. Robust cloud management tools and platforms enable organizations to operate and manage their cloud environment seamlessly with maximum efficiency.

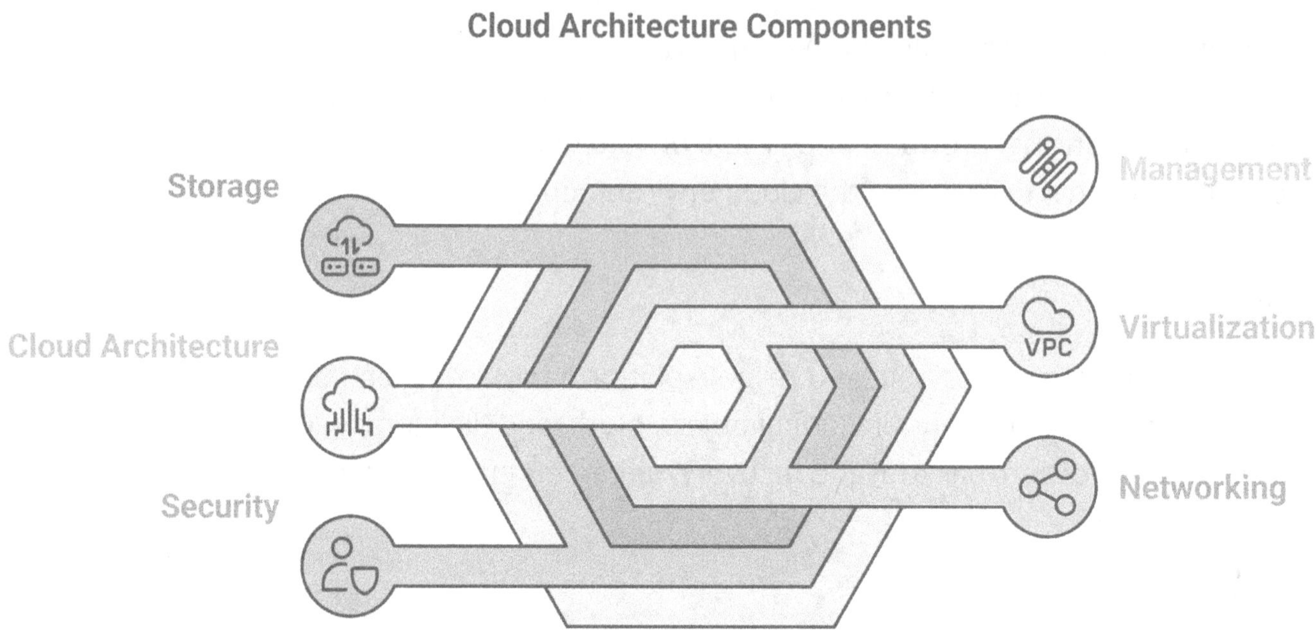

Cloud Logical Model

The Cloud Logical Model provides comprehensive categorization for understanding and organizing terminology related to cloud computing. It encompasses four layers:

1. Infrastructure Layer (Infrastructure Security)

The infrastructure layer represents the cloud environment's physical resources and infrastructure protection seamlessly with maximum efficiency, including servers, storage devices, and networking equipment. Infrastructure security measures are implemented on this layer to prevent unauthorized access, data breaches, and service disruption. Infrastructure security measures are implemented on this layer. Physical security setups, network segmentation, and systematic vulnerability management practices ensure a robust infrastructure security posture.

2. Metastructure Layer (Virtual Environment Security)

The metastructure layer encompasses virtualization technology and facilitates the creation and operation of virtual resources within the cloud. Virtual environment security is paramount in this layer, protecting virtual infrastructure, including virtual machines, networks, and hypervisors.

Essential virtualization security measures include isolation mechanisms, access controls, and comprehensive virtual machine hardening.

3. Infostructure Layer (Data Security)

The infostructure layer focuses on the storage and processing of data within the cloud environment. Data security measures demand protecting sensitive information against unauthorized access, data loss, or corruption. Data-centric measures such as data encryption, access controls, data backup, and classification ensure a fortified data security posture.

4. Applistructure Layer

The applistructure layer encompasses the applications and services built upon the cloud infrastructure and offered to end-users. Application security measures in this tier safeguard applications against security vulnerabilities, enforce stringent authentication and authorization mechanisms, and protect against application-level attacks.

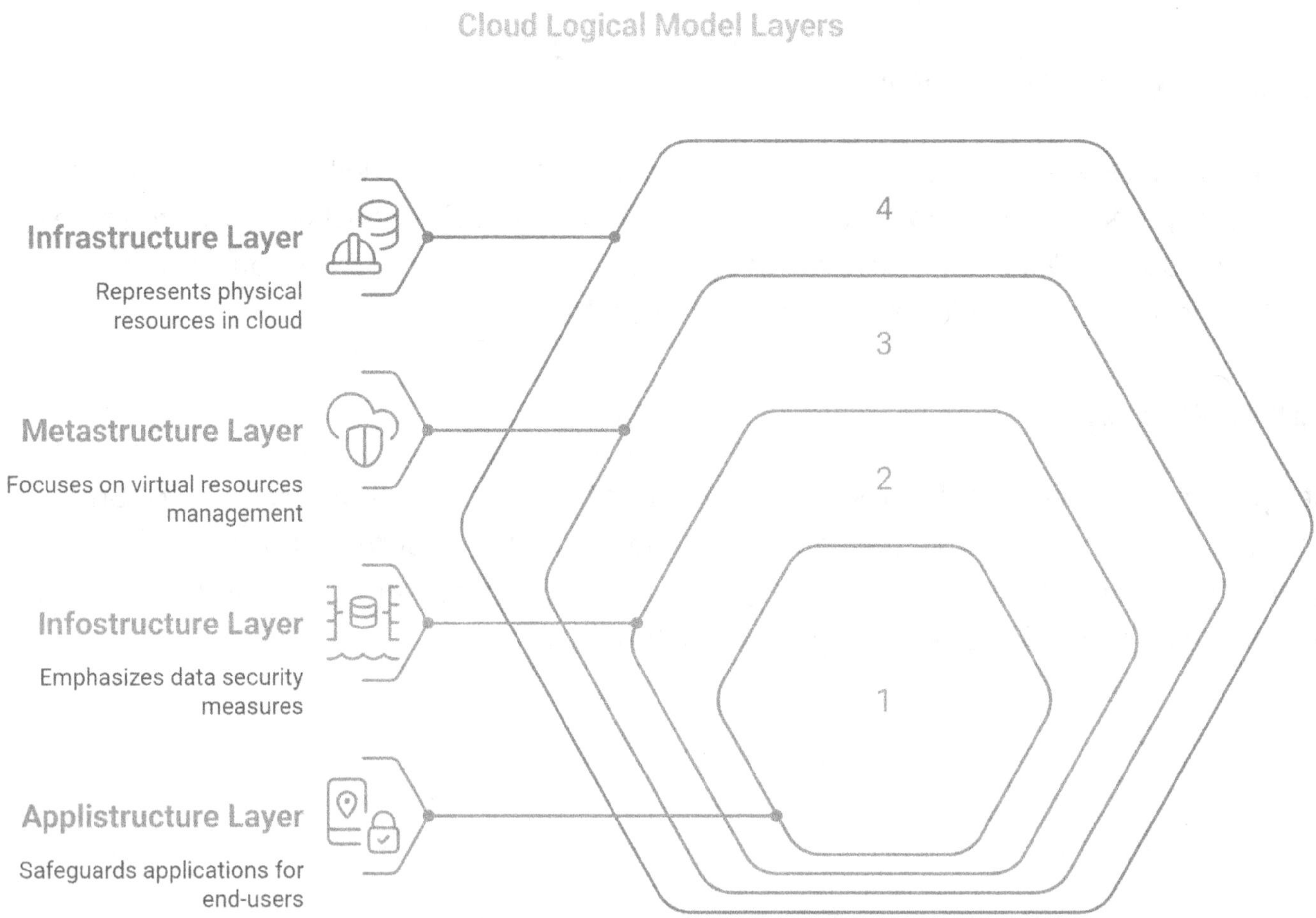
Cloud Logical Model Layers
Infrastructure Layer
Represents physical resources in cloud
Metastructure Layer
Focuses on virtual resources management
Infostructure Layer
Emphasizes data security measures
Applistructure Layer
Safeguards applications for end-users
4
3
2
1

1.3 Cloud Security Scope, Responsibilities, & Models

This section of Domain 1 discusses the critical aspects of cloud security, focusing on the scope of security measures, the delineation of responsibilities, and the models that govern cloud security practices.

Cloud Security Considerations in Architecture

To ensure data and services' confidentiality, integrity, and availability, various security considerations must be meticulously factored in when designing and implementing cloud architectures. Key security considerations are as follows:

1. Data Protection:

Sensitive data must be protected through encryption during transmission and while at rest. Implementing stringent access controls and authentication mechanisms helps ensure that only authorized users can access and modify data.

2. Identity and Access Management:

Proper identity and access management (IAM) practices prevent unauthorized entry and misuse of cloud resources. Sound IAM includes user provisioning, streamlined role-based access controls, multi-factor authentication, and regular access reviews.

3. Network Security:

Network security measures, such as firewalls, intrusion detection systems, and virtual private networks (VPNs), should be implemented to prevent unauthorized access, safeguard against malware, and curb network-based attacks within the cloud environment.

4. Incident Response and Forensics:

Cloud architectures ought to have a well-defined incident response and forensics capabilities for immediate identification and mitigation of security incidents. Essential measures like detailed incident response plans, comprehensive logging, and monitoring, accompanied by robust forensic investigative procedures, ensure swift, targeted action.

5. Compliance & Auditing:

Cloud architectures must conform to the relevant regulatory requirements and industry standards. Regular audits and thorough assessments that identify latent vulnerabilities strengthen confidentiality, integrity, and the overall security posture.

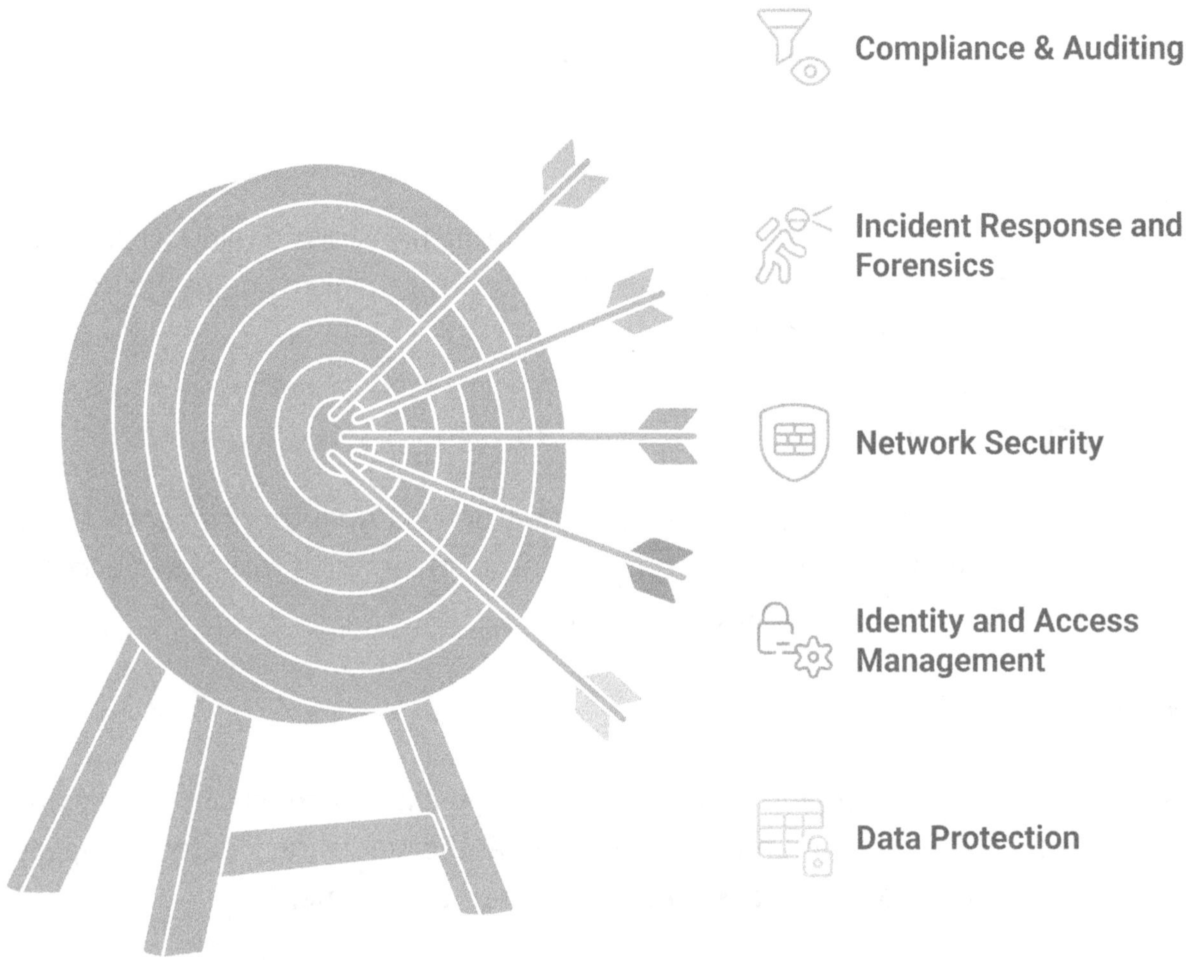

Cloud Security Considerations in Architecture

By carefully reflecting on these core security considerations during the cloud architecture creation phase, organizations establish secure and resilient cloud environments that protect their data and applications from potential threats.

1.3.1 Shared Security Responsibility Model

The Shared Security Responsibility Model defines how security responsibilities are divided between a cloud provider and the customer. It ensures both parties understand their roles in protecting data, applications, and infrastructure.

Cloud Provider's Responsibilities:

Cloud providers secure the underlying **cloud infrastructure**. This includes:

- Physical hardware (servers, storage devices).
- Networking components.
- Data centers (physical access controls like locks or cameras).
- Virtualization layers that run virtual machines or containers.

For example: In AWS, Azure, or Google Cloud Platform (GCP), they ensure servers stay patched against vulnerabilities at the host level and maintain uptime for services.

Customers Responsibilities:

Customers manage what they put into the cloud—this is often referred to as "security *in* the cloud." Their duties include securing things such as:

1. **Data:** Encrypt sensitive information during transit and at rest.
2. **Applications:** Keep software updated with patches; prevent insecure coding practices.
3. **Access Management:** Use strong identity management policies like multi-factor authentication (MFA) for users accessing resources.
4. **Network Configuration:** Set up firewalls properly; restrict unnecessary ports using security groups or network ACLs.

For instance: If you deploy an application on a virtual machine in AWS EC2 but leave it open to all IP addresses without encryption—you're responsible if it's breached because that's part of your configuration choices within their platform tools.

Key Differences by Service Type

Responsibilities vary depending on whether you're using IaaS, PaaS, SaaS:

1. For Infrastructure-as-a-Service (**IaaS**, e.g., Amazon EC2):

   The provider secures physical hosts/networking/virtualization layers only—you handle OS patching/configuration/security entirely yourself!

2. For Platform-as-a-Service (**PaaS**, e.g., Azure App Services):

   Providers take care of runtime environments/framework updates while customers focus solely upon app code/data protection configurations.

3. Software-As-A-service(Saas): customers primarily manage data protection and user access, while the provider handles everything else, including application security and infrastructure maintenance.

The diagram below illustrates the evolving responsibilities across the three cloud service models: Infrastructure as a Service (IaaS), Platform as a Service (PaaS), and Software as a Service (SaaS).

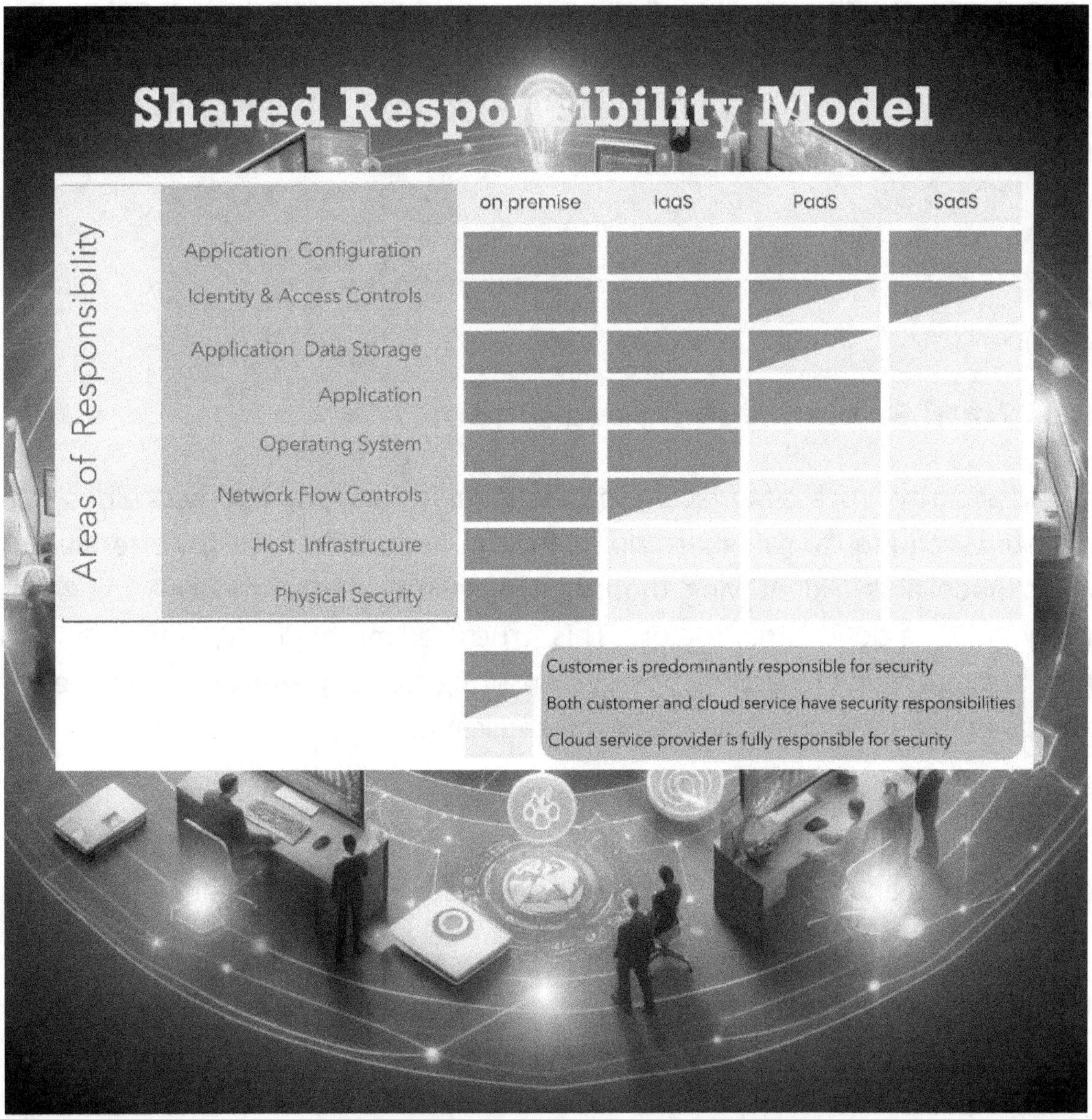

This model emphasizes collaboration between the CSP and the customer to achieve effective security. Both parties must be aware of their roles and responsibilities to mitigate risks and protect their assets.

Importance of the Shared Responsibility Model

Understanding this model is crucial for organizations as it helps them clearly define which security controls and practices they must enforce within their cloud environments. It ensures that both parties are aligned on their security posture, which is vital for compliance, risk management, and overall cybersecurity effectiveness.

Application in Cloud Security Practices

Organizations using cloud services should establish security frameworks that define their responsibilities based on this model. They should conduct regular assessments to identify potential areas of risk and create action plans for addressing those risks, ensuring that they leverage both the protections offered by the CSP and the controls they need to implement themselves.

A Simple Cloud Security Process Model

A Simple Cloud Security Process Model is a foundational framework that meticulously outlines the essential steps required to safeguard cloud environments effectively. By offering a systematic approach, this model aids in identifying, thoroughly assessing, and strategically mitigating potential security risks within the cloud infrastructure. This structured methodology empowers organizations to proactively strengthen their security posture, ensuring robust protection against evolving cyber threats and vulnerabilities in the dynamic cloud landscape.

1. Identify: The first step is identifying the potential security risks and threats that may affect the cloud environment. This includes understanding the assets, data, and applications stored or processed in the cloud and assessing the potential vulnerabilities and attack vectors.

2. Assess: Once the risks are identified, they must be assessed regarding their potential impact and likelihood. This involves evaluating the possibility of a threat occurring and its potential impact on cloud resources' confidentiality, integrity, and availability.

3. Mitigate: After assessing the risks, appropriate security controls and measures must be implemented to mitigate the identified risks. This may include implementing encryption, access controls, intrusion detection systems, data loss prevention mechanisms, and regular security patching and updates.

4. Monitor: Once the security controls are in place, it is essential to continuously monitor the cloud environment for any security incidents or anomalies. This involves implementing security monitoring tools and techniques to detect and respond to real-time security breaches or unauthorized activities.

5. Review: Regular reviews and audits should ensure that the security controls and measures are adequate and aligned with the changing threat landscape. This includes evaluating the effectiveness of the security controls, identifying any gaps or weaknesses, and making necessary improvements or adjustments.

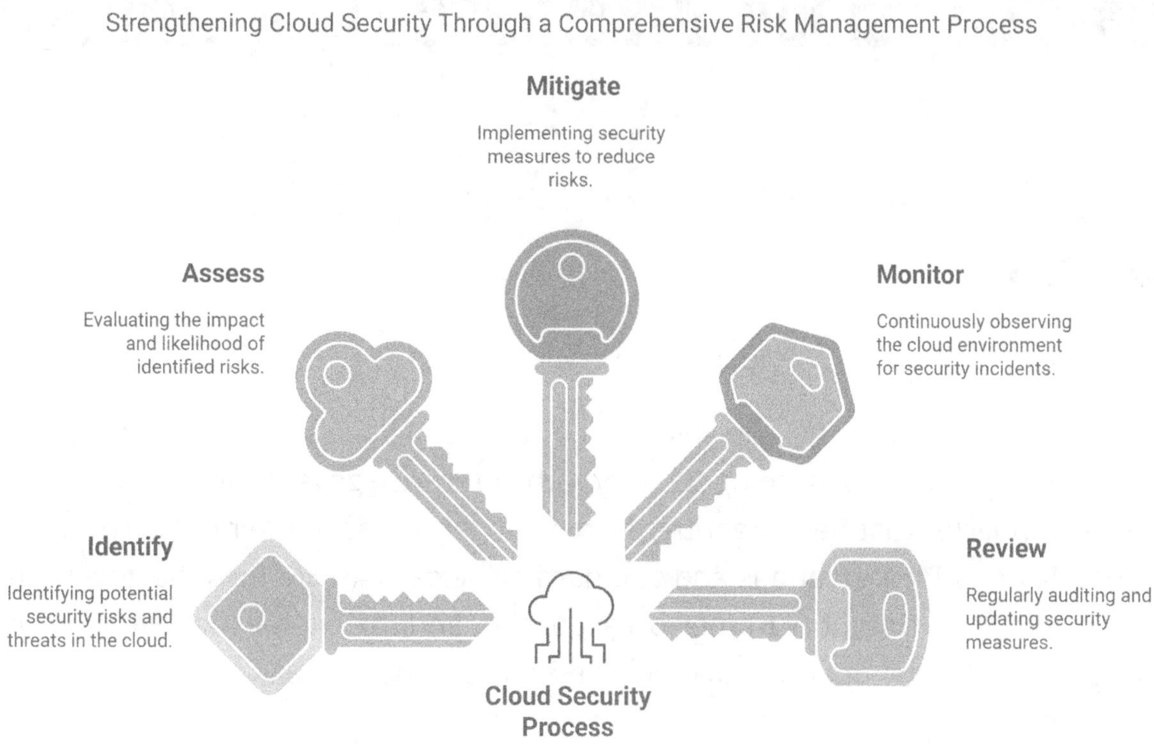

Organizations can manage and mitigate security risks in their cloud environments by following this simple cloud security process model. It provides a systematic approach to ensuring the confidentiality, integrity, and availability of cloud resources and helps organizations maintain a strong security posture in the cloud.

Chapter Five

Domain 2: Cloud Governance and Strategies

Introduction

Cloud Governance focuses on the principles and practices of governing cloud environments, emphasizing the importance of aligning security with enterprise governance. It involves establishing frameworks and policies that help organizations effectively manage their cloud resources while ensuring compliance with regulations and standards. The domain outlines the governance hierarchy, including cloud security frameworks, policies, and the overall management required to meet strategic, tactical, and operational objectives in the cloud context.

Learning Objectives

The learning objectives for Domain 2: Cloud Governance are designed to provide participants with a comprehensive understanding of how to manage and govern cloud environments effectively. The specific objectives include:

1. **Understanding Cloud Governance**: Participants will learn the fundamental principles of cloud governance and its significance in the context of organizational strategy.
2. **Governance Hierarchy**: The objectives include familiarizing learners with the governance hierarchy in cloud environments, highlighting the various levels of governance, and the roles and responsibilities involved.
3. **Cloud Security Frameworks**: Learners will explore different cloud security frameworks that provide guidelines and structures for implementing governance measures.

4. **Policies**: The objectives emphasize the importance of developing and implementing policies that guide organizations in their cloud governance practices to ensure compliance and security.

These objectives aim to equip participants with the necessary skills to align cloud governance with the strategic and operational goals of their organizations, ultimately contributing to more effective management of cloud resources and risks

2.1. Cloud Governance

Cloud governance is a set of principles and practices that ensure the effective and efficient management of cloud resources. By implementing cloud governance, organizations can establish control, reduce risks, and optimize the value they derive from their cloud investments.

The following are some essential cloud governance principles:

1. Clear Roles and Responsibilities: Clearly define the roles and responsibilities of individuals and teams involved in cloud management. This includes roles such as cloud administrators, security officers, and compliance officers.

2. Policy and Standards Framework: Establish a framework to define and enforce policies and standards for cloud usage. This includes policies for data security, access control, and compliance with regulations and industry best practices.

3. Risk Management: Implement a risk management framework to identify, assess, and mitigate risks associated with cloud adoption. This involves regular risk assessments, vulnerability management, and incident response planning.

4. Asset Inventory and Configuration Management: Maintain an accurate inventory of cloud assets and configurations. This includes tracking virtual machines, storage resources, and network components. Regularly review and update configurations to ensure compliance with security requirements.

5. Compliance and Audit: Establish processes and controls to ensure compliance with relevant regulations and industry standards. Regularly conduct audits to assess compliance and identify areas for improvement.

6. Training and Awareness: Provide training and awareness programs to educate employees about cloud security best practices. This helps to foster a security-conscious culture and reduce the likelihood of human error.

7. Incident Response and Recovery: Develop and test incident response and recovery plans to ensure a timely and effective response to security incidents. This includes procedures for detecting, containing, and recovering from security breaches.

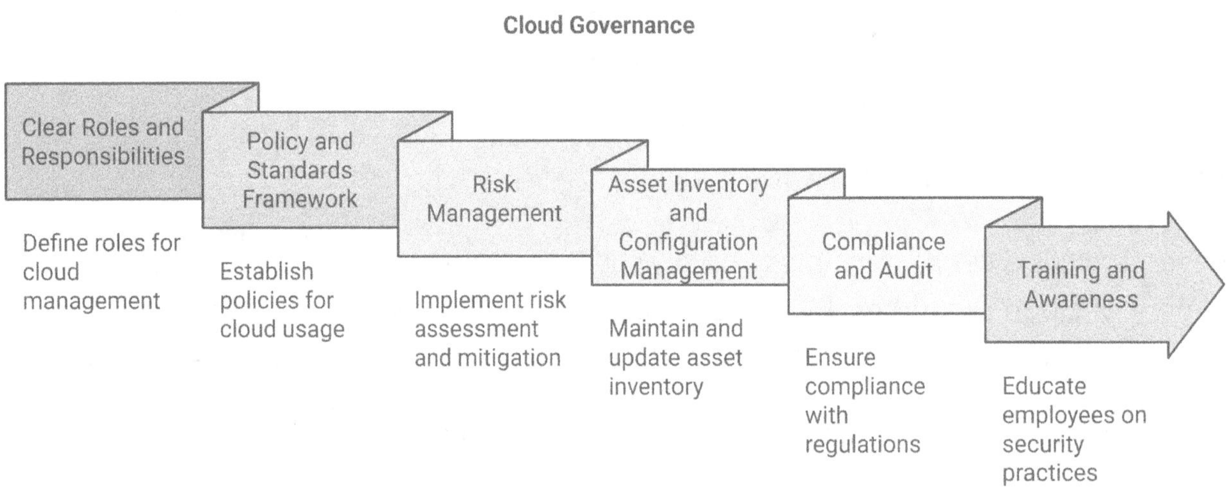

By adopting these cloud governance principles, organizations can achieve better control and governance over their cloud resources, reduce risks, and maximize the benefits of cloud computing.

2.2 The Governance Hierarchy

Governance Hierarchy in the context of cloud computing refers to the structured framework that defines the roles, responsibilities, and relationships among various stakeholders involved in managing and overseeing cloud resources and services. This hierarchy ensures that governance mechanisms are effectively implemented to align with an organization's strategic objectives and regulatory requirements.

Governance Levels

1. **Enterprise Governance**:
   - This is the highest level of governance that encompasses the organization as a whole. It focuses on aligning cloud strategies with business goals and involves executive leadership decisions.

- **Roles and Responsibilities**:
  - C-Level Executives (e.g., CIO, CTO): Ultimately responsible for ensuring that cloud governance aligns with the organization's strategic objectives and risk appetite.

2. **Cloud Governance Framework Governance**:
   - This level pertains to the creation and maintenance of the governance framework designed specifically for cloud services. It involves defining the policies, standards, and processes for cloud adoption and management.
   - **Roles and Responsibilities**:
     - Governance Teams: Develop and update the cloud governance framework, ensure adherence to regulations, and assess risk management strategies.
3. **Operational Governance**:
   - This level deals with the day-to-day management and operational oversight of cloud resources. It ensures that the cloud environment is managed effectively and securely.
   - **Roles and Responsibilities**:
     - Cloud Administrators/Managers: Responsible for executing governance policies, monitoring operational performance, and managing cloud services.
4. **Technical Governance**:
   - This level focuses on the technical aspects of cloud governance, including security measures, compliance, and data management.
   - **Roles and Responsibilities**:
     - IT Security and Compliance Teams: Implement security controls, conduct audits, and ensure compliance with policies and regulations.
5. **Project Governance**:
   - This is often ad-hoc and project-specific governance, which may be required for specific cloud initiatives or deployments. It involves defining project objectives, roles, and timelines.

- **Roles and Responsibilities**:
    - Project Leads and Managers: Oversee project execution within the cloud framework, ensuring that resources meet organizational governance standards.

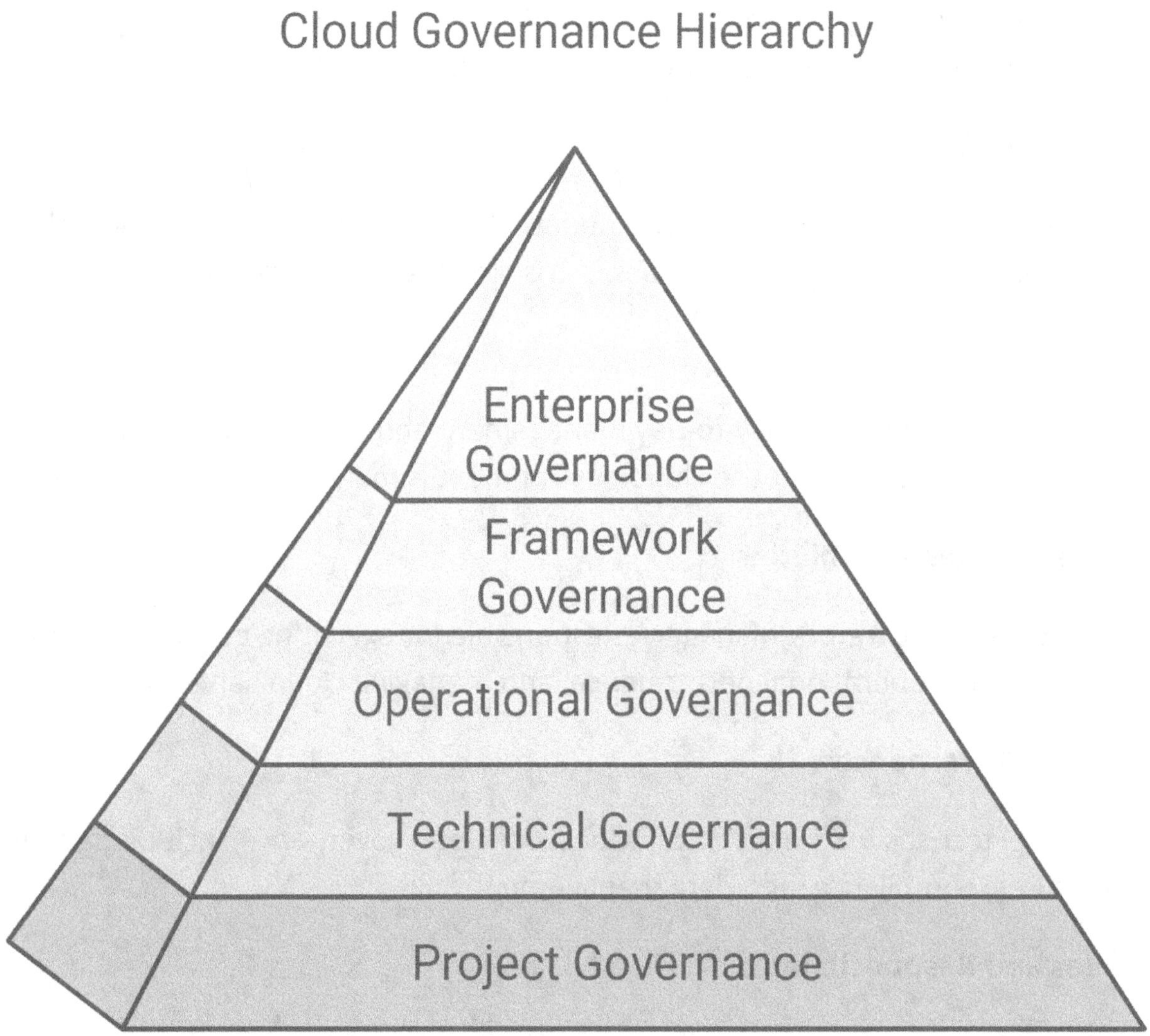

2.2.1 Cloud Security Frameworks

Focuses on the various structures and guidelines that organizations can adopt to establish effective security measures in cloud computing environments. These frameworks help in aligning cloud security practices with business objectives, regulatory requirements, and industry best practices.

Key Aspects of Cloud Security Frameworks:

1. **Definition and Purpose**: Cloud security frameworks provide a structured approach for managing cloud security risks. They outline the principles, standards, and practices necessary to secure cloud operations and protect sensitive data.
2. **Standardization**: Frameworks often include standardized protocols and methodologies that organizations can follow to ensure consistency in securing cloud environments. This standardization aids in compliance with regulatory requirements and helps in managing security across multiple cloud services and providers.
3. **Best Practices**: They incorporate industry best practices that have been established by security experts, regulatory bodies, and industry associations. These practices help organizations to identify vulnerabilities and implement appropriate security controls.
4. **Assessment and Compliance**:

Cloud security frameworks assist organizations in conducting risk assessments and compliance checks. They provide a basis for evaluating current security postures and identifying areas requiring improvement.

5. **Types of Frameworks**:
    - Various frameworks exist, including:
        - **NIST Cybersecurity Framework**: Provides guidelines for managing and reducing cybersecurity risks and emphasizes a risk-based approach.
        - **ISO/IEC 27001**: An international standard focusing on information security management systems (ISMS), relevant to cloud security.
        - **CIS Controls**: A set of best practices for securing IT systems, which can be applied to cloud environments.

- **Cloud Security Alliance (CSA) Cloud Controls Matrix (CCM)**: Specifically designed for cloud security, it helps organizations assess the security risk of cloud providers.

6. **Implementation**: Organizations can use these frameworks to develop tailored security policies and procedures that fit their specific cloud usage and business requirements. Effective implementation of the frameworks enhances security posture and resilience against threats.

By leveraging cloud security frameworks, organizations can establish a robust security strategy that not only protects their cloud resources but also aligns with their overall governance and risk management objectives.

2.2.2 Policies

Refers to the formalized guidelines and principles that govern the use, management, and security of cloud resources within an organization. These policies are essential for establishing a clear framework under which all cloud-related activities are conducted, ensuring compliance with legal, regulatory, and organizational standards.

Key Aspects of Cloud Security Policies:

1. **Definition and Scope**: Cloud security policies are written documents that outline the standards, rules, and practices that personnel must follow while utilizing cloud services. They define roles and responsibilities, security measures, and protocols for handling cloud resources.
2. **Purpose and Importance**: The primary purpose of cloud security policies is to mitigate risks associated with cloud computing by clearly defining acceptable use, data protection, and incident response procedures. They provide a foundation for effective governance, risk management, and compliance efforts.
    - **Access Control Policies**: Define who can access specific cloud resources and under what circumstances. This includes authentication mechanisms, role-based access controls, and user permissions.
    - **Data Protection Policies**: Outlines how data is classified, managed, and protected in cloud environments. This includes encryption standards, data retention, and data loss

prevention measures.

- **Incident Response Policies**: Detail the procedures for responding to security incidents, including detection, containment, eradication, and recovery processes, ensuring timely and effective responses to potential breaches.
- **Compliance Policies**: Ensure adherence to relevant laws and regulations, industry standards, and organizational policies. This includes policies for managing privacy, legal compliance, and audit requirements.

Components of Cloud Security Policies

Development and Implementation

- Developing effective cloud security policies involves assessing organizational needs, understanding regulatory requirements, and engaging stakeholders to ensure that policies are practical and enforceable.
- Implementation requires ongoing training for personnel, communication of the policies, and consideration for continuous updates to adapt to changing security landscapes and emerging threats.

Enforcement and Review: Policies must be enforced through monitoring and auditing practices. Organizations should regularly review and update policies to ensure they remain relevant and effective against evolving threats and compliance requirements.

By establishing and implementing comprehensive cloud security policies, organizations can create a structured approach to managing security risks and ensure that all stakeholders align with the organization's cloud governance objectives.

Chapter Six

Domain 3: Risk, Audit and Compliance

Introduction

This domain is a critical area focused on understanding and managing the security risks associated with cloud computing. This domain emphasizes the importance of evaluating cloud service providers (CSPs) and establishing robust cloud risk registries. It provides a framework for organizations to effectively assess, audit, and ensure compliance with various regulatory requirements and industry standards.

Learning Objectives

The learning objectives for Audit, & Compliance focus on enabling professionals to effectively manage risks, ensure compliance, and conduct audits in cloud computing environments. The key objectives include:

1. **Understand Cloud Risks**: Identify and articulate the specific risks associated with various cloud service models (IaaS, PaaS, SaaS).
2. **Evaluate Cloud Risk Management Practices**: Assess and develop effective risk management strategies tailored for cloud environments, including the creation of cloud risk registers.
3. **Assess Cloud Services**: Learn to evaluate cloud service providers based on their security measures, compliance status, and risk profiles during the vendor selection process.
4. **Compliance & Audit Requirements**: Familiarize with relevant legal, regulatory, and industry

compliance requirements, as well as auditing standards applicable to cloud services.

5. **Understand Governance Tools**: Gain knowledge of governance, risk management, and compliance (GRC) tools that facilitate audits and ensure compliance in cloud settings.

6. **Develop Policies and Procedures**: Create and implement effective policies and procedures that align with risk management and compliance objectives.

These objectives provide a structured approach to understanding and managing the complexities of risk and compliance in cloud computing.

3.1. Cloud Risk Management

Cloud Risk Management involves identifying, assessing, and mitigating risks associated with using cloud services. It ensures organizations can securely operate in the cloud while protecting data, maintaining compliance, and minimizing disruptions. This process includes evaluating unique cloud-specific threats like shared responsibility challenges, misconfigurations, or unauthorized access. Effective risk management helps align security practices with business goals to safeguard assets in dynamic cloud environments.

3.1.1 Cloud Risks

Cloud risks refer to potential threats or vulnerabilities that could impact an organization's use of cloud services. These risks arise from shared responsibility models, dynamic environments, and unique characteristics of the cloud.

Key categories include:

1. **Data Breaches**: Unauthorized access to sensitive data stored in the cloud.

2. **Misconfigurations**: Incorrect setup of resources leading to exposure or exploitation.

3. **Account Hijacking**: Compromise of user credentials granting attackers control over accounts.

4. **Insider Threats**: Malicious actions by employees with legitimate access.

5. **Service Downtime/Outages**: Disruption caused by provider failures or attacks like DDoS (Distributed Denial-of-Service).

6. **Compliance Risks**: Failure to meet legal/regulatory requirements due to improper controls.

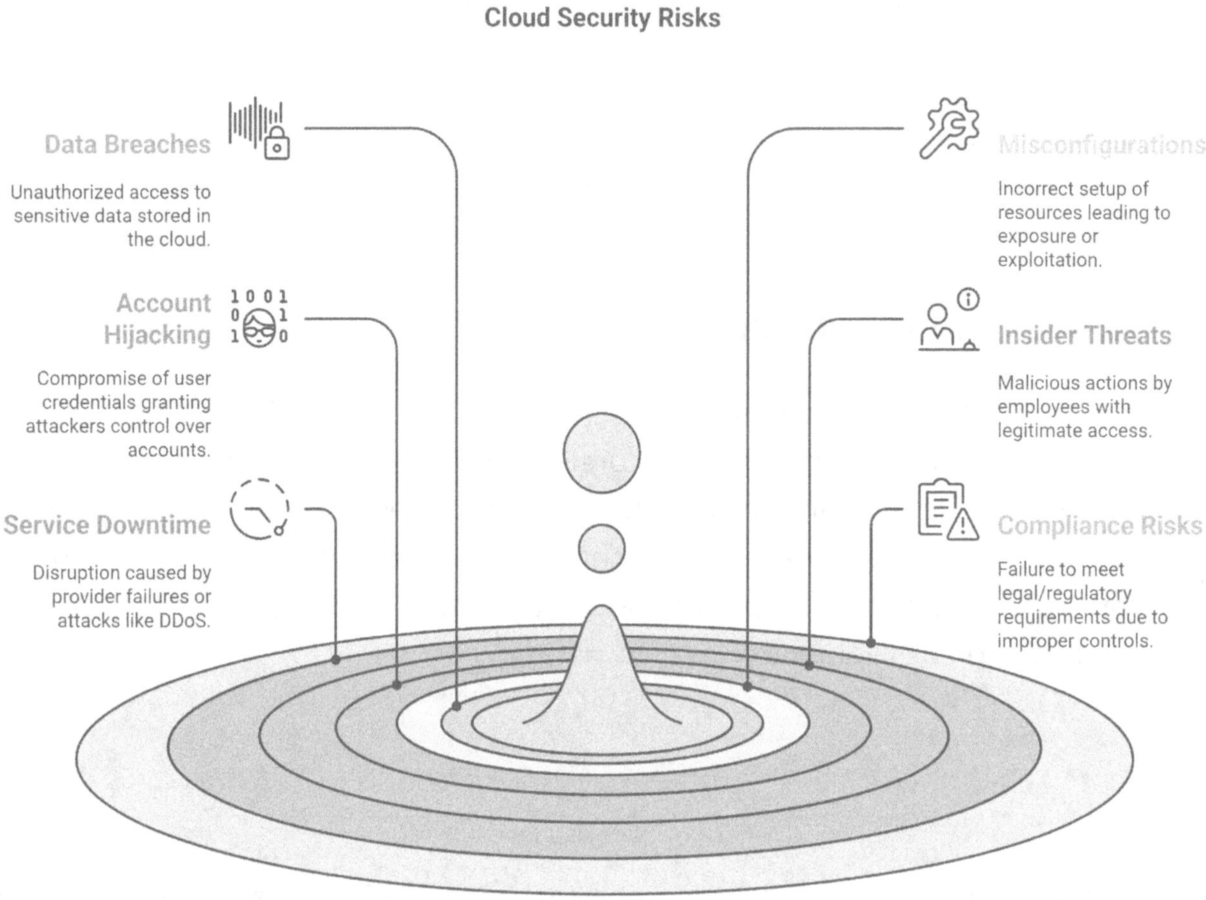

CCSK v5 emphasizes understanding these risks and implementing strategies such as encryption, monitoring tools, identity management systems (IAM), regular audits, and secure configurations for mitigation efforts tailored specifically for a shared-responsibility model in the cloud environment.

3.1.2 Understanding Cloud Risk Management

Cloud risk management involves identifying, assessing, and mitigating risks associated with cloud services. Organizations can minimize the likelihood and impact of potential threats to their cloud environments by implementing effective risk management strategies.

Here are some key cloud risk management strategies:

1. Risk Assessment: Conduct a comprehensive risk assessment to identify potential risks and vulnerabilities in the cloud environment. This involves evaluating the security controls provided by cloud service providers and assessing the impact and likelihood of possible risks.

2. Risk Mitigation: Implement appropriate controls and countermeasures to mitigate identified risks. This may include encryption, access controls, and regular vulnerability scanning and patching.

3. Data Classification: Classify data based on its sensitivity and criticality. This helps determine the appropriate security controls and level of protection required for different data types.

4. Vendor Due Diligence: Perform due diligence when selecting cloud service providers. This includes evaluating their security practices, certifications, and track record in managing security incidents.

5. Service Level Agreements (SLAs): Ensure SLAs with cloud service providers include appropriate security and risk management provisions. This includes requirements for incident response, data retention, and disaster recovery.

6. Continuous Monitoring: Implement a continuous monitoring program to detect and respond to real-time security incidents. This involves monitoring system logs, network traffic, and user activities to identify potential threats.

7. Incident Response Planning: Develop an incident response plan to respond to security incidents effectively. This includes establishing roles and responsibilities, defining incident-handling procedures, and conducting regular drills and exercises.

8. Security Awareness and Training: Provide ongoing security awareness and training programs to educate employees about cloud security risks and best practices. This helps in reducing the likelihood of human error and insider threats.

By following these risk management strategies, organizations can proactively identify and address cloud security risks, ensuring their cloud-based resources' confidentiality, integrity, and availability.

3.1.3 Assessing Cloud Services

In CCSK v5, assessing cloud services focuses on evaluating the security and suitability of cloud services before adoption or during ongoing use. This process ensures that chosen services align with an organization's risk tolerance, compliance requirements, and operational needs.

Key steps include:

1. **Understanding Provider Capabilities**: Review the cloud provider's offerings, including their security controls (e.g., encryption, logging) and certifications (e.g., ISO 27001).
2. **Evaluating Shared Responsibility Model**: Identify which responsibilities lie with the provider versus your organization to avoid gaps in protection.
3. **Risk Assessment Frameworks**: Use frameworks like CSA STAR or NIST to assess risks related to data confidentiality, integrity, availability, legal obligations (GDPR/HIPAA), etc.
4. **Review Contracts & SLAs**:
    - Ensure Service Level Agreements define uptime guarantees.
    - Confirm terms address liability for breaches or outages.
5. **Technical Testing/Validation Tools:** Conduct penetration testing where permitted by agreements; verify configurations meet organizational standards using tools like CSPM solutions.

Assessing cloud services is essential for informed decision-making when adopting new platforms while ensuring they support secure operations within regulatory boundaries outlined under CCSK v5 principles effectively

3.1.4 The Cloud Register

The Cloud Register is a centralized inventory or record of all cloud services an organization uses. This register helps track and manage the risks associated with these services by providing visibility into their usage, configurations, and security posture.

Key Components:

1. **Service Details**: Includes information about each cloud service in use (e.g., provider name, purpose of the service).
2. **Data Classification**: Identifies what type of data is processed or stored within each service (e.g., sensitive data like PII or financial records).
3. **Risk Assessment Results**: Documents any identified risks from assessments conducted on

the specific cloud services.

4. **Compliance Requirements**: Tracks regulatory obligations tied to certain datasets or operations using that particular service.
5. **Ownership & Responsibility Mapping**:
   - Defines who owns/uses the resource internally.
   - Maps responsibilities based on shared responsibility models between providers and users.

Purpose:

The Cloud Register ensures transparency across departments regarding which tools are being used while enabling better governance over them through periodic reviews/audits aligned under risk mitigation frameworks outlined throughout other sections discussed previously within CCSK standards effectively ensuring safer practices overall.

3.2 Compliance & Audit

Compliance & Audit focuses on ensuring cloud environments meet regulatory, legal, and organizational requirements while maintaining transparency through regular audits. It involves understanding applicable laws (e.g., GDPR, HIPAA), aligning with industry standards (e.g., ISO 27001), and verifying that security controls are implemented effectively. This process helps organizations manage risks, avoid penalties, and build trust by demonstrating accountability in their use of cloud services.

3.2.1 Jurisdictions

Understanding Jurisdictions refers to the legal and regulatory environments that govern data stored or processed in specific geographic locations within cloud services. When using cloud providers, organizations must understand how laws from different jurisdictions impact their operations, especially regarding data privacy, security, and compliance.

Key Considerations:

1. **Data Residency Requirements**: Some regulations (e.g., GDPR) mandate that sensitive data remain within certain countries or regions.
2. **Cross-Border Data Transfers**: Moving data between jurisdictions may require adherence to international agreements like Standard Contractual Clauses (SCCs).
3. **Conflicting Laws**: Different jurisdictions may impose conflicting requirements on access control or government requests for information.
4. **Provider Location & Subcontractors**:
    - Understand where your provider operates its infrastructure.
    - Identify third-party subcontractors who might handle your organization's data across borders.
5. **Legal Risks of Multi-Jurisdictional Clouds**:
    - Be aware of risks such as differing breach notification timelines or liability issues under local law enforcement demands.

Purpose in Cloud Security

Understanding jurisdictional impacts helps organizations ensure compliance with global standards while mitigating risks tied to unauthorized disclosures due to varying regional laws governing cloud service usage outlined effectively under principles discussed further throughout CCSK frameworks comprehensively

3.2.2 Cloud-Relevant Laws & Regulations Examples

Here are some examples of cloud-relevant laws and regulations:

1. **General Data Protection Regulation (GDPR)**: This European Union regulation sets guidelines for the collection and processing of personal information of individuals within the EU. It is crucial for cloud service providers to comply with GDPR to ensure data protection and privacy.

2. **Health Insurance Portability and Accountability Act (HIPAA)**: In the United States, HIPAA sets national standards for protecting the privacy and security of individuals' medical records and personal health information. Cloud services handling healthcare data must adhere to HIPAA regulations.

3. **Payment Card Industry Data Security Standard (PCI DSS)**: This standard applies to organizations that handle card information for the major debit, credit, prepaid, e-purse, ATM, and POS cards. Cloud services that process payment card information must comply with PCI DSS to ensure secure handling of sensitive financial data.

These examples illustrate the types of laws and regulations that are relevant to cloud security and compliance.

3.2.3 Understanding Compliance Inheritance in Cloud Services

Compliance inheritance plays a crucial role in managing regulatory responsibilities within cloud environments. This concept, part of Domain 3 in the CCSK curriculum, highlights how compliance duties are distributed and shared between cloud service providers (CSPs) and their customers. By grasping this framework, organizations can better manage risks and ensure they meet legal and security standards.

Shared Responsibility Model: Who Does What?

In cloud services, compliance isn't a one-sided effort. The shared responsibility model defines how tasks are divided between CSPs and their customers. For example, while a CSP might handle physical security measures or infrastructure-level protections, customers must focus on securing their data, applications, and user access controls.

Think of it like renting an apartment. The landlord ensures the building structure is safe and up to code, but tenants need to lock their doors and keep their belongings secure. Similarly, CSPs provide foundational safeguards while customers maintain control over what they store or run within that environment.

Borrowing Compliance Controls from Providers

One significant advantage of working with reputable CSPs is inheriting some of their compliance efforts. Many top-tier providers invest heavily in meeting regulations such as GDPR or HIPAA. When you use these services, you're essentially tapping into those certifications without starting from scratch.

For instance, if your provider complies with PCI DSS for payment processing or ISO 27001 for information security management systems, your organization may already meet parts of those requirements by association. However, it's not automatic—you'll still need to confirm which aspects apply to your specific operations.

Balancing Risk Management with Responsibility

While inheriting compliance controls can ease some burdens, it doesn't mean you're off the hook entirely. Organizations must carefully assess which areas fall under the provider's scope versus where they remain accountable.

This requires asking critical questions: Are shared controls adequately managed? Do internal teams understand what's expected on their end? How will audits be handled when responsibilities overlap? Addressing these concerns helps ensure nothing slips through the cracks during implementation or review processes.

Why It Matters for Your Organization

Understanding compliance inheritance isn't just about ticking boxes—it's about protecting your business from potential fines or reputational damage due to non-compliance. Beyond that risk mitigation aspect lies another benefit: operational efficiency. By leveraging pre-existing frameworks offered by CSPs, businesses can save time and resources while focusing on core activities instead of duplicating efforts unnecessarily.

For example:

- A healthcare company using a HIPAA-compliant cloud platform can streamline patient data storage without worrying about encryption protocols.
- An e-commerce brand relying on PCI DSS-certified services avoids redundant payment security checks during annual reviews.

These scenarios highlight how strategic partnerships with compliant providers simplify complex regulatory landscapes without compromising accountability.

Final Thoughts on Navigating Compliance Inheritance

Navigating compliance inheritance effectively requires collaboration between all parties involved—CSPs providing robust frameworks and customers taking ownership where needed. Clear communication ensures everyone understands their roles while reducing gaps that could lead to vulnerabilities or audit failures down the line.

By approaching this process thoughtfully rather than assuming everything "just works," organizations position themselves for long-term success in maintaining both trustworthiness and legal integrity within cloud environments.

3.2.4 Artifacts of Compliance

Artifacts of Compliance are the tangible outputs and documentation that serve as evidence of compliance with various regulatory and security standards in a cloud environment. The key components of this concept include:

1. **Definition of Compliance Artifacts**: Artifacts of compliance are the documents and records that demonstrate that an organization has met certain regulatory and industry standards. These can include policies, procedures, reports, and other documentation that provide proof of compliance efforts.
2. **Types of Compliance Artifacts**:

- **Security Policies**: Documents outlining the security frameworks and protocols in place to protect data and manage risks.
- **Audit Reports**: Independent assessments conducted by third parties to evaluate whether an organization meets specific compliance requirements.
- **Risk Assessments**: Evaluations that identify and analyze potential risks that could affect compliance status.
- **Control Assessments**: Documentation verifying that specific security controls are functioning as intended.
- **Compliance Certificates**: Certificates provided by regulatory bodies or industry standards organizations (e.g., ISO 27001, SOC 2), validating compliance.

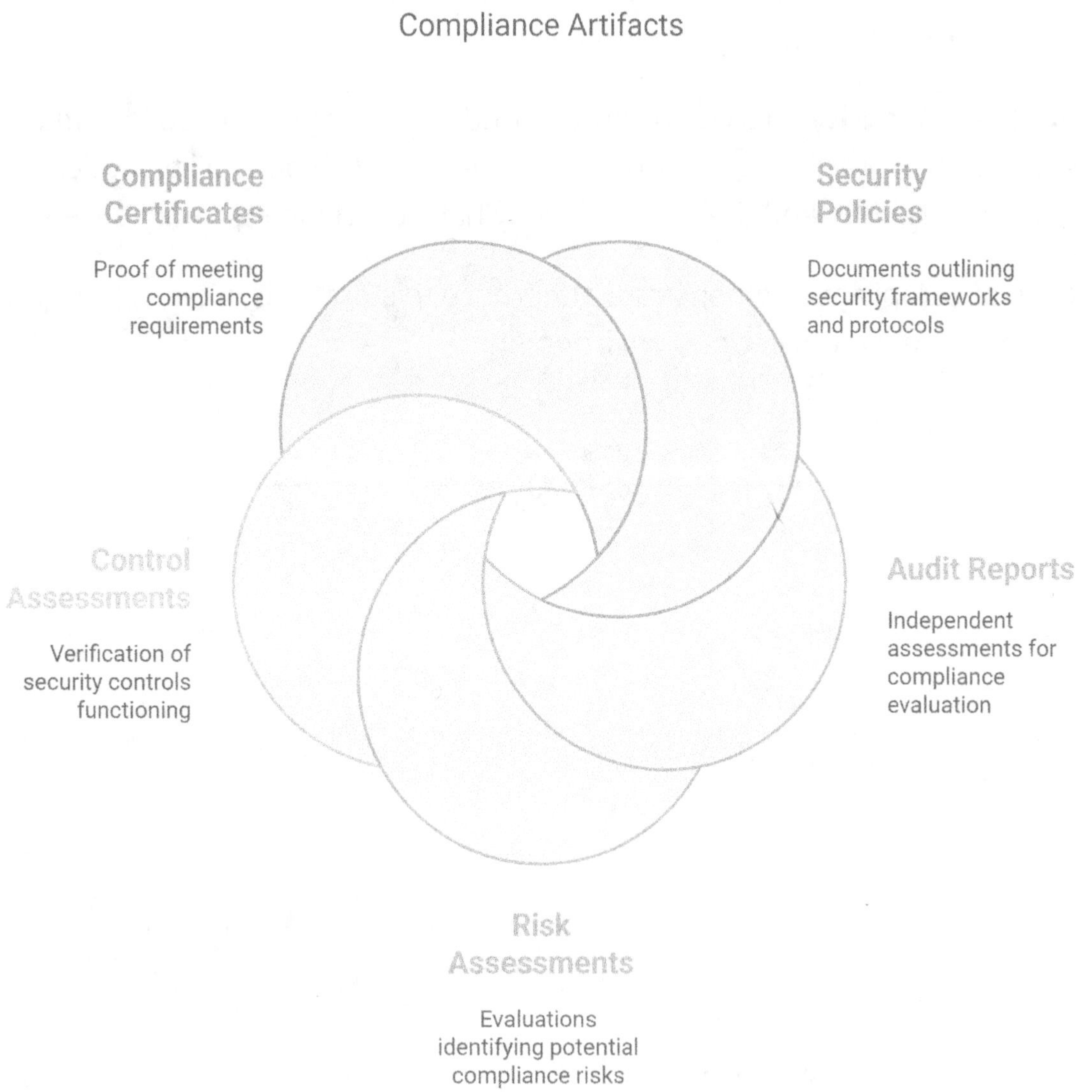

1. **Importance of Compliance Artifacts**:
    - **Demonstrating Compliance**: These artifacts are essential for proving to regulators, auditors, and stakeholders that an organization adheres to required standards.
    - **Supporting Audits**: During audits, organizations present these artifacts to substantiate their compliance posture. Well-organized artifacts can facilitate smoother audit processes.
    - **Risk Management**: Having clear documentation allows organizations to manage compliance risks effectively and see a clearer picture of their compliance landscape.

2. **Lifecycle of Compliance Artifacts**: Emphasizes the need for maintaining, updating, and reviewing compliance artifacts regularly to ensure they reflect the current state of security and compliance within the organization.

3. **Role in Cloud Security**: In a cloud context, understanding how to collect, manage, and present compliance artifacts is crucial due to the shared responsibility model, where both the cloud service provider and the customer may have overlapping compliance requirements.

Overall, artifacts of compliance demonstrate adherence to standards, aiding in risk management, and supporting audit readiness in cloud environments.

3.3 Governance, Risk, Compliance Tools & Technologies

Governance, Risk, Compliance Tools & Technologies focuses on the various tools and technologies that assist organizations in managing governance, risk, and compliance (GRC) within cloud environments. This section is essential because it addresses the complexities of ensuring that cloud services operate within the bounds of regulatory requirements and organizational policies. Here's a detailed exploration of what this section may cover:

1. Overview of GRC in Cloud Computing:

- **Governance**: Refers to the frameworks, policies, and processes that ensure an organization's strategies align with its objectives, particularly regarding cloud usage.
- **Risk Management**: Involves identifying, assessing, and prioritizing risks associated with cloud computing, including security, compliance, and operational risks.
- **Compliance**: Encompasses adhering to laws, regulations, and internal policies relevant to the organization's cloud operations.

2. Importance of GRC Tools and Technologies:

- **Streamlined Processes**: GRC tools help automate and streamline processes associated with risk assessments, audits, compliance checks, and governance, leading to increased efficiency.
- **Improved Visibility**: These tools provide dashboards and reporting capabilities that enhance the visibility of compliance status and risk posture across cloud environments.
- **Facilitating Decision Making**: By analyzing risk data, governance tools assist executives in making informed decisions regarding cloud strategy and risk appetite.

3. Types of GRC Tools:

- **Governance Tools**: These tools may include policy management software, which aids organizations in defining, communicating, and enforcing governance policies.
- **Risk Management Tools**: Such tools help in conducting risk assessments, managing risk registers, and performing risk analysis, often integrating with other security tools.
- **Compliance Management Tools**: These include tools designed to monitor compliance with

specific regulations, generate compliance reports, and track remediation efforts.

- **Integrated GRC Platforms**: Comprehensive tools that provide a unified interface for managing governance, risk, and compliance processes in an integrated manner, promoting collaboration across departments.

4. Key Features of GRC Tools:

- **Automated Workflows**: Creation of automated workflows for risk assessments, compliance checks, and incident management to improve response times and reduce human error.
- **Document Management**: Features for storing and managing compliance artifacts, with version control and auditing capabilities to track changes over time.
- **Reporting and Analytics**: Tools provide real-time analytics and reporting functionalities to track compliance status and risk exposure, enabling proactive decision-making.
- **Continuous Monitoring**: Some GRC solutions offer continuous monitoring capabilities to detect compliance violations or risks as they develop in real-time.

5. Integration with Cloud Providers:

- Discussion on how these GRC tools can be integrated with cloud service providers to leverage APIs and data sharing for automated compliance checks and risk assessments.
- Understanding how cloud provider-specific tools (e.g., AWS Config, Azure Policy) can be used alongside enterprise GRC tools for comprehensive management.

6. Challenges in Implementing GRC Tools:

- **Complexity**: Navigating different compliance requirements across jurisdictions and industries can be challenging.
- **Integration Difficulties**: Integrating GRC tools with existing security and IT processes may require substantial effort and resources.
- **Data Privacy and Security**: Managing sensitive data within GRC tools, especially in cloud environments, raises security and privacy concerns.

7. Best Practices for Utilizing GRC Tools:

- **Define Clear Objectives**: Organizations should clearly outline their goals and objectives for using GRC tools to align them with business strategies.
- **Regular Training**: Continuous training for personnel involved in compliance and risk management is essential to ensure effective tool utilization.
- **Continuous Improvement**: Organizations should regularly assess the effectiveness of their GRC tools and processes to adapt to changing regulations and risks.

In summary, Section 3.3 provides a comprehensive view of the tools and technologies available to manage governance, risk, and compliance within cloud environments, emphasizing their importance in creating a robust security posture and facilitating compliance efforts.

Chapter Seven

Domain 4: Organization Management

Introduction

Domain 4 of the CCSK curriculum highlights managing and securing an organization's cloud environment, focusing on organizational structures, tenancy models, and enterprise management. As cloud adoption grows, effective governance becomes essential for maintaining security and compliance.

Learning Objectives

This domain covers organization hierarchy models, secure identity and access controls, and managing hybrid or multi-cloud deployments. It emphasizes best practices for navigating shared environments to protect data and applications throughout their lifecycle.

4.1 Organization Hierarchy Models

4.1.1 Definitions

Definitions refer to the foundational terminology and concepts used in managing organizations within cloud environments.

This section is essential as it lays the groundwork for understanding how to effectively organize and manage cloud resources, roles, and security policies. It may include definitions of key terms related to organizational structure in the cloud, such as:

1. **Organization Hierarchy**: This refers to how organizations are structured within the cloud service provider. It typically details how different departments or units are organized and how they relate.

2. **Cloud Service Provider (CSP)**: The definitions might encompass what constitutes a CSP, including their roles, services offered, and responsibilities.

3. **Tenancy**: This could refer to how resources are allocated and shared among different users or groups within the cloud environment.

4. **Role-based Access Control (RBAC)**: Terms like this may be defined to explain how permissions and access are managed within cloud services based on user roles.

5. **Identity and Access Management (IAM)**: IAM definitions will clarify how identities are authenticated and authorized to access various resources in the cloud.

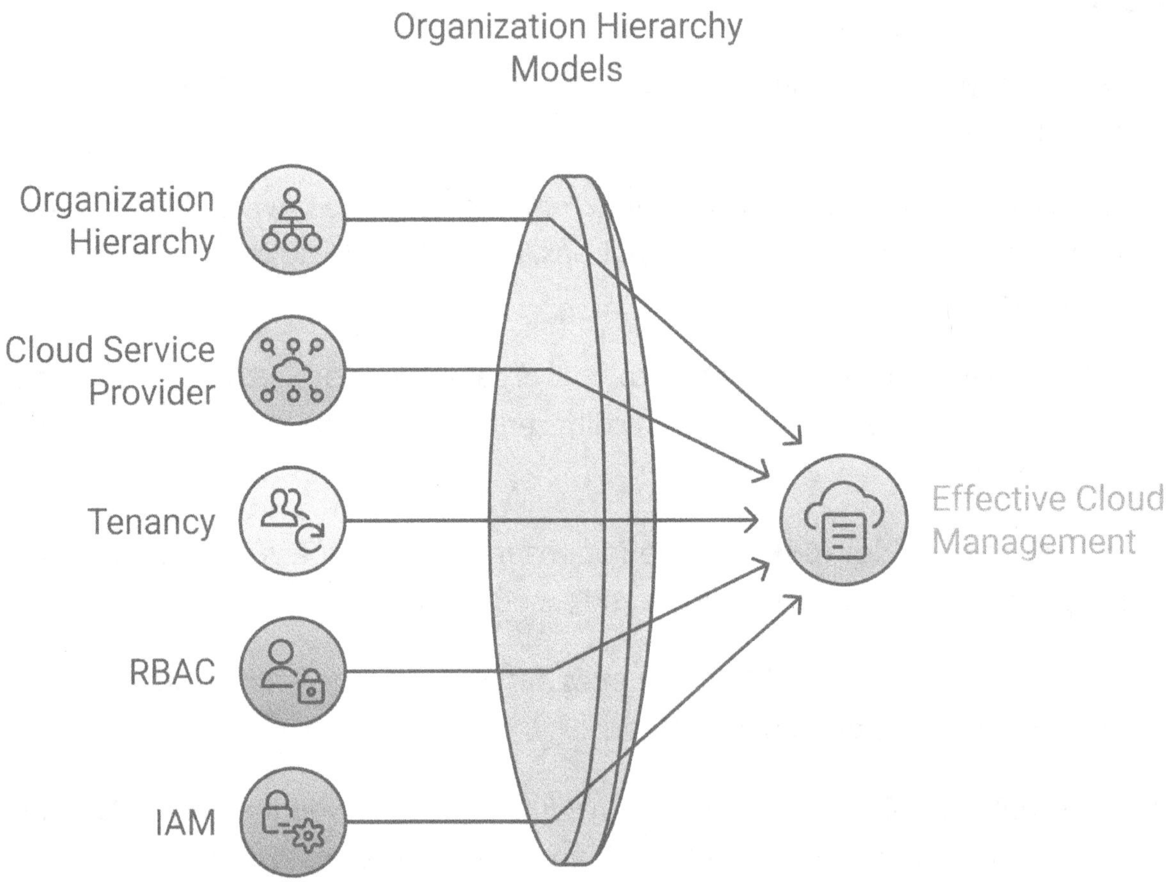

By understanding these definitions, stakeholders within an organization—such as IT teams and security professionals—can better implement and manage cloud resources, ensuring compliance with security standards and effective utilization of the cloud infrastructure.

4.1.2 Organization Capabilities Within a Cloud Service Provider

Organization Capabilities Within a Cloud Service Provider focuses on the functionalities and capabilities an organization can leverage when utilizing services offered by a Cloud Service Provider (CSP). Understanding these capabilities is crucial for effectively managing resources, ensuring security, and aligning technical operations with business strategies.

Key Capabilities Provided by CSPs

1. **Resource Management**:
    - **Provisioning and Deprovisioning**: Organizations can quickly provision new

resources—like virtual machines, databases, or storage—on demand and de-provision them when no longer needed, optimizing cost-efficiency.

- **Scaling**: CSPs offer vertical and horizontal scaling capabilities, allowing organizations to adapt resource allocation based on current demands without significant downtime.

2. **Identity and Access Management (IAM)**:
    - **User Management**: CSPs provide tools for managing user accounts, ensuring only authorized individuals can access resources.
    - **Role-Based Access Control (RBAC)**: Organizations can define roles and permissions within the CSP environment, ensuring that users only have access to the information and resources necessary for their roles.
3. **Security and Compliance**:
    - **Built-in Security Features**: Cloud providers invest in advanced security measures, including encryption, threat detection, and compliance certification, which organizations can leverage to enhance their own security posture.
    - **Compliance Tools**: Many CSPs offer tools that help organizations comply with relevant laws and regulations, simplifying the compliance process.
4. **Monitoring and Analytics**:
    - **Resource Monitoring**: CSPs provide monitoring capabilities that allow organizations to track resource usage, performance metrics, and security events.
    - **Analytics and Reporting**: Through dashboards and reports, organizations can gain insights into their cloud usage patterns, which can help them make capacity planning and optimization decisions.
5. **Disaster Recovery and Backup Solutions**:
    - **Backup Services**: CSPs typically offer automated backup solutions to protect data against loss.
    - **Disaster Recovery Plans**: Managed disaster recovery services enable organizations to quickly recover following an outage, minimizing downtime and data loss.
6. **Networking Services**:

- **Virtual Networking**: CSPs provide virtual networks that organizations can configure to connect their various resources securely.
- **Content Delivery**: Many CSPs offer Content Delivery Network (CDN) capabilities to enhance performance for localized content delivery.

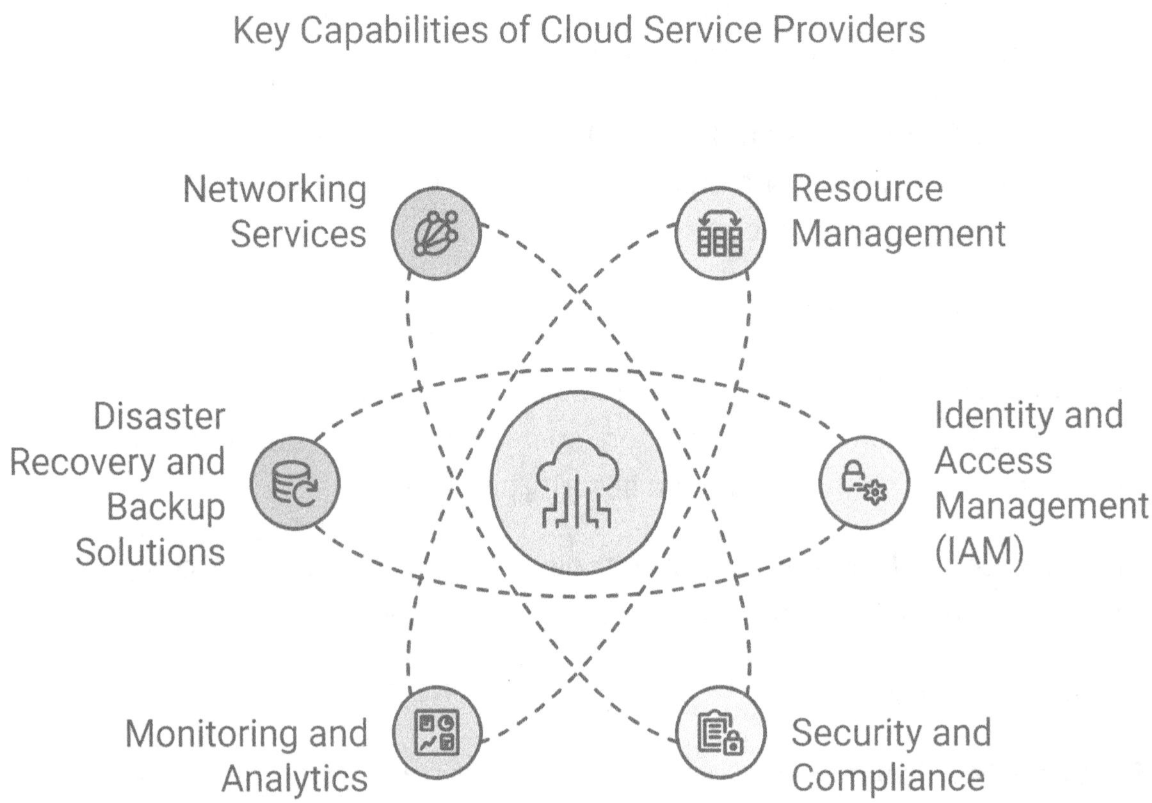

Strategic Considerations

Flexibility and Agility:

Organizations benefit from the flexibility to quickly adapt their IT resources to changing business needs. This can lead to faster innovation and the ability to respond promptly to market demands.

Cost Management: Understanding CSPs' billing models and cost structures helps organizations manage their cloud spending effectively by preventing resource sprawl and ensuring budget adherence.

Multi-Cloud and Hybrid Capabilities: Addresses how organizations can utilize capabilities across multiple cloud providers (multi-cloud) or integrate on-premises resources with cloud services (hybrid cloud).

Mastering the organization's capabilities within a cloud service provider empowers businesses to leverage the full potential of cloud technology. Organizations can align their cloud strategy with their operational and security goals, leading to enhanced efficiency, improved performance, and a robust security posture. This understanding is foundational for establishing effective cloud governance and risk management strategies.

4.1.3 Building a Hierarchy Within a Provider

Section 4.1.3, titled "Building a Hierarchy Within a Provider," in Domain 4 of the CCSK curriculum, focuses on the structured management of resources and roles within a cloud service provider (CSP) environment. Establishing a clear hierarchy is crucial for organizations to manage their cloud resources effectively, ensure security, and promote operational efficiency. Here's a comprehensive breakdown of this section:

Understanding Hierarchy in the Cloud

1. **Definition of Hierarchy**:
    - A hierarchy within a cloud service provider refers to the organized structure that categorizes resources, roles, and permissions. It sets the framework for managing access and delineating responsibilities among various components and users within a cloud environment.
2. **Importance of Hierarchy**:
    - Establishing a hierarchy helps implement controls and governance practices, enabling organizations to manage data security, compliance, and organizational policies effectively. A well-defined hierarchy also simplifies resource management and ensures that appropriate permissions are granted to users or systems.

Components of Building a Hierarchy

1. **Organizational Units**:

- **Departments or Teams**: Organizations can create units that mirror their internal structure (e.g., finance, HR, development). These units help segment resources and apply specific policies and access controls.
- **Business Units**: In larger organizations, separate business units can be created within the cloud, allowing for distinct governance and resource management tailored to each unit's needs.

2. **Resource Grouping**:
   - **Tags and Naming Conventions**: Implementing naming conventions and tagging strategies allows organizations to logically group cloud resources for easier identification and management.
   - **Resource Groups**: CSPs allow the formation of resource groups to bundle related resources (like virtual machines, databases, and networking components), which can be managed collectively.
3. **Role Definition and Management**:
   - **User Roles**: Identifying and defining roles within the organization—such as administrators, developers, users, and auditors—enables precise access rights assignment.
   - **Role-Based Access Control (RBAC)**: Utilizing RBAC ensures users are granted permissions based on their roles within the hierarchy, helping to mitigate security risks and facilitating compliance requirements.
4. **Policy Application**:
   - **Policy Inheritance**: Hierarchies allow policies to be inherited from higher-level organizational units. For instance, security policies set at the department level can cascade down to the department's resources and users.
   - **Custom Policies**: Specific policies can also be applied to individual resources or groups, allowing for customization in governance while maintaining overarching organizational standards.

Implementation Strategies

1. **Mapping Organizational Structure to Cloud Infrastructure**:
    - It is vital for organizations first to map their internal structures to the CSP's capabilities. This often involves aligning business processes with available cloud services while being mindful of security, compliance, and operational efficiencies.
2. **Automation Tools**:
    - Many CSPs provide automation tools and management interfaces that facilitate hierarchy implementation. This can simplify setting up user permissions, managing resources, and applying policies.
3. **Consistent Review and Adjustment**:
    - Regularly auditing the hierarchy and access controls is essential to ensure they align with organizational needs, industry standards, and compliance regulations. This may involve adjusting permissions or re-evaluating the structure in response to changes within the organization or the cloud services used.
4. **Training and Awareness**:
    - Providing staff with training on the CSP's structure and processes helps ensure that users understand their roles and responsibilities, enhancing governance and compliance.

Building a hierarchy within a cloud service provider is fundamental in ensuring organized management of resources, roles, and policies, enhancing operational efficiency and security. By strategically establishing organizational units, defining roles, and implementing consistent policies, organizations can effectively govern their cloud environments, reduce risks, and achieve business objectives with clarity and purpose.

4.2 Managing Organization-Level Security Within a Provider

4.2.1 Identity Provider & User/Group/Role Mappings

This section focuses on managing identities within cloud environments, emphasizing the significance of identity providers (IdPs) and the relationships between users, groups, and roles. This section is critical for implementing strong identity and access management (IAM) practices, which are essential for securing cloud resources and ensuring compliance with governance frameworks. Here's an in-depth explanation:

Identity Providers (IdPs)

1. **Definition**:
    - An Identity Provider (IdP) is a system or service that manages user identities and provides authentication services. IdPs create, maintain, and manage identity information while offering user authentication and authorization services.
2. **Role of IdPs**:
    - **Authentication**: IdPs verify an individual's identity by requiring credentials (like usernames and passwords) and can implement multi-factor authentication (MFA) to enhance security.
    - **Single Sign-On (SSO)**: Many IdPs support SSO, allowing users to access multiple applications or services with one set of credentials, streamlining the user experience.
    - **User Management**: IdPs enable administrators to create, modify, and delete user accounts, manage passwords, and update profile information centrally.
3. **Examples of IdPs**: Common Identity Providers include Microsoft Active Directory, Google Identity, Okta, and AWS IAM. Each serves as a central authority for managing user identities and access within its respective ecosystems.

User/Group/Role Mappings

1. **User Mappings**:
    - **Individual Users**: In cloud environments, each user should have a unique identity

authenticated through the IDP. User mappings refer to how these identities are connected to cloud resources and services.

- **Attributes**: Users often have attributes (like email, department, and job title) associated with their identities, which can be leveraged for role assignments and access control.

2. **Group Management**:

   - **Definition of Groups**: Groups are collections of users that can be managed collectively, simplifying administration. For instance, a group can be created for all IT department employees.
   - **Group Assignments**: Permissions can be assigned to groups rather than individuals. This allows an administrator to grant access to cloud resources to all group members without needing to set permissions for each user individually.

3. **Role-Based Access Control (RBAC)**:

   - **Roles Definition**: Roles are specific permissions assigned to users or groups, encapsulating what actions users with that role can perform on designated resources.
   - **Role Mappings** entail linking roles to users and groups through the IdP. For instance, an "Administrator" role may have full access to various resources, while a "Viewer" role might only have read access.
   - **Granularity**: RBAC allows organizations to enforce the principle of least privilege by granting users only those permissions necessary to perform their job functions.

Implementation Considerations

1. **Mapping Strategy**:

   - Organizations should develop a mapping strategy that aligns user roles and permissions with business functions and security requirements. This may involve categorizing users based on their roles in the organization and mapping those groups to appropriate access levels in the cloud.

2. **Automation Tools**:

   - Many cloud providers offer tools to automate the process of provisioning and deprovisioning users, managing groups, and assigning roles, making identity management more efficient.

3. **Regular Audits**:
    - Regular audits of user, group, and role mappings are crucial for maintaining an organization's security posture. This involves reviewing who has access to what resources and ensuring that roles and permissions are still relevant and necessary.
4. **Compliance and Security Policies**:
    - Organizations must ensure their identity provider and mapping practices align with compliance requirements and security policies. This may include guidelines for password complexity, MFA requirements, and guidelines surrounding sharing access rights among users.

Identity Provider and User/Group/Role Mappings are foundational components of an effective identity and access management strategy in cloud environments. By establishing a clear structure for identities, leveraging identity providers for authentication, and implementing role-based access control, organizations can ensure that they securely manage access to their resources. This helps mitigate unauthorized access risks while supporting compliance with various regulations and policies.

4.2.2 Common Organization Shared Services

This addresses the fundamental services that organizations utilize to manage their cloud environments effectively and securely. Shared services are crucial in enhancing efficiency, maintaining security, and ensuring consistency across various organizational departments and teams. Below is a detailed explanation of this section.

Definition of Common Organization Shared Services

Common Organization Shared Services refer to centralized services that all teams or departments can leverage. These services aim to streamline IT operations, foster collaboration, and enforce security policies across the cloud ecosystem. By centralizing these services, organizations can improve resource utilization, reduce redundancy, and ensure consistent implementation of policies and procedures.

Key Components of Common Organization Shared Services

1. **Identity and Access Management (IAM)**:
    - **Overview**: IAM is a foundational service that oversees user identities, authentication, and access control across cloud resources.
    - **Functionality**: IAM entails managing user roles, permissions, and policy enforcement to ensure that only authorized individuals access specific resources and data. To enhance security, IAM tools often support Single Sign-On (SSO) and multi-factor authentication (MFA).
    - **Benefits**: Centralized IAM reduces administrative overhead, provides better visibility into user activities, and enhances the organization's security posture.
2. **Virtual Private Network (VPN) Services**:
    - **Overview**: VPN services allow secure remote access to an organization's cloud resources by establishing encrypted connections over the Internet.
    - **Functionality**: Users can connect to the organization's network on-site, enabling secure access to applications and data while ensuring data integrity and confidentiality.
    - **Benefits**: Centralized VPN services help protect sensitive information while allowing flexibility and mobility for users accessing resources remotely.
3. **Resource Management and Orchestration**:
    - **Overview**: This encompasses tools and platforms that enable efficient deployment, management, and scaling of cloud resources. These can include services for managing compute instances, databases, and storage solutions.
    - **Functionality**: Orchestration services automate the provisioning and management of cloud services, improving operational efficiency and enabling infrastructure as code (IaC) practices.
    - **Benefits**: By centralizing resource management, organizations can reduce the likelihood of misconfigurations and optimize resource utilization.
4. **Monitoring and Logging Services**:

- **Overview**: Shared monitoring and logging services provide visibility into the health and status of cloud infrastructure and applications.
- **Functionality**: These services collect and analyze logs, metrics, and events to identify performance issues, detect security incidents, and facilitate troubleshooting.
- **Benefits**: A centralized approach to monitoring ensures that all teams have access to consistent data, supporting proactive management and timely incident response.

5. **Data Loss Prevention (DLP)**:
   - **Overview**: DLP services help organizations protect sensitive data from unauthorized access and breaches, ensuring regulatory compliance.
   - **Functionality**: DLP tools monitor and control data movement across the cloud environment, identifying potential risks and enforcing policies to prevent data leaks.
   - **Benefits**: Central DLP solutions streamline the administration of data protection policies across different departments, boosting the organization's overall security.
6. **Backup and Disaster Recovery Services**:
   - **Overview**: These services are critical for ensuring the availability and integrity of organizational data in the event of data loss or disasters.
   - **Functionality**: Centralized backup solutions automate data backup processes and facilitate disaster recovery planning to ensure quick service restoration.
   - **Benefits**: Organizations can improve data resilience and ensure business continuity by implementing these shared services.

Implementation Considerations

Shared Responsibility: Organizations must clearly delineate responsibilities between the cloud service provider (CSP) and the organization itself. This includes understanding what services are managed by the CSP and what the organization's responsibility is.

Standardization: To maximize the efficiency of shared services, organizations should aim to standardize processes and policies across departments. This reduces complexity and ensures that all teams follow consistent procedures for accessing and managing cloud resources.

Cost Management: Centralized shared services should be monitored for usage and cost-effectiveness. Organizations can implement tools for tracking resource consumption to control costs and identify areas for optimization.

Security Policies: It is crucial to establish robust security policies that apply across all shared services. These policies include access control measures, data protection guidelines, and compliance with relevant regulations.

Training and Support: Providing employees with training and resources on how to utilize shared services effectively promotes adoption and maximizes the benefits of these centralized functions.

Common Organization Shared Services are integral to managing an efficient, secure, and compliant cloud environment. By centralizing services such as IAM, VPN, resource management, monitoring, DLP, and disaster recovery, organizations can enhance operational efficiencies, maintain security integrity, and foster collaboration across departments. Implementing these shared services requires careful planning, standardization, and adherence to best practices to unlock their full potential in the cloud.

4.3 Considerations for Hybrid & Multi-Cloud Deployments

4.3.1 Organization Management for Hybrid Cloud Security

This section focuses on the strategies and practices for managing security within a hybrid cloud environment. A hybrid cloud seamlessly integrates on-premises infrastructure with public and private cloud services, offering organizations flexibility and scalability but introducing unique security challenges. Below is a comprehensive explanation of this section.

Understanding Hybrid Cloud Security

Hybrid Cloud Overview: A hybrid cloud combines private cloud (used by a single organization) and public cloud services (offered by third-party providers) to create a unified infrastructure. This model allows organizations to maintain sensitive workloads on-premises while utilizing the public cloud for less-sensitive operations, temporary workloads, or to scale resources.

Key Security Challenges in Hybrid Clouds

Data Security: Data distribution across multiple environments raises data confidentiality, integrity, and availability concerns. Organizations must ensure that data is encrypted both at rest and in transit.

Access Management: Managing user identities and access controls across disparate environments can complicate security. Inconsistent access policies may lead to unauthorized access or data breaches.

Compliance and Regulatory Requirements: Ensuring compliance with regional and industry-specific regulations (such as GDPR or HIPAA) can become complex when data is spread across multiple locations, both on-premises and in the cloud.

Visibility and Monitoring: Organizations often struggle with visibility issues across hybrid environments, making it difficult to monitor security incidents or manage logs effectively.

Network Security: Establishing secure connections between on-premises and cloud environments is crucial to prevent data interception or unauthorized access.

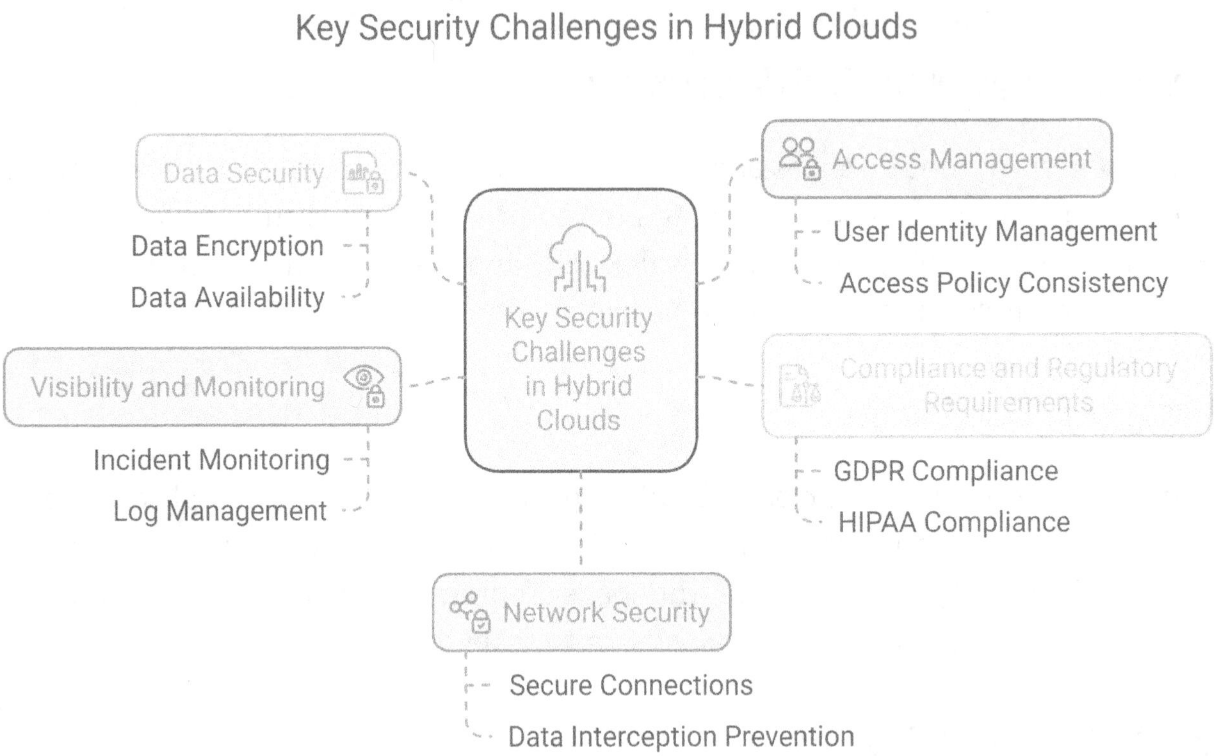

Organization Management Strategies for Hybrid Cloud Security

1. **Unified Security Policy Framework**:
    - **Overview**: Develop a comprehensive security policy that applies uniformly across both on-premises and cloud resources. This framework should define security standards, protocols, and compliance requirements.
    - **Importance**: A unified policy ensures consistency in security practices, reduces vulnerabilities, and provides clear user guidance.
2. **Identity and Access Management (IAM)**:
    - **IAM role**: Implement a centralized IAM system that manages access controls and user roles across the hybrid environment. Solutions should support Single Sign-On (SSO) and enforce multi-factor authentication (MFA).
    - **Implementation**: Use role-based access controls (RBAC) to ensure users have the minimum necessary permissions to perform their duties and mitigate the risk of

unauthorized access.

3. **Encryption and Data Protection**:
   - **Data Encryption**: Ensure that all sensitive data is encrypted in transit and at rest, regardless of where it is stored. This includes utilizing securely managed encryption keys.
   - **Backup and Recovery**: Establish robust data backup and disaster recovery protocols encompassing the hybrid environment to ensure data can be restored promptly and securely in the event of loss.
4. **Network Security Controls**:
   - **Secure Connectivity**: Use Virtual Private Networks (VPNs) or private connections (e.g., AWS Direct Connect or Azure ExpressRoute) to establish secure communication channels between on-premises and cloud resources.
   - **Firewall and Security Groups**: Implement firewalls and security groups to control traffic flow and prevent unauthorized access between different environments.
5. **Continuous Monitoring and Threat Detection**:
   - **Centralized Monitoring Tools**: Utilize security information and event management (SIEM) tools that provide visibility across both on-premises and cloud environments, enabling real-time threat detection and incident response.
   - **Logging and Auditing**: Maintain comprehensive logging and auditing processes to track user activities and changes across the hybrid environment. This can facilitate forensic analysis in the event of a security incident.
6. **Compliance and Risk Management**:
   - **Regular Audits**: Conduct security audits and assessments to ensure compliance with legal and regulatory requirements. This includes reviewing access logs and security configurations.
   - **Risk Management Framework**: Implement a risk management framework to identify, assess, and mitigate security risks associated with the hybrid cloud architecture.
7. **Training and Awareness Programs**:
   - **User Education**: To foster a security-aware culture, provide employees with training on

cloud security best practices, potential threats, and organizational policies.

- **Incident Response Training**: Prepare teams for incident response through simulations and training that enable them to handle security incidents effectively.

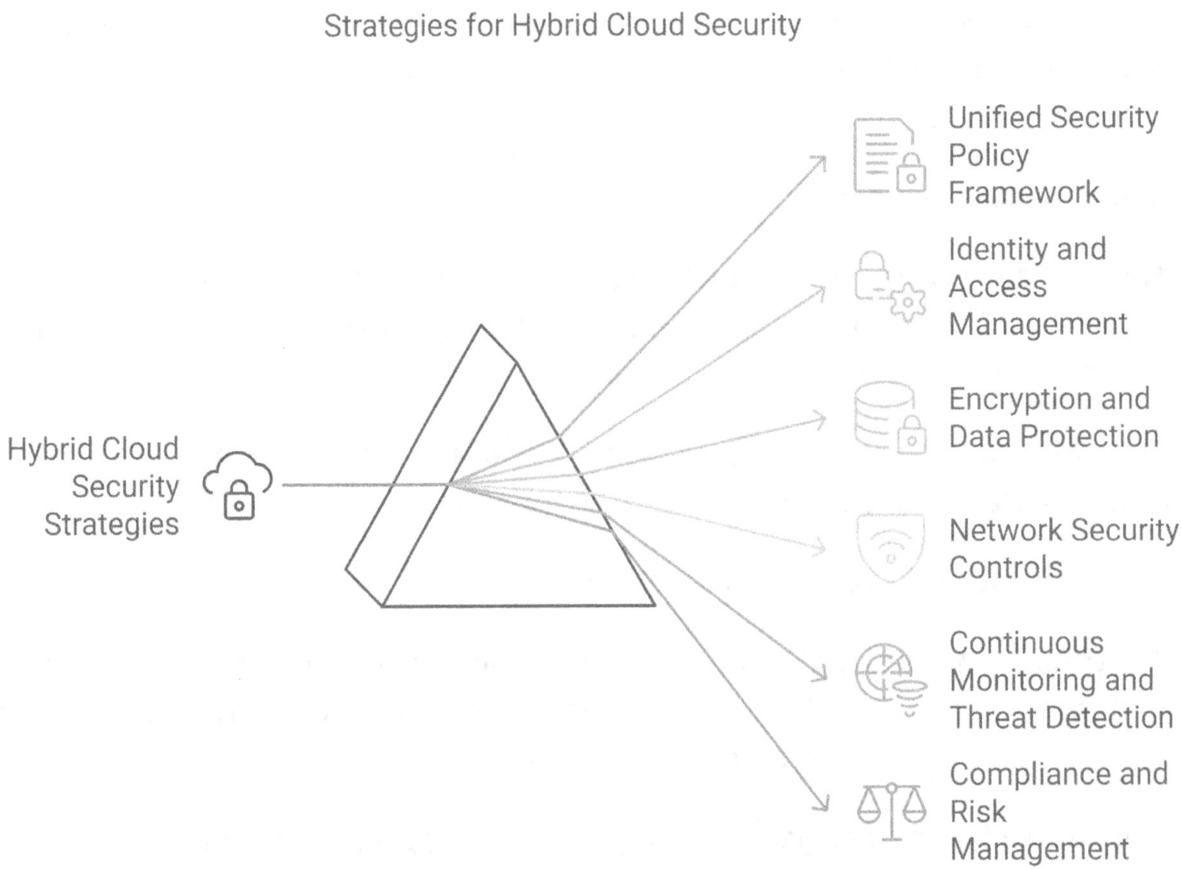

Managing security in a hybrid cloud environment requires a thoughtful approach that combines robust policies, advanced technologies, and continuous monitoring. Organizations can effectively mitigate risks associated with hybrid cloud deployments by implementing a unified security framework, enhancing data protection measures, establishing secure network connections, and fostering a culture of security awareness. These practices protect sensitive data, ensure regulatory compliance, and bolster overall organizational resilience in the face of evolving cyber threats.

4.3.2 Organization Management for Multi-Cloud Security

Organization Management for Multi-Cloud Security addresses the complexities and security challenges that arise when organizations utilize multiple cloud service providers (CSPs). A multi-cloud strategy offers businesses the flexibility to choose the best services and features from various providers, but it also creates unique security risks that must be managed effectively. Below is a detailed explanation of this section.

Understanding Multi-Cloud Security

Multi-Cloud Overview: Multi-cloud refers to using multiple cloud computing services in a single architecture. Typically, this involves integrating different public and private cloud services from various vendors, such as AWS, Microsoft Azure, and Google Cloud Platform. This approach can help avoid vendor lock-in, enhance performance, and optimize costs.

Key Security Challenges in Multi-Cloud Environments

1. **The complexity of Security Management**: Managing security policies across multiple cloud platforms can be cumbersome and often leads to inconsistencies in security practices and controls.

2. **Inconsistent Compliance**: Different CSPs may have varying compliance certifications and security features. Ensuring consistent compliance across these platforms can be challenging, leading to potential regulatory violations.

3. **Data Protection and Security**: Data is often distributed across various clouds, complicating data protection strategies. Ensuring data confidentiality, integrity, and availability becomes a multi-faceted challenge.

4. **Identity and Access Management (IAM)**: Managing user identities and access permissions in a multi-cloud environment can lead to security gaps if not properly coordinated, as each provider may have its own IAM policies and tools.

5. **Visibility and Monitoring**: Achieving holistic visibility across multiple cloud environments can be difficult, making detecting security incidents challenging and assessing the overall security posture challenging.

Organization Management Strategies for Multi-Cloud Security

1. **Centralized Security Policy Framework**:
    - **Overview**: Develop and implement a centralized security policy framework that consistently applies to all cloud environments. This framework should uniformly outline security standards, processes, and compliance requirements across all platforms.
    - **Importance**: A consistent policy framework helps reduce vulnerabilities and ensures all teams understand their security responsibilities.
2. **Unified Identity and Access Management (IAM)**:
    - **Role of IAM**: Establish a centralized IAM solution with a single control point for managing user identities and access across different CSPs. This could involve adopting identity federation and SSO capabilities.
    - **Implementation**: Implement role-based access controls (RBAC) to manage user permissions depending on their roles, ensuring users have the least privilege necessary to perform their tasks.
3. **Data Protection Strategies**:
    - **Data Encryption**: Utilize encryption for data at rest and in transit across all cloud environments. Implementing strong encryption methods helps safeguard sensitive data from unauthorized access.
    - **Data Governance**: Establish clear policies to classify, manage, and protect data appropriately across all platforms, considering where it resides and how it is accessed.
4. **Consistent Compliance Management**:
    - **Compliance Framework**: Create a compliance framework that ensures adherence to industry regulations and corporate policies across all cloud providers. This framework should include regular audits and assessments.
    - **Cross-Provider Compliance Tools**: Leverage tools that support compliance assessments across multiple environments and automate reporting to streamline the process.
5. **Integrated Security Monitoring and Response**:

- **Holistic Monitoring Solutions**: Deploy Security Information and Event Management (SIEM) solutions that aggregate logs and security events from all cloud environments, providing comprehensive visibility.
- **Incident Response Planning**: Develop coordinated incident response plans that address how to respond to security incidents across multiple cloud providers efficiently.

6. **Network Security Architectures**:
   - **Secure Communication Links**: To establish secure links between environments, use secure communication protocols such as VPN or private connection services for each CSP.
   - **Firewalls and Access Controls**: Implement unified firewalls and security group configurations that enforce consistent access policies across all connected clouds.
7. **Visibility and Threat Detection**:
   - **Centralized Monitoring Tools**: Utilize integrated security monitoring solutions that provide insights into the security posture of all cloud environments, allowing for real-time threat detection and response.
   - **Regular Security Audits**: Conduct periodic security audits and assessments to evaluate each cloud provider's security posture and ensure compliance with organizational policies.
8. **Training and Awareness Programs**:
   - **User and Administrator Training**: Provide ongoing training for users and administrators on cloud security best practices, including recognizing phishing attempts and adhering to security policies across different cloud platforms.
   - **Incident Response Drills**: Conduct drills to prepare teams for responding to multi-cloud security incidents and help them understand the specific protocols and tools involved.

Managing security in a multi-cloud environment requires an organized approach that involves cohesive policies, integrated IAM strategies, and robust data protection efforts. A centralized security policy framework, effective access management, and enhanced visibility and monitoring are crucial to mitigating risks and ensuring compliance across various cloud platforms. By implementing these strategies, organizations can effectively secure their multi-cloud environments, protect sensitive data, and maintain compliance with regulatory standards.

4.3.3 Organization Management for SaaS Hybrid & Multi-Cloud

Organization Management for SaaS Hybrid & Multi-Cloud focuses on the specific organizational and security management challenges that arise when integrating Software-as-a-Service (SaaS) applications within a hybrid and multi-cloud environment. This framework addresses the need for effective governance, risk management, and compliance while leveraging the benefits of SaaS solutions alongside various cloud infrastructures.

Understanding SaaS in Hybrid and Multi-Cloud Environments

SaaS Overview: SaaS refers to software solutions delivered over the internet on a subscription basis. Users can access these applications via a web browser without installing or maintaining them locally. Examples include customer relationship management (CRM) tools like Salesforce, email services like Google Workspace, and collaboration platforms like Microsoft Teams.

Hybrid and Multi-Cloud Strategies:

- **Hybrid Cloud**: This involves integrating on-premises infrastructure with public or private cloud environments. Organizations may choose this approach to maintain control over sensitive data while benefiting from the scalability of cloud solutions.
- **Multi-Cloud** refers to using multiple cloud service providers concurrently, allowing organizations to leverage various features and services from different providers.

Key Security and Management Challenges

1. **Integration of SaaS with Existing IT Infrastructure**: Ensuring seamless interoperability between SaaS applications and internal systems or other cloud services can be complex and require careful planning.
2. **Data Security and Compliance**: Managing data privacy and compliance becomes more challenging when sensitive information is distributed across SaaS applications and cloud environments. Organizations must ensure consistent data protection strategies are applied across all services.
3. **Identity and Access Management (IAM)**: Controlling who has access to SaaS applications and ensuring secure authentication mechanisms are critical to safeguarding against unauthorized access.
4. **Visibility and Monitoring Across Multiple Platforms**: Gaining holistic visibility into user activities, data flows, and security incidents across different cloud environments, including SaaS platforms, can be difficult.
5. **Cost Management**: Accumulating multiple SaaS subscriptions and cloud services can lead to unanticipated costs, necessitating effective tracking and optimization strategies.

Management Strategies for SaaS in Hybrid & Multi-Cloud

1. **Unified Governance Framework**:
    - **Overview**: Develop and implement a unified governance framework encompassing policies for managing SaaS applications alongside other cloud environments, ensuring consistency in security policies, compliance standards, and operational practices.
    - **Importance**: A cohesive framework helps organizations manage risks effectively, align security practices across platforms, and ensure accountability.
2. **Centralized Identity and Access Management**:
    - **Single Sign-On (SSO)**: Implement SSO mechanisms that allow users to access multiple SaaS applications and other cloud services with a single set of credentials. This reduces credential fatigue and enhances security.
    - **Role-Based Access Control (RBAC)**: Establish RBAC configurations for SaaS applications to ensure users have restricted access based on their organizational roles.
3. **Data Protection and Governance**:
    - **Data Encryption**: When sensitive data is stored in SaaS applications, encryption should be utilized both in transit and at rest to protect against unauthorized access and data breaches.
    - **Data Classification and Governance Policies**: Implement data classification protocols to identify sensitive information and establish governance policies for handling across all cloud environments.
4. **Compliance Management and Risk Assessment**:
    - **Regulatory Framework**: Create a comprehensive compliance framework that addresses specific regulatory requirements across various regions and cloud environments. Regularly update this framework to adapt to new regulations.
    - **Third-Party Risk Management**: To minimize risks, assess the compliance posture of SaaS providers, and establish security requirements for third-party services.
5. **Comprehensive Security Monitoring**:

- **Integrated Security Solutions**: Deploy tools that provide comprehensive visibility and monitoring capabilities across both SaaS applications and on-premises systems. This helps detect anomalous activities and potential security incidents effectively.

- **User Activity Monitoring**: Implement monitoring solutions to track user activity within SaaS applications. This will enable organizations to identify suspicious behavior and respond promptly.

6. **Cost Management Strategies**:

   - **Subscription Monitoring**: Develop practices for regularly reviewing SaaS subscriptions and usage to optimize costs and ensure that only necessary services are used.

   - **Resource Allocation and Budgeting**: Create budgetary processes to allocate resources effectively while considering the costs associated with SaaS solutions and various cloud services.

7. **Incident Response and Management**:

   - **Comprehensive Incident Response Plan**: Establish an incident response plan tailored to address potential security incidents in SaaS applications and across cloud environments, including defined roles and responsibilities.

   - **Regular Drills and Training**: Conduct periodic drills to prepare teams for responding to security incidents involving SaaS applications, ensuring they are familiar with the protocols and tools utilized.

8. **User Education and Training**:

   - **Security Awareness Programs**: Implement ongoing training programs to educate users about the risks associated with SaaS applications and best practices for maintaining security.

   - **Guidelines for Secure Usage**: Provide clear guidelines on securely accessing and using SaaS applications, including awareness of phishing attempts and data handling procedures.

Effectively managing SaaS applications in a hybrid and multi-cloud context requires organizations to adopt a comprehensive approach that integrates governance, security, compliance, and cost management strategies. By implementing these practices, organizations can enhance their security posture, protect sensitive data, and derive maximum value from their SaaS investments while mitigating associated risks.

Chapter Eight

Domain 5: Identity and Access Management

Introduction

Identity & Access Management (IAM) is pivotal in securing interactions between organizations and cloud service providers. It involves managing identities, controlling Access, and implementing robust authentication and authorization protocols. Key aspects include the creation of identity federations, strong authentication methods, and comprehensive access management strategies.

Effective IAM ensures secure user identity handling across diverse cloud environments while addressing the complexities of cloud-based systems. By adopting best practices, organizations can enhance compliance, reduce risks tied to unauthorized Access, and streamline operations between their infrastructure and cloud services or even among multiple cloud providers.

Learning Objectives

The learning objectives of **Domain 5: Identity & Access Management (IAM)** are tailored to build expertise in this essential area of cloud security. Key goals include:

- Gaining a clear understanding of foundational IAM terms relevant to cloud environments.
- Exploring federation concepts and standards that support federated identity management.
- Mastering user and identity management processes specific to cloud computing.

Additionally, you will explore advanced topics such as strong authentication methods, effective authorization processes, entitlement management strategies, and privileged user management. By achieving these objectives, individuals will acquire the skills to manage identities confidently and enforce access controls within complex cloud systems.

By mastering these principles, professionals can ensure secure interactions within their organization's digital ecosystem while aligning with industry best practices for IAM in the cloud.

5.1 Fundamental Terms

This section covers essential vocabulary and concepts that form the backbone of IAM in cloud environments. It helps you familiarize yourself with key terms critical for understanding IAM practices.

- **Identity**: The representation of an individual or entity within a system—often linked to user accounts or devices.
- **Authentication**: Verifying a user's or entity's identity using credentials like passwords, tokens, or biometrics.
- **Authorization**: Granting or denying access rights based on established policies and user roles.
- **Access Control** is a Mechanism that restricts who can access or manipulate data or systems. Common models include Role-Based Access Control (RBAC), Attribute-Based Access Control (ABAC), and Discretionary Access Control (DAC).
- **Identity Providers (IdPs)**: Services responsible for creating, maintaining, and managing user identity information. These often facilitate authentication while supporting federated identity management.
- **Federation**: A framework enabling users to log in once and gain seamless Access across multiple systems or applications without repeated logins—based on trust relationships between IdPs.

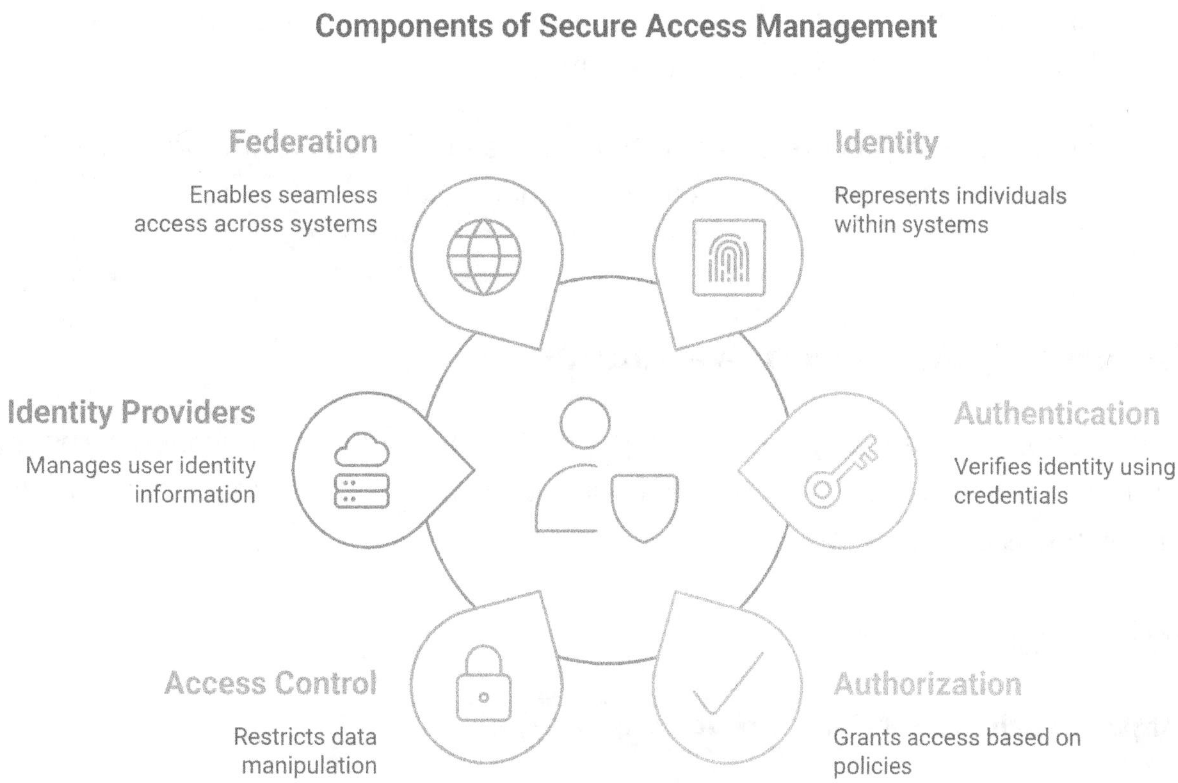

Understanding these fundamental terms is crucial for security professionals navigating the complexities of IAM within cloud infrastructures. These concepts provide the foundation for ensuring proper user identity governance and effectively enforcing robust access controls.

5.2 Federation

Federation in cloud systems is a framework that allows users to access multiple applications or systems with one set of login credentials. It eliminates the need for repeated logins by establishing trust between different Identity Providers (IdPs) and service providers.

For example, suppose your organization uses an external IDP like Google or Microsoft Azure AD. In that case, federation enables employees to use their company credentials to securely access third-party apps without creating separate accounts. This approach enhances user convenience while maintaining strong security controls.

Key benefits include:

- **Simplified Access:** Users log in once (Single Sign-On - SSO) and gain seamless Access across trusted platforms.

- **Improved Security:** Reduces password fatigue and minimizes risks tied to weak passwords.
- **Centralized Management:** Administrators can manage identities from one system instead of handling individual accounts on each platform.

In short, federation supports secure collaboration across diverse environments by leveraging shared identity management practices based on mutual trust.

5.2.1 Common Federation Standards

Common federation standards enable secure identity sharing and authentication across systems. These standards ensure compatibility between Identity Providers (IdPs) and service providers, supporting seamless user access.

Key Federation Standards:

1. **SAML (Security Assertion Markup Language):**
   - The XML-based protocol is used to exchange authentication and authorization data.
   - Commonly supports Single Sign-On (SSO) in enterprise environments.
2. **OAuth 2.0:**
   - Open standard for delegated AAccesswithout sharing passwords.
   - Often paired with APIs to grant limited permissions securely.
3. **OpenID Connect (OIDC):**
   - Built on top of OAuth 2.0, adding user authentication capabilities.
   - It provides a simple way to verify identities while enabling SSO.
4. **WS-Federation:**
   - Microsoft designed the protocol for federated trust relationships using web services.
   - Used primarily within Windows ecosystems like Active Directory Federation Services (ADFS).

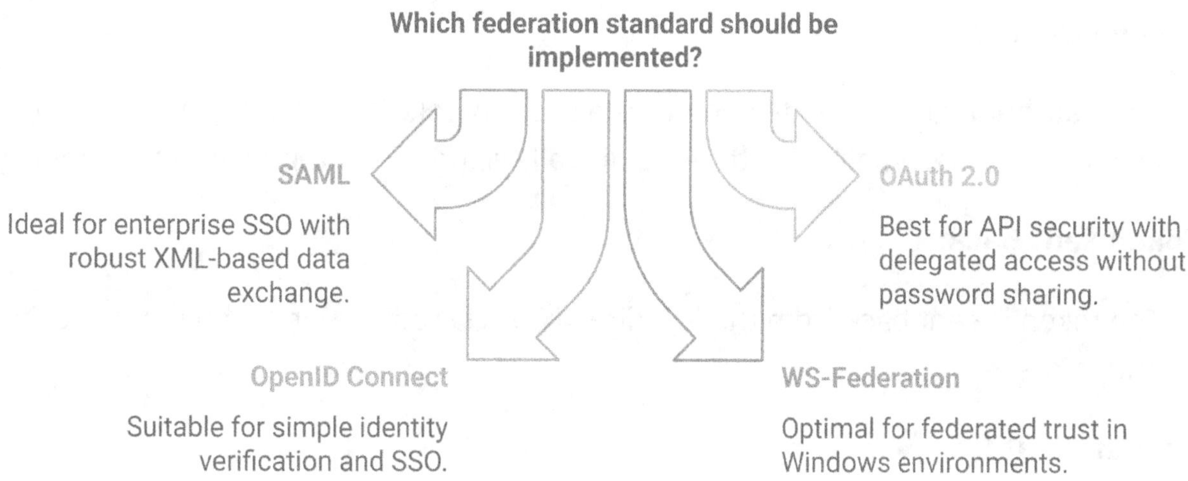

These standards allow organizations to implement secure, scalable identity management solutions tailored to their needs while enhancing interoperability among cloud platforms or applications, effectively managing user credentials across trusted domains globally!

5.2.2 How Federated Identity Management Works

Federated Identity Management (FIM) allows users to access multiple systems or applications using a single set of credentials. It establishes trust between an **Identity Provider (IdP)** and various **Service Providers (SPs)** through secure protocols.

Step-by-Step Process:

1. **User Requests Access:**
    - A user attempts to log in to an application or service hosted by the Service Provider.
2. **Redirect to IdP:**
    - The Service Provider redirects the user's authentication request to the trusted Identity Provider.
3. **Authentication at IdP:**
    - The Identity Provider verifies the user's Identity via username/password, multi-factor

authentication, or other methods.

4. **Token Issuance:**
   - Once authenticated, the IdP generates a security token containing information about the user (e.g., name, email). This token is digitally signed for integrity and authenticity.
5. **Token Sent Back:**
   - The token is sent back from the IDP directly or via redirection through SP-specific endpoints.
6. **Validation at SP:**
   - The Service Provider validates that:
     i. The token comes from a trusted source.
     ii. User details match its requirements for granting Access
7. **Access Granted:** After successful validation, the user gains seamless entry into requested services without creating separate login accounts.

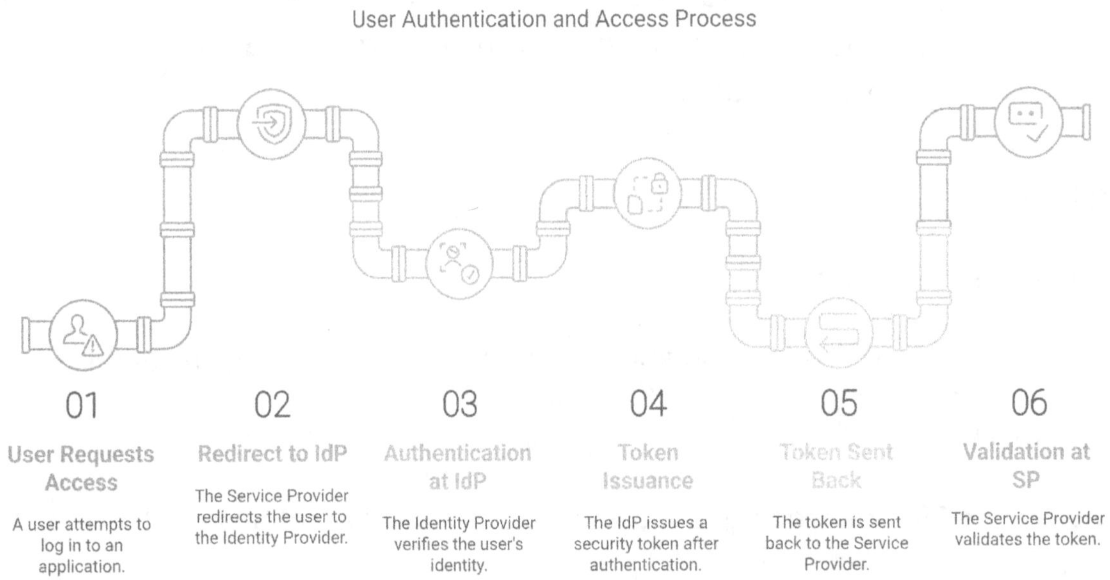

5.2.3 Managing Users & Identities for Cloud Computing

Cloud IAM, short for Identity and Access Management, is critical in overseeing user identities, defining roles, and managing permissions within a cloud infrastructure. In this framework, users must verify their Identity through various means, such as passwords, multi-factor authentication (MFA), or biometrics, before gaining Access. Once authenticated, users are granted authorization based on established roles and policies. The advantage of centralized IAM solutions lies in providing a unified platform for efficiently controlling access to diverse cloud services and resources. This centralized approach enhances security and simplifies Access management across multiple cloud platforms.

Cloud Identity and Access Management Policies

IAM policies play a crucial role in defining access rules for cloud resources. By following the principle of least privilege, these policies grant or restrict users' permissions based on their specific job requirements. IAM policies offer granular control over access privileges, whether assigned at the user, group, or resource level. It is essential to regularly review and update these policies to adapt to changing security landscapes and ensure that access rights remain aligned with evolving security requirements. By proactively managing IAM policies, organizations can enhance their overall security posture and mitigate potential risks associated with unauthorized access to sensitive data.

Cloud Identity and Access Management Technologies

Various technologies are leveraged to implement Identity and Access Management (IAM) in the cloud. Identity Providers (IdPs) are crucial in handling user authentication and ensuring secure AAccess Single Sign-On (SSO) solutions enhance the user experience by providing seamless access to multiple cloud services with just one set of credentials. Role-based access Control (RBAC) assigns permissions based on predefined roles, simplifying management and ensuring the least privileged access. Additionally, Attribute-Based Access Control (ABAC) dynamically adjusts AAccessbased on specific attributes for more granular control. Cloud Access Security Brokers (CASBs) further enhance security by monitoring and enforcing policies, offering visibility and control across cloud environments for robust protection against threats.

5.3 Strong Authentication & Authorization

Strong authentication and **authorization** are critical to securing access to systems, applications, and data. They ensure that only legitimate users gain entry and can perform the actions they're permitted to.

1. Authentication: Verifying Identity

Authentication confirms a user's identity before granting Access. "Strong" authentication uses multiple layers of security beyond just passwords.

Types of Strong Authentication:

- **Multi-Factor Authentication (MFA):** Combines two or more factors:
  - *Something you know* (password/PIN).
  - *Something you have* (smartphone/token).
  - *Something you are* (fingerprint/face recognition).
- **Biometric Verification:** Uses physical traits like fingerprints, retina scans, or voice for identification.
- **Passwordless Methods:** Relies on secure tokens sent via email/SMS or hardware keys instead of traditional passwords.

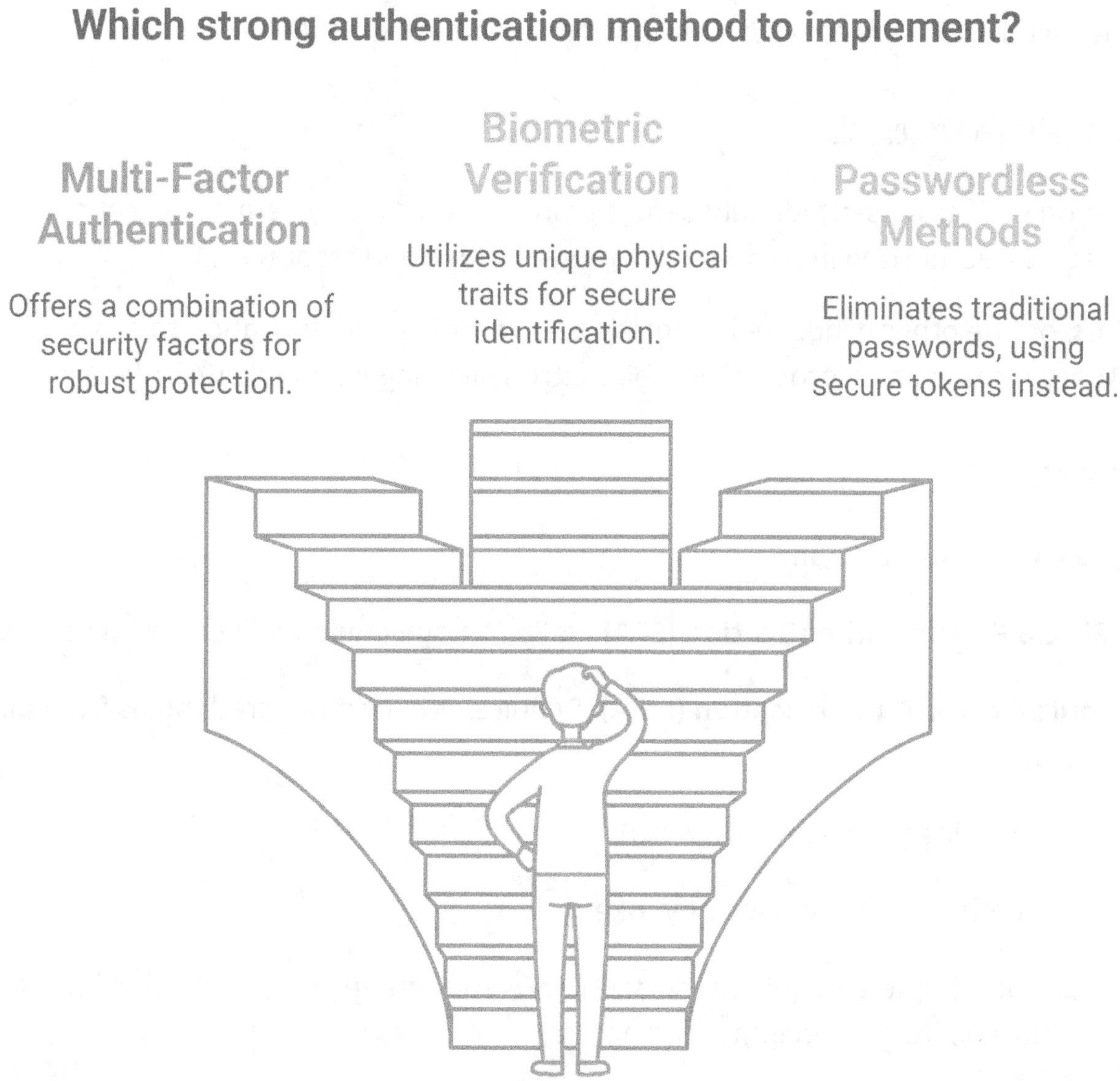

2. **Authorization:** Controlling access once authenticated, authorization determines what resources the user can access based on predefined permissions.

Key Principles in Authorization:

- **Role-Based Access Control (RBAC):** Assigns permissions based on organizational roles.

Example: An HR manager may view employee records; other staff cannot.

- **Least Privilege Principle:** Users receive the minimum needed for their tasks, reducing risk if accounts are compromised.

Examples of tools include OAuth 2.0 protocols that allow fine-grained permission delegation securely between apps/services without exposing credentials directly.

5.3.1 Authentication & Credentials

Authentication verifies a user's Identity before granting Access to systems, applications, or data. It ensures that only authorized individuals can interact with cloud resources.

Credentials, on the other hand, are information used during authentication to prove a user's Identity. These include passwords, tokens, biometrics (like fingerprints), or certificates.

Key Components:

1. **Types of Authentication:**
    - **Single-Factor Authentication (SFA):** Relies on one credential type like a password.
    - **Multi-Factor Authentication (MFA):** Requires two or more credentials from different categories:
        - Something you know (password).
        - Something you have (security token).
        - Something you are (biometric data). MFA strengthens security by making it harder for attackers to gain unauthorized access
2. **Common Credential Types:**
    - Passwords/PINs
    - Security Tokens/One-Time Passcodes
    - Biometric Data such as facial recognition and fingerprints
    - Digital Certificates issued by trusted authorities
3. **Secure Management Practices:** To protect credentials:
    - Use strong passwords—long combinations including letters/numbers/symbols.

- Enable MFA wherever possible to add protection against breaches.
- Avoid sharing/storing plain text versions; use encrypted vault solutions instead.

4. **Importance in Cloud Environments:** Without proper authentication mechanisms combined with secure handling practices around sensitive info (Credential misuse risks escalated, especially across distributed multi-user setups).

5.3.2 Entitlement & Access Management

Entitlement and access management control who can access specific resources in a system, what actions they are allowed to perform, and under what conditions. It ensures that users only have the permissions necessary for their roles, nothing more.

Key Concepts:

1. **Entitlements:**

These define
what
a user or group can do within an environment.

2. **Access Control Mechanisms:**

Two main models manage entitlements:

3. **Under the principle of Least Privilege (PoLP),** Users should receive the minimum Access required for their job functions—no unnecessary rights should be granted beyond what's essential.
4. **Identity Federation Integration:**
Centralized systems such as Identity Providers (IdPs)—like Azure AD or Okta—can streamline entitlement assignments across multiple cloud services through Single Sign-On (SSO).
5. **Regular Reviews & Audits:** Periodically reviewing all active entitlements helps identify outdated/unused privileges, significantly reducing insider threat risks.

5.3.3 Privileged User Management

Privileged User Management is crucial for securing accounts with elevated permissions in cloud environments. These privileged accounts - typically held by system administrators or database managers - require careful oversight due to their potential impact on organizational security.

Strategic Importance

Security Risk Management

- Privileged accounts are prime targets for cybercriminals
- The high level requires stringent monitoring and control
- Critical for preventing unauthorized system changes

Compliance and Governance

- Meets regulatory requirements (GDPR, HIPAA, etc.)
- Supports audit trail documentation
- Ensures accountability for privileged actions

Zero Trust Implementation

- Verifies all users, even those with elevated privileges
- Enforces continuous authentication
- Maintains least privilege principles

Core Components

1. Privileged Access Management (PAM)

PAM solutions provide comprehensive security controls:

- Secure password vaults

- Session monitoring and recording
- Time-based access controls
- Automated privilege elevation

Key Features:

- **PASM** (Privileged Account & Session Management)
  - Credential protection
  - Activity monitoring
  - Audit logging
- **PEDM** (Privilege Elevation & Delegation Management)
  - Just-in-time Access
  - Temporary privilege elevation
  - Role-based delegation

2. Least Privilege Implementation

Best practices include:

- Granting minimal necessary Access and

Regular access reviews

- Time-limited privileges
- Role-based access control

Example: Development teams receive temporary elevated access for debugging rather than permanent administrative privileges, reducing security risks while maintaining operational efficiency.

This approach ensures robust security while enabling necessary business functions through controlled, monitored privilege elevation.

Why Is It Important?

1. **High-Risk Targets:** Privileged accounts have extensive control over critical resources, making them prime targets for attackers.
2. **Minimizing Insider Threats:** Insiders could intentionally or unintentionally abuse their privileges without proper controls.
3. **Compliance Requirements:** Many regulatory frameworks (e.g., GDPR, HIPAA) require strict oversight of privileged user activities.
4. **Zero Trust Alignment:** Adopting Zero-Trust principles ensures no implicit trust exists—even for privileged users—and enforces rigorous verification before granting resource access.

Key Components

Privileged Access Management (PAM)

A cybersecurity strategy explicitly designed to secure the use of privileged credentials:

- Stores sensitive passwords securely in a vault.
- Monitors and records all actions taken during sessions by these users.
- Enforces policies such as time-limited privilege elevation through tools like PAM solutions (e.g., CyberArk or BeyondTrust).

Subcomponents:

a) *Privileged Account & Session Management* (**PASM**): This position manages account credentials and monitors/records session activity for accountability.
b) *Privilege Elevation & Delegation* (**PEDM**): This method temporarily elevates standard user rights only when needed instead of using permanent admin roles.

Principle Of Least Privilege (*PoLP*)

Ensures each individual has the minimum level necessary based solely upon job function requirements rather than broad unrestricted default entitlements granted unnecessarily otherwise.

Cloud Identity and Access Management Best Practices

Implementing IAM best practices is crucial for a secure cloud environment:

1. **MFA Implementation:** Enforcing multi-factor authentication enhances security.

2. **Regular User Access Reviews:** Periodic reviews of user access rights help identify and address unauthorized AAccess

3. **Principle of Least Privilege:** Grant users the minimum necessary access level to reduce the risk of privilege escalation.

4. **Monitoring and Logging:** Continuous monitoring of user activities and access attempts aids in timely detection and response to security incidents.

5. **Encryption:** Encrypting data at rest and in transit ensures sensitive information remains protected even in case of unauthorized access.

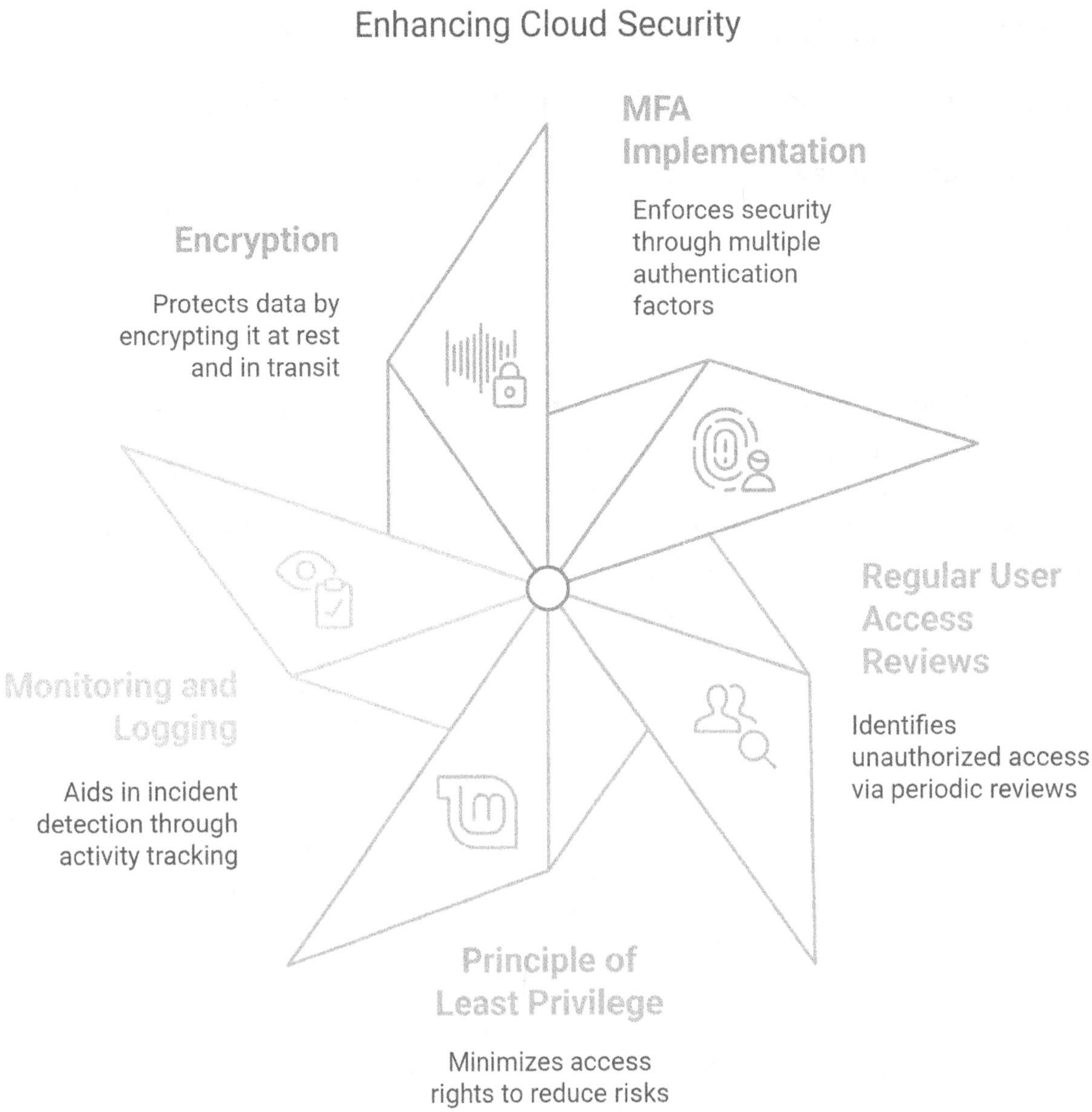

Enhancing Cloud Security
MFA Implementation
Enforces security through multiple authentication factors
Encryption
Protects data by encrypting it at rest and in transit
Regular User Access Reviews
Identifies unauthorized access via periodic reviews
Monitoring and Logging
Aids in incident detection through activity tracking
Principle of Least Privilege
Minimizes access rights to reduce risks

Chapter Nine

Domain 6: Security Monitoring

Introduction

Security Monitoring addresses the unique challenges of monitoring cloud environments effectively. As organizations increasingly migrate to the cloud, they face distinct security monitoring needs that differ from traditional infrastructures. This domain emphasizes the importance of cloud telemetry, which includes collecting and analyzing management plane logs, service logs, and resource logs. Additionally, it explores advanced monitoring tools that enhance visibility and security oversight. By understanding these unique aspects, security professionals can better implement strategies to detect, respond to, and mitigate potential threats within cloud environments, ensuring a robust security posture.

Learning Objectives

Security Monitoring is vital for protecting cloud environments and addressing challenges unique to cloud-based operations. It emphasizes mastering cloud telemetry and implementing effective monitoring strategies.

Key learning objectives include understanding core cloud monitoring concepts like log types and event tracking, leveraging diverse telemetry sources, and adopting beyond-log techniques for continuous security assessment. Professionals also focus on building efficient collection architectures and utilizing AI-powered tools to enhance threat detection and analytics.

These skills empower security professionals to detect, respond to, and mitigate threats effectively, ensuring a robust security posture in complex cloud ecosystems.

6.1 Cloud Monitoring

Cloud monitoring continuously observes and analyzes cloud environments to ensure security, performance, and reliability. It involves collecting data from various sources, such as management plane logs, service logs, and resource logs. This helps detect unusual activity, identify potential threats, and maintain system health. By using advanced tools such as AI-powered analytics or telemetry techniques beyond traditional logging methods, organizations can gain better visibility into their cloud systems for proactive threat detection and response.

By analyzing logs and events:

1. **Detect Threats**: Spot unusual patterns signaling potential attacks.
2. **Investigate Issues**: Trace the root cause of problems quickly.
3. **Ensure Compliance**: Prove adherence to regulatory requirements through audit trails.
4. **Monitor Performance**: Identify bottlenecks affecting system efficiency.

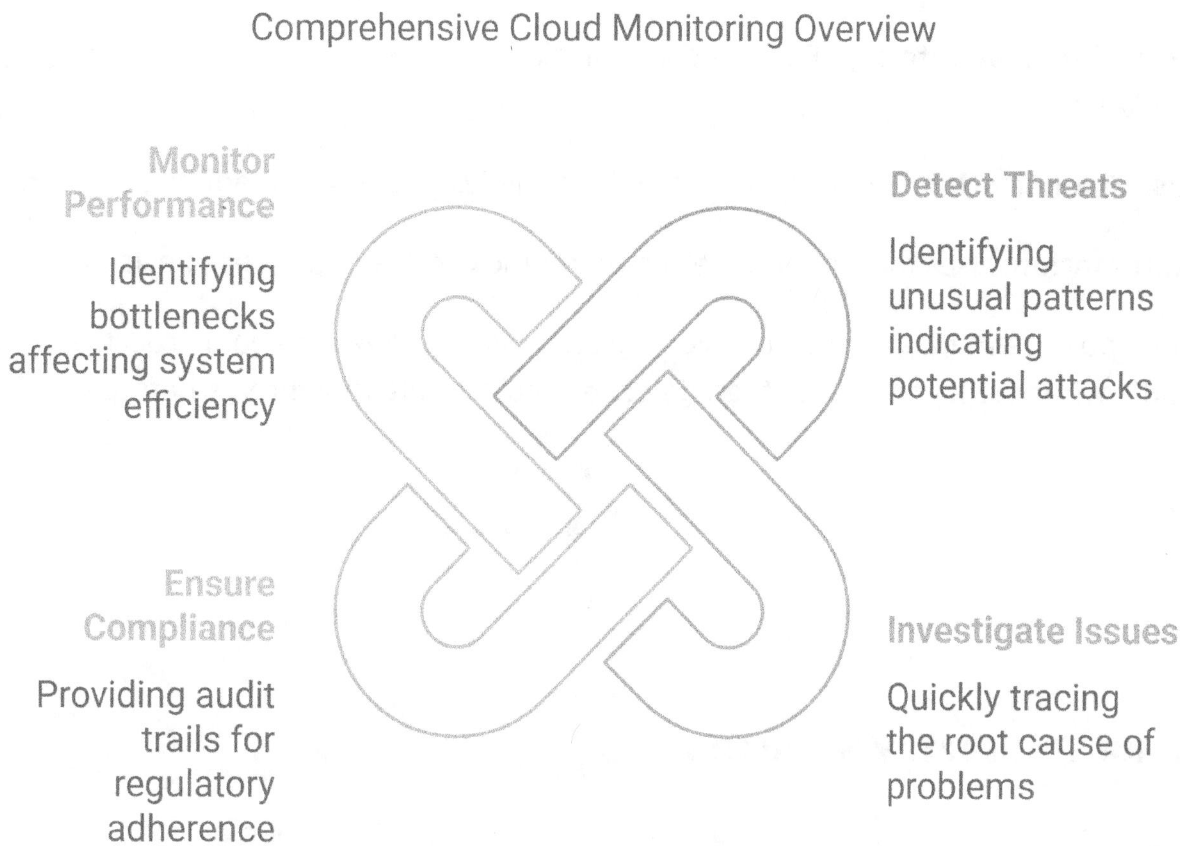

Together, they help maintain a secure and well-functioning cloud environment by offering visibility into operations in real-time or historically for analysis purposes.

6.2 Beyond Logs - Posture Management

Beyond logs, posture management focuses on maintaining the overall security health of a cloud environment. While logs provide detailed activity data, posture management takes a broader approach by continuously assessing and improving an organization's cloud configuration to reduce risks.

Key aspects include:

1. **Misconfiguration Detection**: Identifies weak settings like open storage buckets or overly permissive access controls.
2. **Compliance Monitoring**: Ensures configurations align with industry standards (e.g., GDPR, HIPAA).
3. **Risk Prioritization**: Highlights critical vulnerabilities needing immediate attention.
4. **Automation**: Uses tools to enforce secure policies across resources consistently.

By adopting posture management alongside log analysis, organizations gain proactive control over their cloud environments and strengthen defenses against potential threats before they occur.

6.3 Cloud Telemetry Sources

Cloud telemetry sources are data streams that provide insights into cloud environments' behavior, performance, and security. These sources collect real-time information from various components to help monitor and manage systems effectively.

Key Cloud Telemetry Sources:

Management Plane Logs: Track administrative actions like user access or configuration changes.

Resource Metrics: Measure system performance (e.g., CPU usage, memory consumption).

Network Traffic Data: Monitor inbound/outbound traffic for anomalies or threats.

Application Logs: Capture application-specific events such as errors or transactions.

Service-Specific Logs: Provide details about specific cloud services (e.g., storage activity logs).

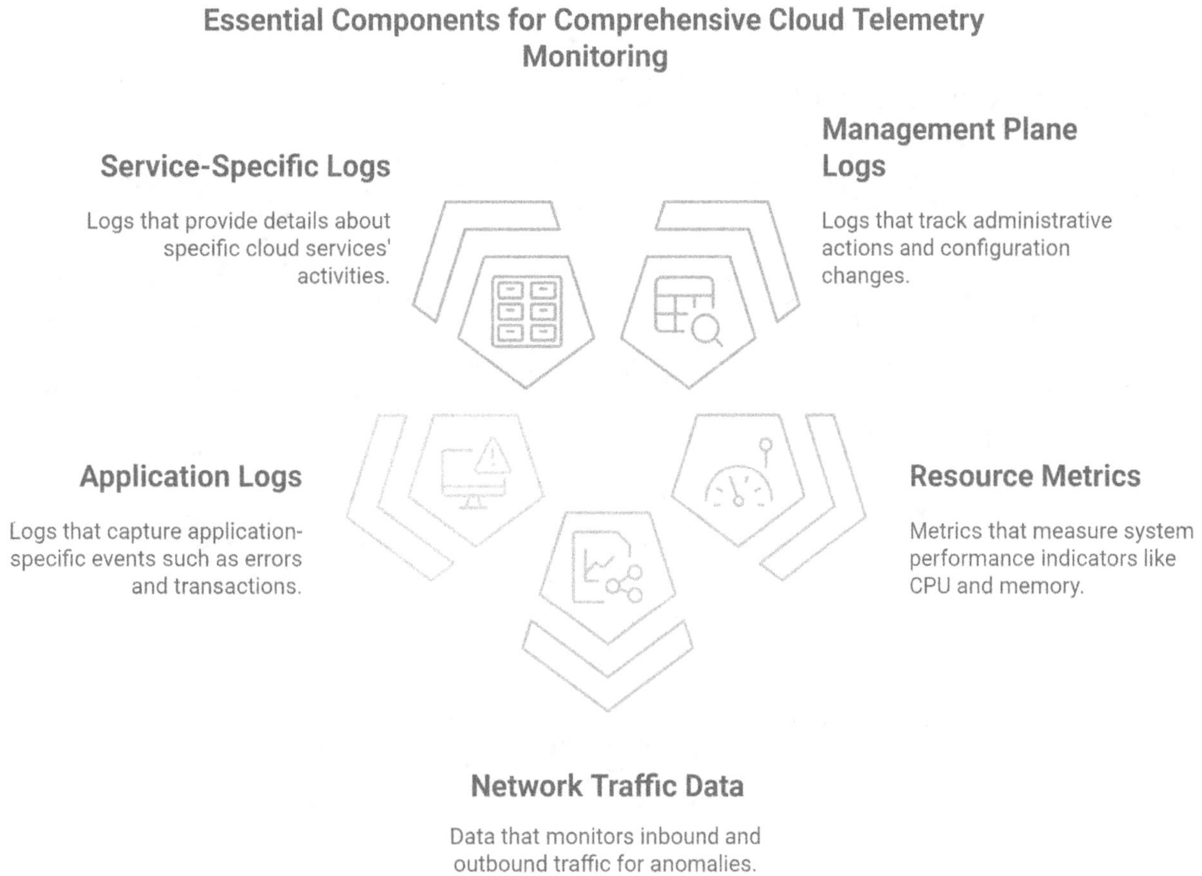

By analyzing these telemetry sources together, organizations can detect issues early, improve operational efficiency, enhance security posture, and ensure compliance with regulations—all while maintaining visibility across their entire cloud environment in real-time.

6.2.1 Management Plane Logs

Management plane logs record activities related to controlling and managing cloud resources. They track actions such as creating or deleting virtual machines, modifying configurations, or managing access permissions.

Cloud providers automatically generate these logs when users interact with the cloud's management interface (e.g., APIs, consoles). The data includes details like who acted (user identity), what was done (action type), where it occurred (resource location), and when it happened (timestamp).

These logs are stored in centralized logging services provided by cloud platforms:

- AWS CloudTrail for AWS
- Azure Activity Log for Microsoft Azure
- Google Cloud Audit Logs for GCP

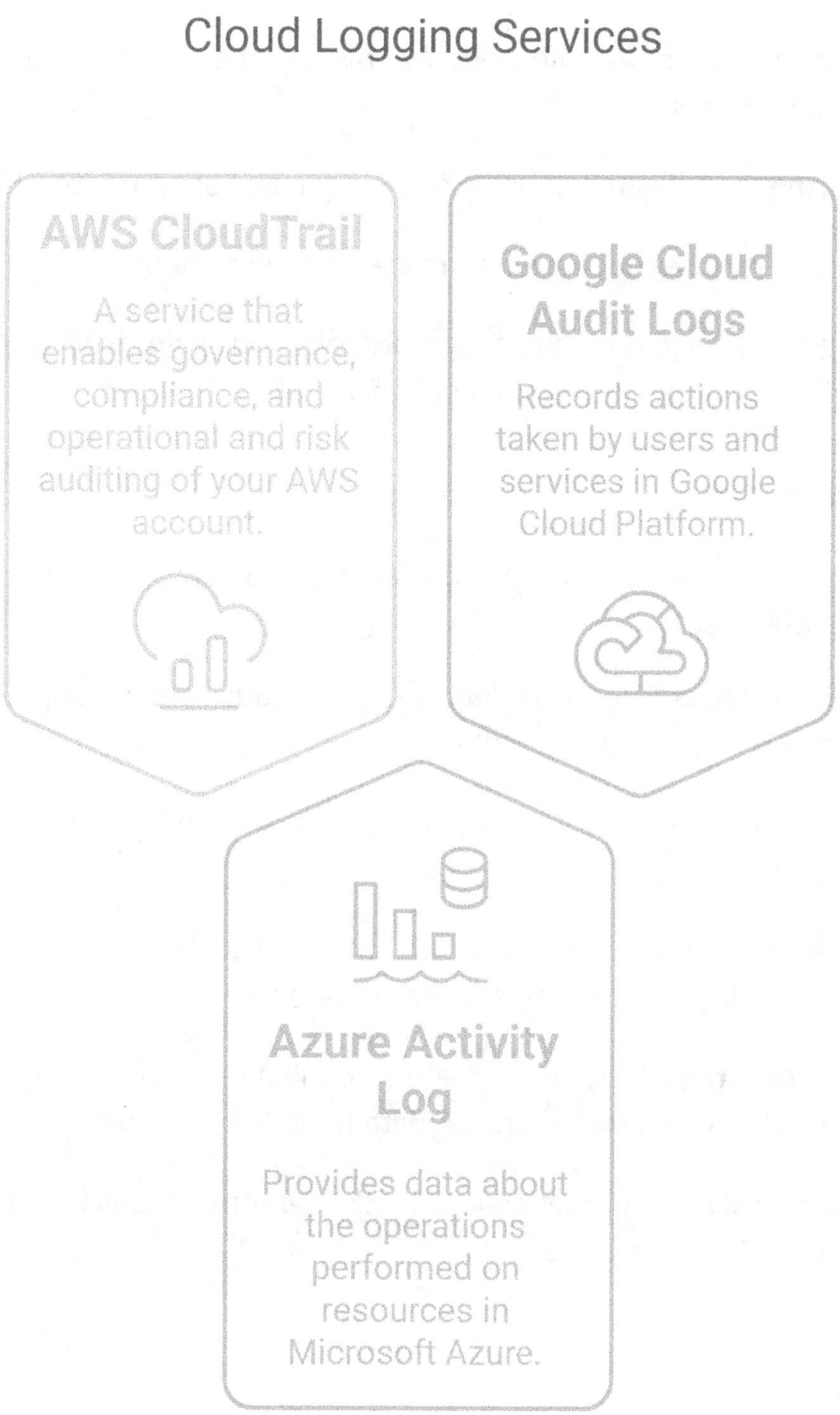

Logs can also be exported to external monitoring tools or SIEM systems for deeper analysis.

Why These Logs Are Required

1. **Security Monitoring:** Detect unauthorized changes or suspicious activity.
2. **Auditing & Compliance:** Maintain a detailed history of administrative actions to meet regulatory requirements.
3. **Troubleshooting:** Investigate issues by reviewing past configuration changes.
4. **Accountability:** Track user behavior across your environment.

By effectively leveraging management plane logs, organizations gain visibility into their operations while enhancing their security posture and compliance efforts.

6.2.2 Service & Application Logs

Service and application logs are essential for maintaining cloud environment visibility, security, and performance. Here's why they matter:

1. **Troubleshooting Issues**: Logs help identify the root cause of errors or failures within services or applications, enabling faster resolution.
2. **Performance Monitoring**: They provide insights into system behavior and resource usage to optimize performance.
3. **Security Detection**: Service logs reveal unauthorized access attempts or suspicious activities, while application logs can expose vulnerabilities being exploited.
4. **Compliance & Auditing**: These logs create a detailed record of operations that support regulatory compliance by proving proper data handling practices.
5. **User Behavior Analysis**: Application logs track user interactions to improve functionality and detect anomalies like misuse patterns.

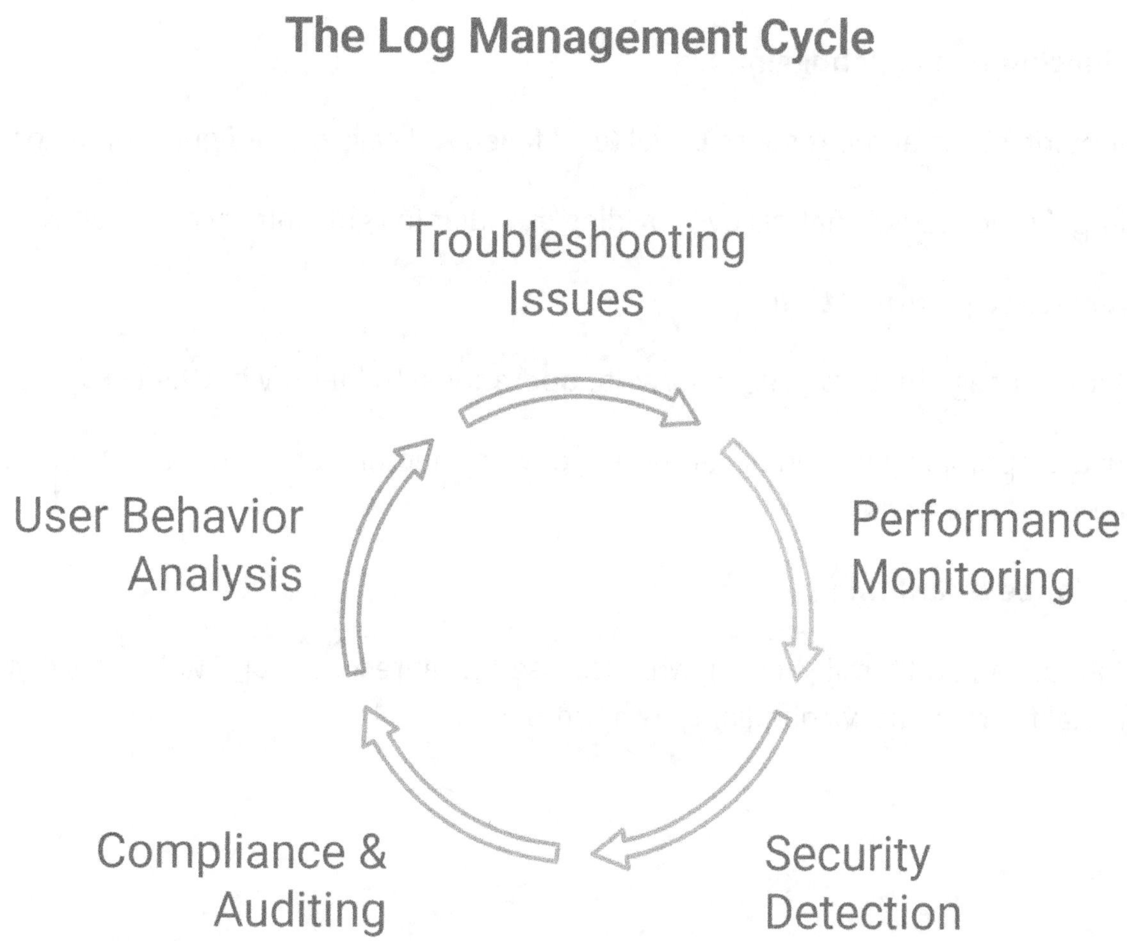

By consistently collecting service and application logs, organizations ensure better control over their systems while proactively addressing risks before they escalate into major problems.

6.2.3 Resource Logs

Resource logs provide detailed information about the operations and activities of specific cloud resources, such as virtual machines, storage buckets, or databases. They are critical for maintaining a secure and efficient cloud environment.

Key Reasons to Have Resource Logs:

1. **Security Monitoring**

- Detect unauthorized access or changes to individual resources.
- Identify potential threats like unusual activity patterns targeting specific assets.

2. **Troubleshooting & Debugging**
   - Pinpoint issues at the resource level (e.g., failed API calls or configuration errors).
   - Simplify root cause analysis by providing granular insights into system behavior.
3. **Performance Optimization**
   - Monitor usage metrics (e.g., read/write operations) to identify bottlenecks.
   - Ensure optimal allocation of computing power, memory, and other resources based on workload demands.
4. **Compliance & Auditing**
   - Maintain an audit trail showing who accessed what resource and when it occurred; this is crucial for regulatory compliance requirements.

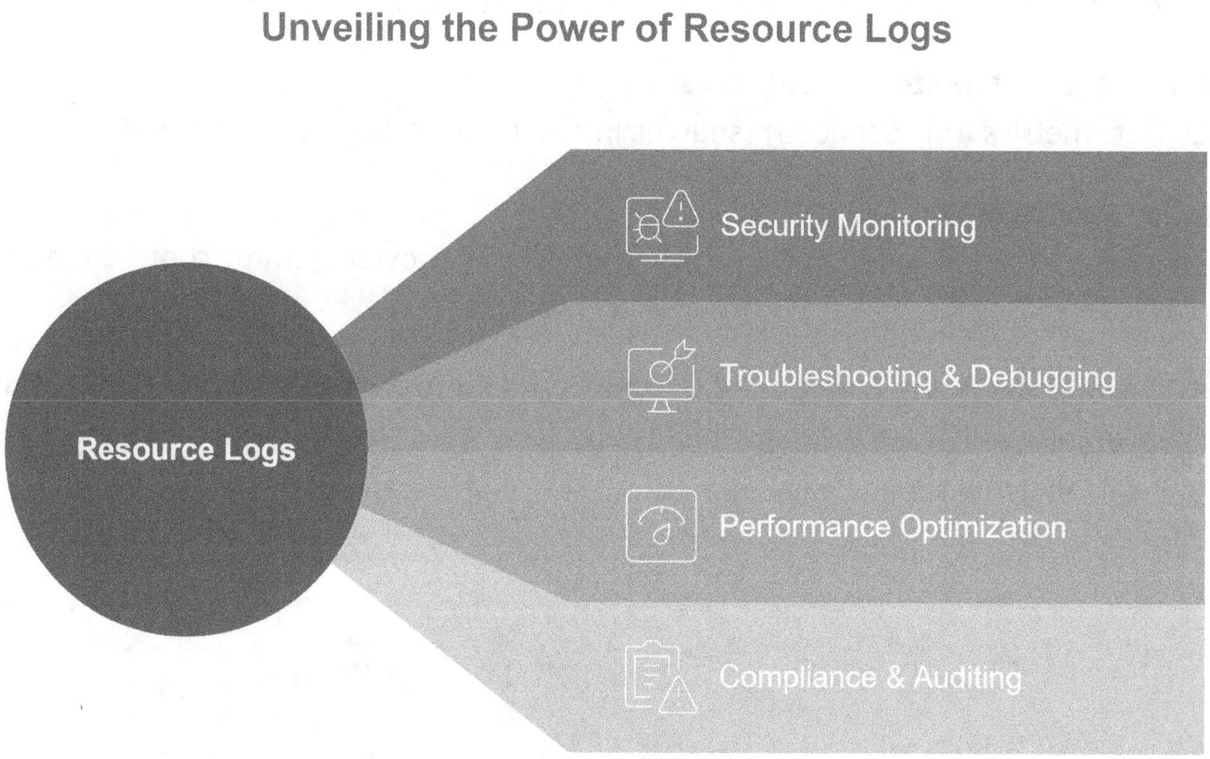

6.2.4 Cloud Native Tools

Cloud-native tools are software solutions designed specifically to operate within cloud environments. These tools leverage cloud platforms' scalability, flexibility, and automation capabilities to optimize development, deployment, monitoring, and management processes.

Key Features:

- **Scalable**: Adapt easily as workloads grow or shrink.
- **Resilient**: Handle failures gracefully with minimal downtime.
- **Automated**: Use built-in features to provision resources or manage infrastructure.

Examples of Cloud Native Tools:

1. **Kubernetes (Orchestration)**
   Manages containerized applications across clusters for scaling and high availability.

2. **Terraform (Infrastructure-as-Code)**
   Automates resource provisioning using declarative configuration files.

3. **Prometheus (Monitoring & Metrics)**
   Collects metrics from services/resources in real-time for performance tracking.

4. **Istio (Service Mesh)**
   Enhances communication between microservices by providing traffic control and security policies.

5. **AWS Lambda / Azure Functions / Google Cloud Functions (Serverless Computing):**
   Execute code without managing servers; ideal for event-driven tasks like APIs processing user requests dynamically.

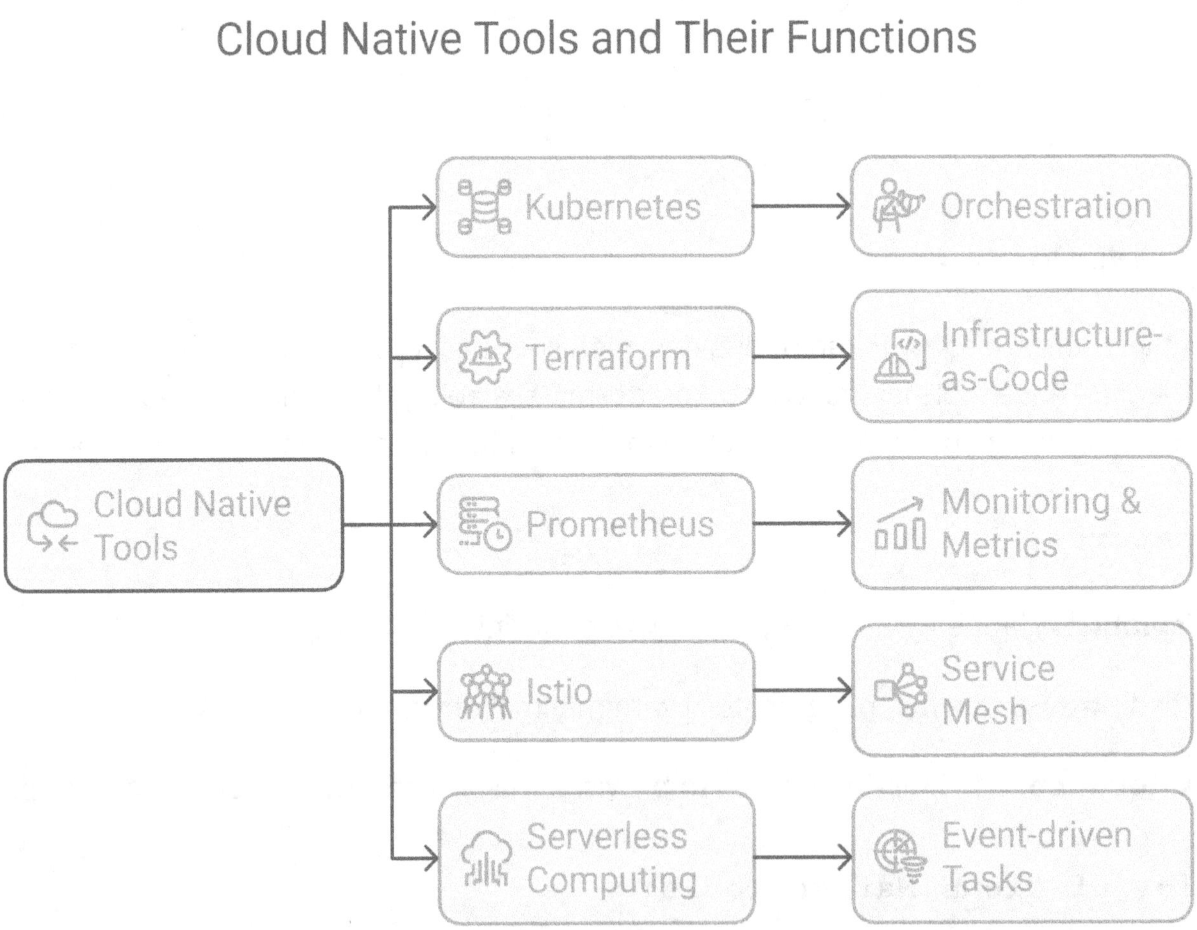

6.4 Collection Architectures

Collection architectures refer to the structured methods and designs used to gather and store security-related data from cloud environments, such as logs and telemetry information. In security monitoring, these architectures are critical for ensuring that data is efficiently collected, retained, and can be analyzed for threat detection and compliance purposes.

Key components of collection architectures include:

1. **Log Storage**
2. **Cascading Log Architecture**
3. **Retention Policies**
4. **Integration with Monitoring Tools**

6.4.1 Log Storage & Retention

Log Storage: Systems and methods for storing collected logs in a way that supports easy retrieval and analysis. This may include centralized logging servers or cloud-native storage solutions.

Retention Policies: Guidelines that dictate how long different logs are stored are based on regulatory requirements and organizational needs. Proper retention helps maintain compliance with laws and regulations while optimizing storage costs.

6.4.2 Cascading Log Architecture

A design where logs are collected from various sources and passed through multiple layers or levels of processing. This approach allows for preliminary filtering and aggregation of logs, ensuring only relevant data is retained for deeper analysis.

Collection architectures must be compatible with various security monitoring tools and technologies that analyze the collected data for anomalies, threats, and other security incidents - in other words; these architectures must be compatible with **integration and monitoring tools**.

By implementing robust collection architectures, organizations can enhance their ability to monitor, analyze, and respond to security events effectively within their cloud environments.

6.5 AI for Security Monitoring

6.5 AI for Security Monitoring focuses on integrating artificial intelligence (AI) technologies into security monitoring processes within cloud environments. This section highlights how AI can enhance the effectiveness of security operations by providing advanced analytical capabilities beyond traditional monitoring methods.

Key aspects of this topic include:

1. **Threat Detection**: AI can analyze large volumes of security data and identify patterns indicative of potential threats or anomalies. Machine learning algorithms can be trained to recognize normal behavior, allowing them to flag unusual activity that may signify a security breach.

2. **Automated Response**: AI can automate responses to certain types of security incidents, reducing the time it takes to react to threats. For instance, if an AI system detects suspicious activity, it can automatically trigger predefined security protocols, such as isolating affected resources or notifying security teams.

3. **Predictive Analytics**: By leveraging historical data and machine learning models, AI can predict future threats and vulnerabilities based on trends and emerging patterns. This proactive approach helps organizations to defend against potential attacks before they occur.

4. **Enhanced Data Correlation**: AI systems can correlate data from various sources and contexts, offering a more comprehensive view of security incidents. This capability allows for better context around alerts and incidents, improving the efficiency and accuracy of incident response.

5. **Continuous Learning**: One of AI's main advantages is its ability to learn and adapt over time. As new threats emerge and data is collected, AI models can refine their algorithms to improve detection capabilities and reduce false positives.

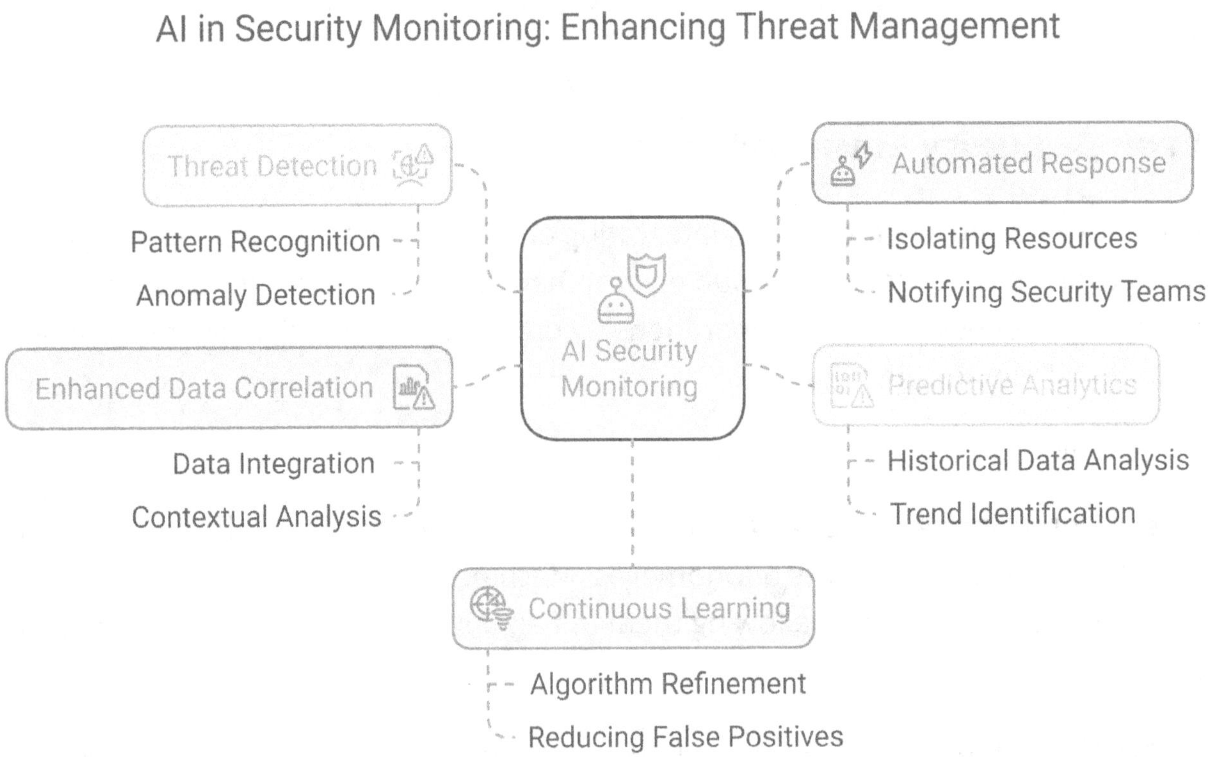

By incorporating AI into security monitoring, organizations can significantly enhance their ability to detect, analyze, and respond to cyber threats in real time, increasing their overall security posture in cloud environments.

Chapter Ten

Domain 7: Infrastructure and Networking

Introduction

Cloud infrastructure and networking are key to secure, efficient operations. With cloud providers managing some security tasks and businesses handling others, understanding these roles prevents vulnerabilities. Modern networks rely on software, demanding strong security principles to block threats like data breaches. Professionals with this knowledge can safeguard connections, ensure smooth data flow, and support growth—empowering organizations to protect sensitive information while achieving their goals in a fast-paced world.

Learning Objectives

The learning objectives for Domain 7: Infrastructure & Networking are designed to provide a comprehensive understanding of the security principles and practices associated with managing cloud infrastructure and networks. The specific objectives include:

1. **Cloud Infrastructure Security**: Understanding the foundational techniques for securing cloud infrastructure, including best practices for protecting assets and ensuring resilience against threats.

2. **CSP Infrastructure Security Responsibilities**: Grasping the security responsibilities of cloud service providers (CSPs) and how they relate to the security posture of the overall cloud environment, including compliance with security frameworks.

3. **Infrastructure Resilience**: Learning how to implement strategies and measures that enhance the resilience of cloud infrastructure, ensuring continuity and the ability to recover from incidents.

4. **Cloud Network Fundamentals**: Gaining insights into the basic concepts of cloud networking, particularly the transition to software-defined networks and the implications for security and performance.

5. **Cloud Connectivity**: Exploring the various methods and mechanisms for establishing secure and efficient connectivity between cloud resources, users, and on-premises environments.

6. **Cloud Network Security & Secure Architectures**: Developing knowledge of secure architectural frameworks and practices that safeguard cloud networks from vulnerabilities and threats.

By achieving these objectives, professionals will be better equipped to address the security challenges associated with cloud infrastructure and networking, ultimately leading to more effective management of cloud environments and enhanced organizational security.

7.1 Cloud Infrastructure Security

Imagine running your business entirely in the cloud—fast, flexible, and efficient. But cyber threats are always lurking, ready to exploit vulnerabilities. Protecting your cloud infrastructure isn't optional; it's critical for safeguarding your data and reputation. Hackers work tirelessly to find weak points, so staying one step ahead means prioritizing security measures that keep your operations safe and resilient. Don't leave your business exposed.

7.1.1 Foundational Infrastructure Security Techniques

Securing cloud infrastructure requires smart strategies to protect data and resources. Professionals focus on access control, encryption, network security, and regular monitoring. These practices help build trust while safeguarding sensitive information. By staying proactive and informed, organizations can reduce risks and ensure a safer environment for their operations.

1. **Defense-in-Depth**: This principle encourages the implementation of multiple layers of security controls throughout the infrastructure. Organizations can better protect against potential breaches and vulnerabilities by having overlapping security measures.

2. **Access Control**: Establishing strict access control policies is vital. This involves implementing

principles such as least privilege, whereby users are granted the minimum level of access necessary to perform their tasks, thus reducing the risk of unauthorized access.

3. **Network Segmentation**: Dividing the cloud network into segments helps contain potential breaches. By isolating critical systems and services, organizations can limit attackers' lateral movement in the event of a security incident.

4. **Monitoring and Logging**: Continuous monitoring and logging of infrastructure activities are essential for identifying and responding to security incidents. This includes deploying tools that can provide visibility into system operations and help detect anomalies.

5. **Configuration Management**: It is crucial to maintain consistent and secure configurations across cloud resources. Automated tools for configuration management can help ensure compliance with security baselines and quickly identify deviations.

6. **Patch Management**: Regularly updating and patching software and systems is vital to protect against known vulnerabilities. An effective patch management strategy ensures that security updates are applied promptly.

7. **Data Encryption**: Implementing encryption for data at rest and in transit is a fundamental practice for protecting sensitive information from unauthorized access or theft.

Mastering foundational infrastructure security techniques strengthens cloud environments and reduces risks tied to cloud computing. These practices create a solid base for advanced security measures, shaping a stronger defense strategy. Professionals can confidently safeguard their systems by prioritizing these methods while staying prepared for future challenges.

7.1.2 CSP Infrastructure Security Responsibilities

Cloud service providers (CSPs) are key in securing the infrastructure they manage. They safeguard servers, storage, and networks while ensuring compliance with industry standards. Organizations must assess how these measures align with their security needs to protect sensitive data effectively. By understanding CSP responsibilities, businesses can make informed decisions and build stronger defenses against potential threats in shared environments.

1. **Shared Security Model**: CSPs operate under a shared responsibility model, which delineates the security responsibilities between the provider and the customer. While the CSP is responsible for securing the underlying cloud infrastructure (e.g., physical security, network, and virtualization layer), the customer is responsible for securing their applications and data in the cloud.

2. **Physical Security**: CSPs are responsible for the physical security of their data centers. This includes controlling physical access to the facilities, implementing environmental controls (like fire suppression and climate control), and ensuring that hardware is protected from tampering or theft.

3. **Network Security**: CSPs must implement robust security measures to protect their infrastructure. This encompasses firewalls, intrusion detection/prevention systems, and secure configurations to safeguard data transit between users and cloud services.

4. **Virtualization Security**: Cloud environments heavily rely on virtualization, so CSPs must secure the hypervisors and virtual machines. This includes preventing unauthorized access to hypervisor controls and ensuring VM isolation to protect against cross-VM attacks.

5. **Compliance and Regulatory Standards**: CSPs are responsible for maintaining compliance with relevant industry regulations and standards (such as GDPR, HIPAA, and PCI-DSS) as they apply to their infrastructure. This includes ensuring that their services meet necessary security certifications and audits.

6. **Monitoring and Incident Response**: CSPs should provide tools and capabilities for continuous infrastructure security monitoring and have robust incident response plans to address security incidents and breaches effectively.

7. **Security Updates and Patch Management**: Providers are responsible for keeping their infrastructure secure through regular updates and patches to address vulnerabilities in hardware and software components.

8. **Data Security Controls**: CSPs must implement data security controls such as encryption and data loss prevention (DLP) mechanisms to protect data stored in their environments from unauthorized access or breaches.

9. **Service-Level Agreements (SLAs)**: CSPs typically specify their security responsibilities in SLAs, outlining the security measures they will implement and the level of support customers can expect. It assists customers in understanding the extent of the CSP's security obligations.

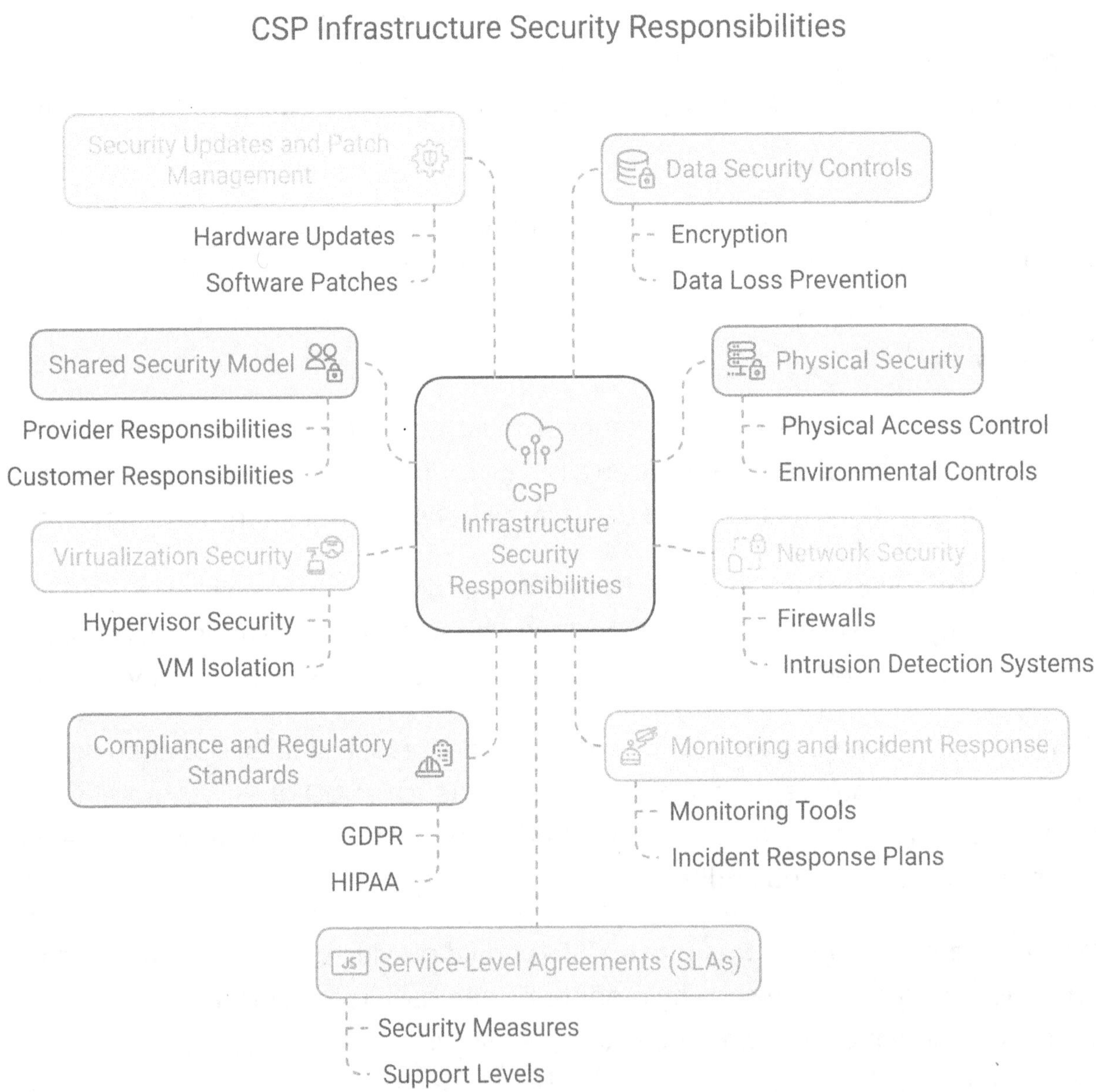

Understanding CSP security responsibilities empowers organizations to make smarter cloud decisions. By aligning provider measures with their own, businesses strengthen protection and meet compliance standards. This collaboration builds trust and boosts overall safety in the cloud.

7.1.3 Infrastructure Resilience

Cloud infrastructure resilience strengthens your systems to handle disruptions like cyberattacks, natural disasters, or hardware failures. By focusing on recovery and adaptability, businesses can keep services running smoothly and protect critical data. This approach ensures you're prepared to tackle challenges head-on while maintaining trust with customers and stakeholders. Strong infrastructure isn't just about technology—it's about building confidence in your ability to stay reliable when it matters most.

Key elements of infrastructure resilience include:

1. **Redundancy**: Implementing redundant systems and components is crucial for resilience. This can involve duplicating critical hardware, software, or network components to eliminate single points of failure. Redundancy ensures that if one component fails, others can take over seamlessly, maintaining service availability.

2. **Geographic Distribution**: Utilizing multiple geographic regions or availability zones helps to mitigate the risk of localized disasters. By distributing workloads across different physical locations, organizations can ensure that a failure in one area does not impact services globally.

3. **Disaster Recovery (DR) Planning**: Developing and regularly updating disaster recovery plans is essential for resilience. DR plans outline procedures for responding to data loss or service outages, including backup strategies, recovery point objectives (RPOs), and recovery time objectives (RTOs) that define acceptable downtime.

4. **Regular Testing and Drills**: Infrastructure resilience relies on testing and validating DR and business continuity plans through simulations and drills. Regular testing helps identify gaps in the plans and ensures that staff know their roles during a disaster.

5. **Monitoring and Analytics**: Implementing real-time monitoring and analytics tools is critical to infrastructure resilience. Continuous monitoring of infrastructure performance enables the detection of potential issues before they escalate into significant problems, allowing for proactive management.

6. **Automated Scaling**: Utilizing cloud capabilities for automated scaling can enhance

resilience. Organizations can maintain application performance and availability during unexpected surges or resource depletion by automatically adjusting resources in response to demand (like increased traffic).

7. **Patch Management and Updates**: Keeping infrastructure components updated and patched is essential for resilience. Regular updates improve security and enhance performance and stability, reducing the likelihood of failures due to outdated software or vulnerabilities.
8. **Incident Response Plans**: Establishing robust incident response plans that outline specific actions to be taken in the face of various incidents contributes to resilience. These plans should include clear roles, communication protocols, and recovery strategies.
9. **Data Backup and Replication**: Implementing regular data backup and replication processes ensures that critical data can be restored quickly during loss or corruption. Organizations should use both on-site and off-site backups to enhance data security.
10. **Continuous Improvement**: Resilience is not a one-time effort but a continuous process. Organizations should regularly review and update their strategies based on lessons learned from incidents, changes in their IT environment, or evolving threats.

Strengthening cloud infrastructure resilience can help organizations reduce disruptions, maintain service reliability, and safeguard critical data. This forward-thinking approach enhances security while fostering trust with customers and stakeholders. Showing a commitment to dependable services protects operations and reinforces confidence in your brand's ability to deliver under pressure. Prioritizing resilience ensures smoother operations and stronger relationships in an increasingly connected world.

7.2 Cloud Network Fundamentals

The cloud is everywhere, powering apps, storing files, and keeping businesses running. But how does it all work? Cloud networks connect everything behind the scenes—securely moving data across the internet like a digital highway system. Understanding these basics can help you stay safe online and make smarter tech choices.

7.2.1 Cloud Networks are Software-Defined Networks

Cloud networks are built on Software-Defined Networks (SDN), a modern way to manage and control network infrastructure. SDN separates the decision-making process (control plane) from traffic forwarding tasks (data plane). This separation enables centralized management, flexibility, and automation.

Key Features of SDN:

1. **Centralized Control:** A single controller oversees all devices in the network. Since everything is managed centrally, changes across large systems become simpler.
2. **Programmability:** Network behavior relies on software instead of hardware configurations. Adjustments can be made dynamically based on business needs or changing traffic patterns.
3. **Decoupling Hardware & Software:** The physical components stay unchanged while logic moves into software layers—reducing reliance on proprietary equipment.
4. **Automation-Friendly:** Tasks like routing updates or load balancing happen automatically through APIs or scripts rather than manual effort.

How SDN Improves Cloud Workloads

1. **Performance Optimization** By adjusting routes dynamically during demand spikes or outages, latency decreases, ensuring better application performance for users when it matters most.
2. **Scalability** Adding virtual networks is easy without touching physical hardware, a perfect match for cloud environments with fluctuating workloads.
3. **Cost Efficiency** Traditional networking gear costs more upfront; replacing this setup with commodity-grade hardware paired alongside intelligent controllers saves money long-term!

7.2.2 Cloud Connectivity

Cloud connectivity ensures smooth, secure communication between users and cloud services or across multiple cloud environments. Strong connections keep applications running efficiently, enhancing user experiences and productivity. Whether streaming data or managing workloads, reliable connectivity makes everything faster and safer. Businesses can stay agile while meeting growing demands by prioritizing secure access and speed. A well-connected cloud keeps your operations moving without interruptions—because staying connected matters more than ever.

Key concepts related to cloud connectivity include:

Types of Connections:

1. **Internet-Based Connectivity**: This is the most common form of cloud connectivity, allowing users to access cloud resources over the public Internet. It is typically achieved through standard protocols such as HTTP/HTTPS. While this method is widely accessible and cost-effective, it may expose organizations to higher security risks and potential latency issues.

2. **Direct Connectivity**: For organizations requiring more reliable and secure connections, direct connectivity options such as dedicated leased lines, MPLS (Multiprotocol Label Switching), or VPN (Virtual Private Network) can be utilized. These connections provide greater bandwidth, lower latency, and enhanced security than Internet-based connections.

3. **Hybrid Cloud Connectivity**: Organizations utilizing hybrid cloud environments need to establish connectivity between on-premises data centers and public or private cloud services. This often involves using secure VPNs or direct connections to ensure that data can be transferred seamlessly between environments while maintaining security and compliance.

4. **Inter-Cloud Connectivity**: Organizations adopting multi-cloud strategies require connectivity between different cloud service providers. Inter-cloud connectivity enables the integration of services and data across various platforms, allowing organizations to leverage the best features from each provider while ensuring interoperability.

APIs and Service Endpoints: Cloud services typically provide APIs (Application Programming Interfaces) to allow applications to communicate with each other or to access cloud services. These APIs act as service endpoints, facilitating secure and efficient interaction between various components of an organization's architecture.

Network Services: Various network services can enhance cloud connectivity, such as:

1. **Load Balancers**: Distributing incoming traffic across multiple servers or services enhances availability and performance.

2. **Content Delivery Networks (CDNs)**: These networks cache data in various locations closer to users, improving access speed and reducing latency.

3. **DNS (Domain Name System) Services**: DNS helps translate human-readable domain names into IP addresses, ensuring users can easily access cloud services.

Security Considerations: Ensuring secure connectivity between cloud services and users is paramount. Organizations should consider implementing:

1. **Encryption**: All data in transit should be encrypted to protect it from interception and unauthorized access.

2. **Firewalls and Security Groups**: These can restrict access to cloud resources, allowing only authorized traffic and protecting against cyber threats.

3. **Identity and Access Management (IAM)**: Proper IAM practices ensure that only authenticated users can access specific resources, maintaining a strong security posture.

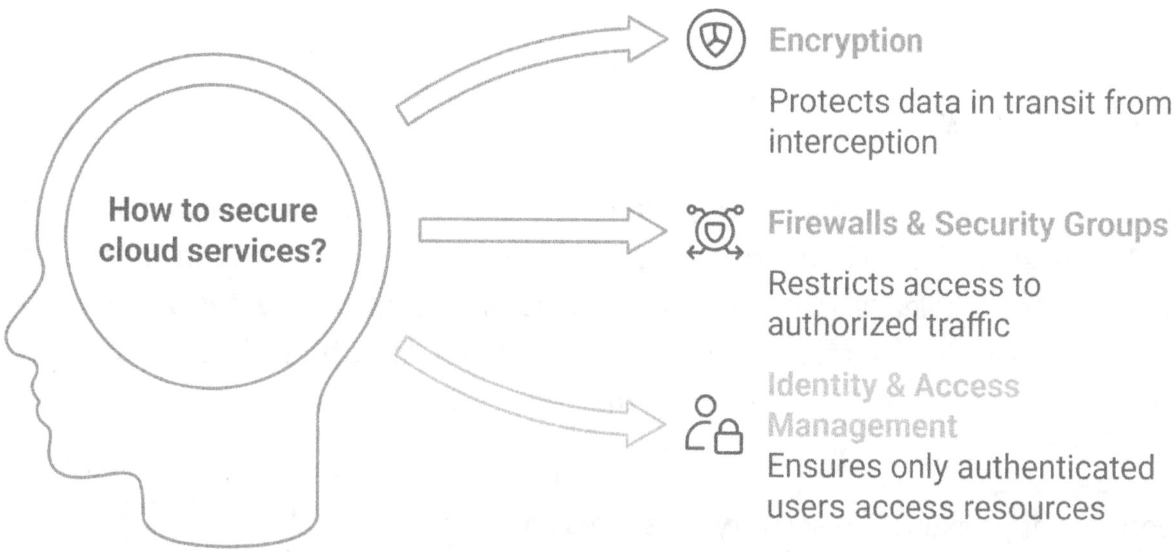

Performance and Optimization: Optimizing cloud connectivity involves monitoring network performance, analyzing latency, and adjusting configurations for better throughput. Tools that provide insights into network performance can help make informed decisions to enhance connectivity.

Latency and Bandwidth Considerations: Understanding and managing latency and bandwidth are critical for effective cloud connectivity. Applications sensitive to delay (like real-time communications) may require dedicated connections or optimization strategies to ensure performance.

To build strong and secure cloud connections, focus on enabling smooth access to resources and reliable communication between applications. This approach ensures organizations can fully harness cloud services while maintaining efficiency and security. By prioritizing these connections, businesses stay agile and prepared for growth in a connected world.

7.3 Cloud Network Security & Secure Architectures

Protecting cloud networks requires proactive strategies tailored to their unique structure, like shared resources and virtualization. As more organizations move to the cloud, securing these environments becomes critical to counter threats and vulnerabilities. Strong security measures, designed with cloud-specific challenges, ensure data integrity and resilience. By prioritizing these practices, businesses can confidently embrace cloud technology while safeguarding sensitive information from potential risks.

7.3.1 Preventative Security Measures

Preventative security measures proactively protect cloud networks by identifying and addressing risks early. These strategies help organizations block cyberattacks, ensuring their resources stay safe, private, and accessible. By staying one step ahead of threats, businesses build trust with users while safeguarding sensitive data. Proactive action not only strengthens defenses but also fosters confidence in the reliability of cloud services—making prevention a smart choice for long-term security success.

Key components of preventative security measures include:

1. **Access Control and Identity Management**:
    - **Least Privilege Principle**: Users and systems should have the minimum level of access necessary to perform their functions. This limits potential damage from compromised accounts.
    - **Multi-Factor Authentication (MFA)**: Requiring multiple forms of verification enhances security by making it more challenging for unauthorized users to gain access to sensitive resources.
    - **Role-Based Access Control (RBAC)**: By assigning permissions based on user roles,

organizations can ensure that users only have access to resources relevant to their responsibilities.

2. **Network Segmentation**:
    - Dividing the network into segments helps contain potential breaches and limits attackers' lateral movement. Critical systems can be isolated from less sensitive ones, reducing the risk of widespread access.
    - Virtual data centers and subnets can enforce segmentation within cloud environments, making it difficult for attackers to traverse from one segment to another.
3. **Firewalls and Intrusion Prevention Systems (IPS)**:
    - Deploying cloud-native or web application firewalls (WAFs) helps filter and monitor incoming and outgoing traffic based on predefined security rules.
    - Intrusion Prevention Systems can detect and respond to potential threats in real-time, preventing malicious traffic from accessing the network.
4. **Security Configuration Management**:
    - Regularly auditing and configuring cloud resources according to best practices is essential for minimizing vulnerabilities. This includes ensuring that only necessary services are active and security settings are aligned with compliance requirements.
    - Implementing automated tools for configuration checks and continuous monitoring can significantly enhance security postures.
5. **Data Encryption and Tokenization**:
    - Encrypting data at rest and in transit protects sensitive information from unauthorized access, even if a security breach occurs.
    - Tokenization replaces sensitive data elements with non-sensitive equivalents, reducing the risk associated with data exposure.
6. **Regular Security Patching and Updates**:
    - Keeping software, applications, and systems updated with the latest security patches is critical to protect against known vulnerabilities.

- Automated patch management processes can streamline the update process and reduce the window of opportunity for attackers.

7. **Security Awareness Training**:

   - Employees play a critical role in maintaining cloud security. Providing regular training on cybersecurity best practices helps raise awareness and fosters a culture of security within the organization.

   - Training topics may include recognizing phishing attempts, password management, and safe browsing behaviors.

8. **Vulnerability Management**:

   - Regularly conducting vulnerability assessments and penetration testing helps identify weaknesses in the cloud infrastructure before they can be exploited.

   - Remediation efforts should be prioritized based on the vulnerabilities' severity and the affected systems' criticality.

9. **Secure Coding Practices**:

   - For organizations developing applications in the cloud, adopting secure coding practices during the software development lifecycle (SDLC) can mitigate vulnerabilities at the source.

   - Techniques such as threat modeling and code reviews should be integrated into the development process to identify and address security issues early.

10. **Incident Response Planning**:

    - Although preventative measures aim to reduce incidents, having a robust incident response plan ensures that organizations can quickly respond to and recover from any security events.

    - Regular drills and updates to the incident response plan help refine the organization's ability to respond effectively.

Strengthening cloud security requires proactive measures to stay ahead of potential threats. Organizations can reduce risks by adopting advanced defenses and monitoring strategies while boosting overall protection. In today's fast-paced tech world, traditional methods often fall short. Staying prepared ensures your data remains safe and your operations remain uninterrupted. Don't wait for vulnerabilities to surface—act now to safeguard your systems and maintain trust with clients and stakeholders alike.

7.3.2 Detective Security Measures

Detective security measures help organizations spot unauthorized activities quickly and uncover cloud environment vulnerabilities. While prevention reduces risks, detection ensures swift responses to incidents, limiting damage and strengthening compliance with policies. By staying alert and proactive, businesses can safeguard their operations effectively.

Key components of detective security measures include:

1. **Security Information and Event Management (SIEM)**:
    - SIEM systems collect, analyze, and correlate security data from various sources across the cloud infrastructure, including logs, events, and security alerts.
    - SIEM solutions help security teams identify anomalies, suspicious activities, and potential threats by providing a centralized view of security events, enabling them to respond quickly to incidents.
2. **Log Management**:
    - Comprehensive log management involves collecting, storing, and analyzing logs generated by cloud services, applications, and network devices.
    - Organizations should establish log retention policies to ensure that logs are retained sufficiently to facilitate incident investigations while complying with regulatory requirements.
3. **Intrusion Detection Systems (IDS)**:
    - IDS solutions monitor network traffic and system activities for suspicious patterns that may indicate a security breach or policy violation.
    - They can be configured to alert security personnel in real time when potential threats are detected, allowing for rapid investigation and response.
4. **Behavioral Analytics**:
    - Implementing user and entity behavior analytics (UEBA) helps organizations establish

baselines for normal activities within their cloud environment.

- Behavioral analytics can detect potential malicious activities, such as insider threats or compromised accounts, by identifying deviations from these baselines.

5. **Vulnerability Scanning**:
   - Regular vulnerability scans help organizations identify known vulnerabilities within their cloud infrastructure before attackers can exploit them.
   - Automated scanning tools can continuously monitor for vulnerabilities and generate reports prioritizing remediation efforts based on the severity and potential impact.
6. **Threat Intelligence Integration**:
   - Integrating threat intelligence into security operations provides organizations with up-to-date information about emerging threats, vulnerabilities, and attack indicators.
   - This intelligence enables security teams to enhance their detection capabilities, recognize attack patterns, and proactively adjust defensive measures.
7. **Anomaly Detection**:
   - Advanced anomaly detection techniques analyze data for unusual patterns and behaviors that may signify a security incident.
   - Machine learning models can enhance the effectiveness of anomaly detection by adapting to evolving usage patterns, thereby improving the detection of malicious activities.
8. **Incident Detection Playbooks**:
   - Developing incident detection playbooks provides a standardized approach for identifying and responding to specific security incidents.
   - Playbooks outline the steps to be taken by security teams when a potential incident is detected, ensuring organized and efficient responses.
9. **User Activity Monitoring**:
   - Monitoring user activities within cloud environments helps detect unauthorized access and potential insider threats.

- Organizations should establish profiling of normal user behavior to identify deviations that may indicate malicious activities or compromised accounts.

10. **Cloud Access Security Brokers (CASBs)**:

    - CASBs operate as intermediaries between users and cloud service providers, providing visibility and control over data and activities within cloud services.
    - They enable organizations to monitor cloud application usage, detect policy violations, and enforce security controls, such as data encryption or access restrictions.

Organizations can monitor cloud environments by adopting strong detection measures, spotting threats early, and responding swiftly to security incidents. Combining proactive prevention with effective detection strengthens overall protection and builds trust. These practices improve incident response and provide valuable insights into security operations and compliance efforts. Staying vigilant helps safeguard sensitive assets from modern cyber risks while reinforcing a reliable and secure foundation for business operations.

7.4 Infrastructure as Code (IaC)

Manage your IT systems with the precision of coding through Infrastructure as Code (IaC). This refers to managing and provisioning computing infrastructure through machine-readable definition files instead of physical hardware configuration. IaC saves time, reduces errors, and strengthens security by automating tasks and improving efficiency, consistency, and reliability. Whether scaling servers or deploying apps faster, this approach simplifies operations while empowering businesses to stay agile and focused on growth. Say goodbye to manual setups and hello to enhanced operational effectiveness.

Here are the key components and concepts surrounding IaC:

1. **Definition and Purpose**:

    - IaC enables the automated management of infrastructure resources such as servers, storage, networks, and services using code. This approach allows teams to define their infrastructure in a high-level configuration language.

   - The primary purpose of IaC is to eliminate manual processes in infrastructure management, reduce errors, enhance deployment speed, and ensure consistent and repeatable configurations across environments.

2. **Declarative vs. Imperative Approaches**:
   - **Declarative**: In this approach, users specify the desired state of the infrastructure (e.g., the configuration and settings). The IaC tool then figures out how to reach that state. Tools such as Terraform are examples of declarative IaC tools.
   - **Imperative**: This approach involves writing commands to achieve a certain state. Users define the specific steps needed to create and manage infrastructure. An example of an imperative tool is AWS CloudFormation.

3. **Benefits of Infrastructure as Code**:
   - **Consistency and Repeatability**: By using code to define infrastructure, organizations reduce the chances of configuration drift, as identical setups can be deployed multiple times across various environments, such as development, testing, and production.
   - **Version Control**: Like application code, infrastructure configurations can be stored in version control systems. This allows changes to be tracked, audited and rolled back if necessary.
   - **Speed and Agility**: IaC enables rapid provisioning of resources, significantly decreasing the time it takes to deploy applications and services. This agility supports DevOps practices and continuous integration/deployment (CI/CD) pipelines.
   - **Automation**: Automated deployments reduce the need for manual intervention, minimizing the risk of human error and increasing operational efficiency.

4. **Tools and Technologies**:
   - There are several popular IaC tools in use today, including:
     - **Terraform**: An open-source tool that allows users to define infrastructure using a high-level configuration language. It supports multiple cloud providers.
     - **AWS CloudFormation**: A service that helps model and set up AWS resources securely and efficiently.

- **Ansible**: Although Ansible is primarily a configuration management tool, It can also be used for IaC by defining infrastructure components in its playbooks.
- **Pulumi**: A relatively newer tool that allows developers to use their programming languages (like JavaScript, Python, or Go) to define infrastructure.

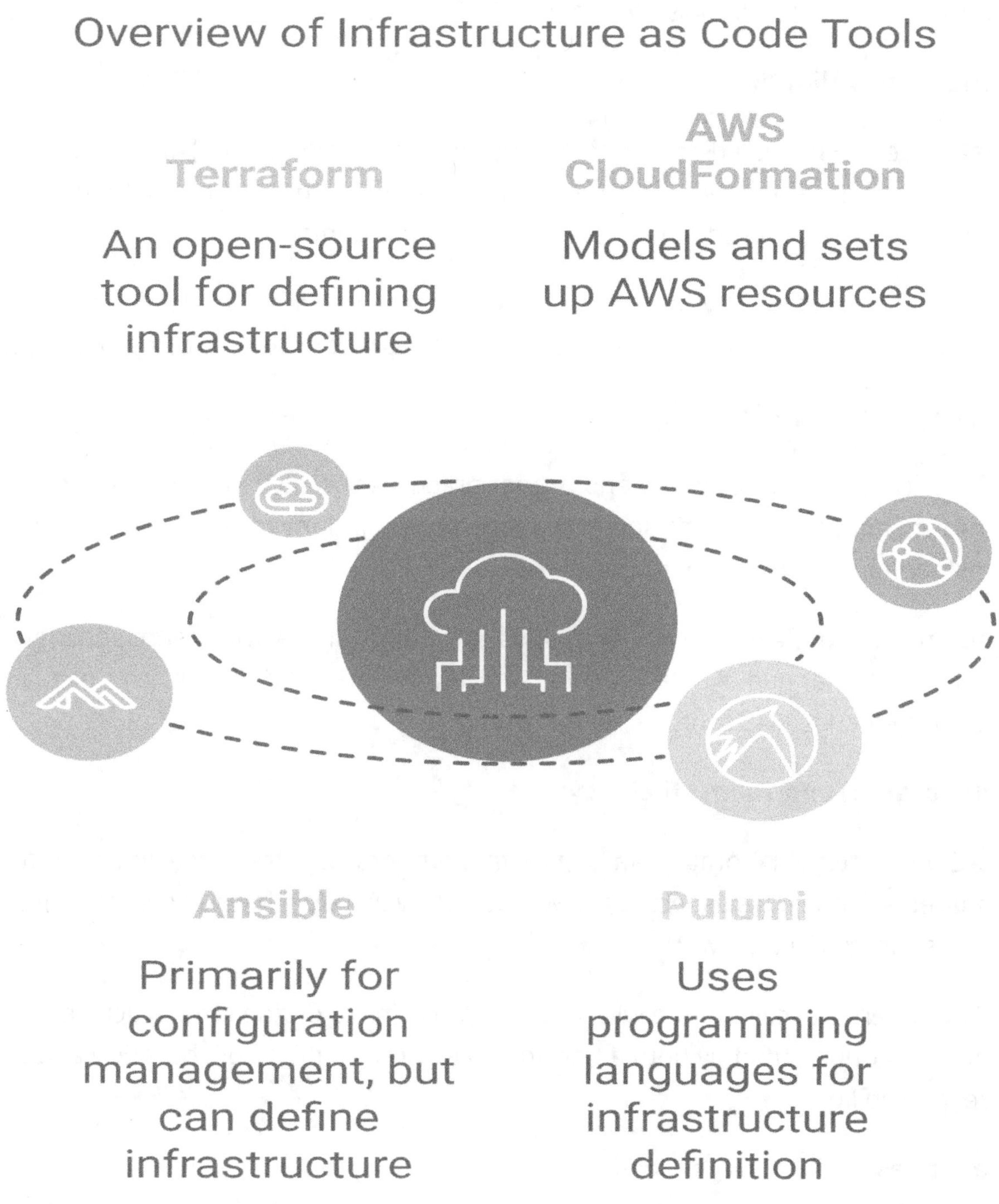

1. **Infrastructure Lifecycle Management**:
   - IaC supports the entire infrastructure management lifecycle, from provisioning to updating and decommissioning. Infrastructure changes can be managed through code, making modifications easier and more reliable.
   - This lifecycle management concept allows for systematic updates and scaling of resources based on the application's demands.
2. **Testing and Validation**:
   - IaC code can be tested and validated just like application code. This testing can include syntax checks, simulation of infrastructure changes without applying them (dry runs), and validation against predefined compliance requirements.
   - Tools such as "Checkov" or "Terraform Compliance" can be employed to check the conformity of IaC scripts to organizational or regulatory standards before deployment.
3. **Security Considerations**:
   - Security in IaC is paramount, and proper practices should be followed to protect sensitive information, such as using secret management solutions for API keys and passwords instead of hardcoding them.
   - To prevent configuration vulnerabilities, it is important to implement security controls, such as regular audits of IaC scripts, applying the principle of least privilege, and using security-focused IaC tools.
4. **Collaboration and Team Efficiency**:
   - IaC promotes collaboration among team members, as infrastructure definitions are shared as code. This aspect aligns well with DevOps principles and encourages cross-functional teamwork.
   - Developers can collaborate with operations teams to define infrastructure requirements in terms understood by both, fostering an environment of collaboration and shared responsibility.
5. **Challenges**:
   - Despite its numerous benefits, adopting IaC can present challenges, such as the

complexity of maintaining large and intricate infrastructure codebases, effectively managing state, and ensuring consistent configurations across different environments and team members.

In conclusion, Infrastructure as Code (IaC) is a transformative approach to managing cloud infrastructure, promoting automation, consistency, and collaboration. By treating infrastructure configuration as code, organizations can achieve greater reliability, faster deployments, and improved alignment with modern software development practices, making IaC an essential component in managing cloud environments.

7.5 Zero Trust for Cloud Infrastructure & Networks

Zero Trust for Cloud Infrastructure & Networks assumes threats can exist anywhere, so it enforces a "never trust, always verify" mindset. Access requests are authenticated, authorized, and encrypted to protect sensitive data and services. Designed for modern cloud environments, this approach prioritizes security at every step—helping businesses stay resilient against evolving risks while ensuring users interact safely with their resources.

Here are the key components and concepts surrounding Zero Trust for Cloud Infrastructure and Networks:

Definition of Zero Trust:

- The Zero Trust model shifts traditional security paradigms by rejecting the assumption that all users and devices inside the network perimeter are trustworthy. Instead, it requires continuous verification of anyone attempting to access resources, whether inside or outside the organization's network.

Core Principles:

- **Least Privilege Access**: Users and devices are given the minimum level of access necessary to perform their tasks. By limiting access permissions, the potential impact of a breach is reduced.

- **Micro-segmentation**: Network segmentation is done at a granular level, allowing for finer control over how resources communicate. This limits lateral movement within the network, encapsulating breaches to small sections.

- **User Authentication and Authorization**: Identity and access management (IAM) systems are essential for verifying user identities through multifactor authentication (MFA) and ensuring meticulously managed user roles and permissions.
- **Continuous Monitoring**: Constantly monitoring network activity allows for detecting suspicious behavior and anomalies, leading to quick responses to potential security incidents.

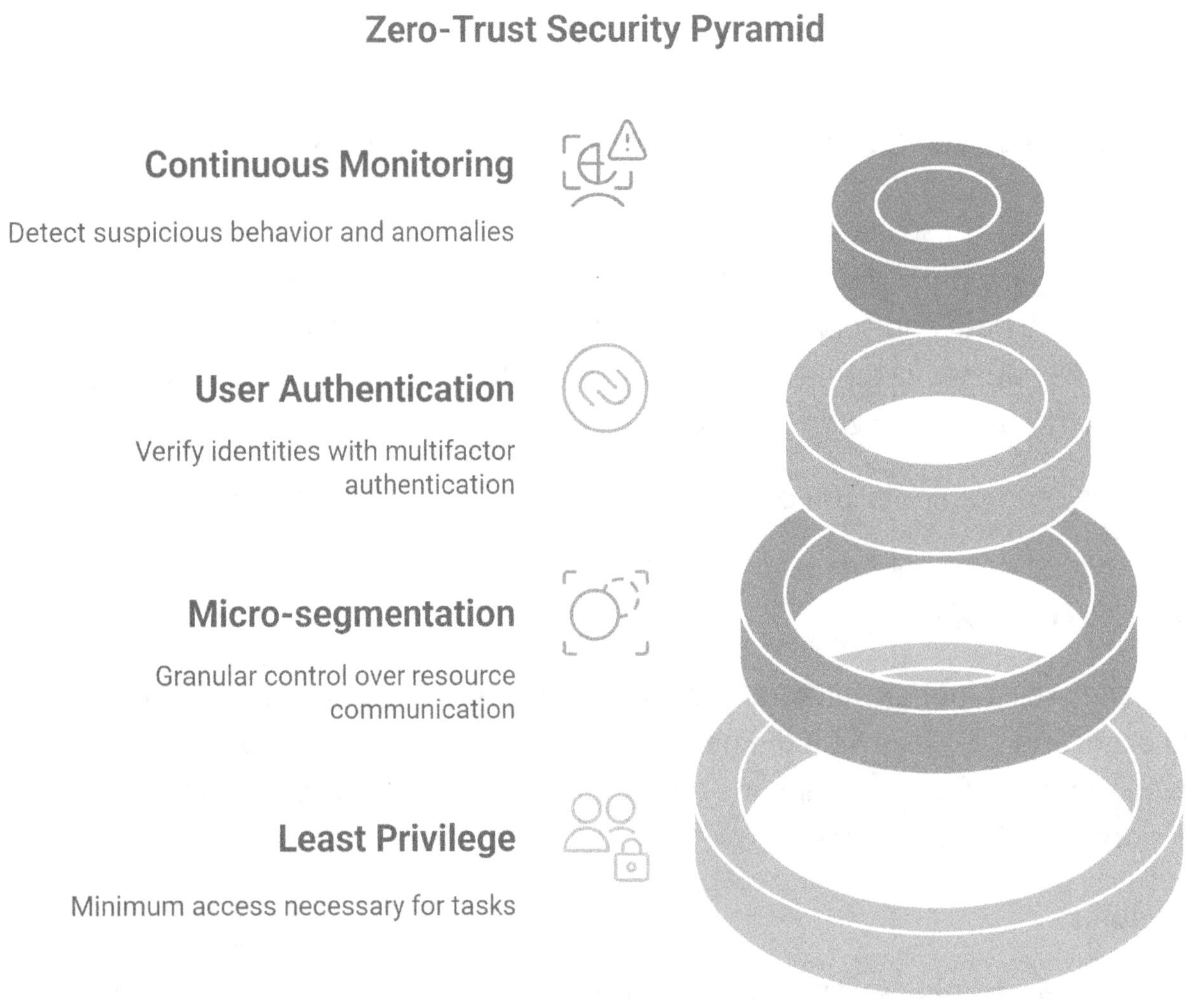

Components of Zero Trust Architecture:

1. **Identity**: Strong identity management is crucial for a Zero-Trust architecture. The system

should authenticate users and devices using methods like MFA before granting access.

2. **Device Security**: It is vital to ensure that devices accessing the cloud infrastructure adhere to security policies. This includes maintaining device health checks and enforcing endpoint security measures.

3. **Network Security**: Network traffic should never be trusted implicitly. Using secure connections, such as Virtual Private Networks (VPNs) or Secure Sockets Layer (SSL)/Transport Layer Security (TLS), is critical to uphold secure communications.

4. **Data and Application Security**: Data classification and encryption protect sensitive information at rest and in transit. Furthermore, applications must be built securely from the ground up, adhering to secure development lifecycle practices.

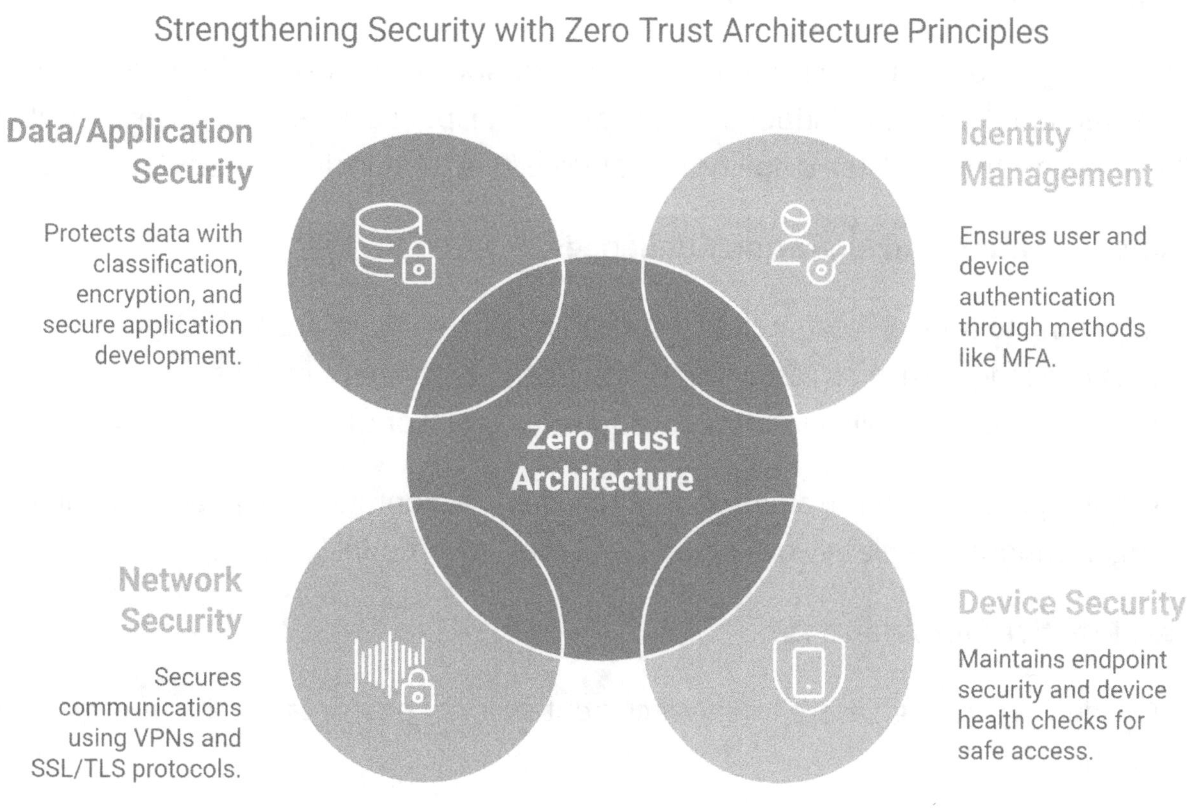

Cloud-Specific Considerations:

- Cloud environments inherently introduce complexities, including dynamic resource allocation and distributed access points. Zero-trust strategies must account for this fluid nature.

- The use of cloud infrastructure services (e.g., IaaS, PaaS) necessitates strict verification of interactions between users, applications, and cloud services.

Zero Trust Network Access (ZTNA):

- ZTNA is a critical component of the Zero Trust model, focusing on securing connections between users and applications. It replaces traditional VPNs by enabling secure, specific access to applications based on user identities and contexts rather than merely network locations.
- With ZTNA, access policies are implemented at a per-application level, ensuring that users can only connect to services they are authorized to use, regardless of location.

Integration with Existing Security Solutions:

- Integrating Zero Trust with security frameworks, such as Security Information and Event Management (SIEM) and Endpoint Detection and Response (EDR), enhances security posture. These integrations bolster visibility, threat detection, and incident response capabilities.
- **Implementation and Migration Challenges**:
    - Migrating to a Zero-Trust architecture can be an intensive process. Organizations often face challenges such as resource constraints, resistance to change, and the need for comprehensive visibility into existing systems and workflows.
    - Careful planning, staff training, and phased implementation strategies can help organizations seamlessly transition to a Zero Trust model.
- **Best Practices for Adoption**:
    - Conduct a thorough assessment of current security postures and identify gaps in trust boundaries.
    - Start with critical assets and applications, applying Zero Trust principles iteratively to broader resources.
    - Utilize automated tools for continuous monitoring and risk assessment, allowing for quick adaptations to evolving threats.

    - Review and update access policies regularly, ensuring they align with the principle of least privilege as roles and requirements change.

- **Benefits of Zero Trust**:
    - **Enhanced Security:** By enforcing strict access controls and continuously monitoring user behavior, organizations can significantly reduce the risk of data breaches and insider threats.
    - **Improved Data Protection:** With strong encryption practices and data classification efforts, sensitive information is better safeguarded against unauthorized access.
    - **Regulatory Compliance:** Many industries face stringent regulatory requirements for data protection. Implementing Zero Trust helps organizations maintain compliance more effectively.
    - **Increased Visibility and Control:** Organizations gain better insights into their network activities, enabling them to respond more swiftly to potential threats.

Zero Trust for Cloud Infrastructure and Networks strengthens security by requiring verification at every step, eliminating default trust. This proactive approach safeguards sensitive data and resources from modern cyber threats. Organizations create a reliable defense system that prioritizes protection and accountability by implementing these principles. Stay secure by adopting zero-trust strategies to keep your cloud environment resilient and prepared for potential risks.

7.5.1 Software-Defined Perimeter & ZT Network Access

Software-defined perimeter (SDP) and Zero Trust Network Access (ZTNA) redefine secure access by enforcing strict verification for every user and device. These architectures prioritize security, ensuring only authorized connections to sensitive resources. By combining Zero Trust principles with advanced networking, organizations strengthen defenses against unauthorized access while maintaining flexibility. This approach empowers businesses to protect assets without compromising efficiency or usability, making it a smart choice for modern security needs.

Here's a detailed explanation of these concepts:

Software-Defined Perimeter (SDP)

1. **Definition**:
    - A Software-Defined Perimeter is a security model that creates a dynamic, secure network boundary utilizing software-defined networking principles. It enables access control to services and applications based on user identity and context rather than physical network locations, effectively cloaking resources from unauthorized access.
2. **Core Components**:
    - **Identity-Aware Access Control**: Access to the network is granted based on the user's identity, device health, and security posture. Identity and access management (IAM) systems are crucial in verifying the user's authenticity before permitting network access.
    - **Dynamic Security Perimeter**: Unlike traditional perimeters, which are static and reliant on firewalls, SDPs create a virtual perimeter that can adapt to user interactions and changing threat landscapes.
    - **Resource Cloaking**: Resources are hidden from the public internet and are only visible to authenticated and authorized users, thus significantly reducing the attack surface.
3. **How SDP Works**:
    - **Authentication and Authorization**: Upon request to access a resource, the user's

identity is authenticated, and their access rights are verified against policies.

- **Secure Connection Establishment**: A secure connection is dynamically established if verification is successful, allowing access to specific applications or services without exposing the entire network to the user.
- **Continuous Monitoring**: Continuous monitoring of user interactions ensures that any anomalous behavior can be detected in real-time, potentially revoking access if suspicious activity is identified.

4. **Benefits of SDP**:
   - **Reduced Attack Surface**: By cloaking resources and allowing only authenticated users to see and access them, the potential entry points for attackers are minimized.
   - **Dynamic Security**: Security measures can be adjusted on the fly in response to emerging threats or changes in user context.
   - **Enhanced User Experience**: Users are more likely to receive seamless access to the needed resources without navigating multiple firewalls or restrictive physical boundaries.

Zero Trust Network Access (ZTNA)

1. **Definition**:
   - **Zero Trust Network Access** is a security framework that enforces strict access controls and continuous monitoring of user activity without assuming trust in any user or device, inside or outside the organization's network.
2. **Core Principles**:
   - **Verify Every Access Attempt**: Users must authenticate each access request, regardless of where they connect, emphasizing a "never trust, always verify" approach.
   - **Least Privilege Access**: Access is limited to the minimum necessary level, ensuring users can only interact with the resources they require for their role.
   - **Micro-segmentation**: ZTNA enhances security by segmenting applications and data access into smaller, manageable zones that restrict lateral movement within the network.
3. **How ZTNA Operates**:

- **Access Control Policies**: Organizations define granular access policies based on numerous factors, including user identity, device status, location, and behavior.
- **Contextual Awareness**: ZTNA considers the context of access requests, including time of day, device compliance, and user behavior patterns, reinforcing security decisions.
- **Non-Perimeter Focus**: ZTNA moves away from a fortress model of security, recognizing that the network perimeter has all but vanished with the proliferation of cloud services and remote access.

4. **Implementation Considerations**:
    - Implementing ZTNA often involves integrating with existing IAM solutions and employing advanced security technologies (e.g., MFA, endpoint monitoring).
    - Organizations must thoroughly assess their security policies and infrastructure to align with ZTNA principles.
5. **Benefits of ZTNA**:
    - **Improved Security Posture**: By adopting Zero Trust principles, organizations can significantly reduce the risk of data breaches and insider threats.
    - **Seamless Remote Access**: ZTNA enables secure access to corporate applications without the complexities and vulnerabilities associated with traditional VPN solutions.
    - **Greater Visibility and Control**: With ZTNA, organizations gain enhanced visibility into user activity and can better detect and respond to security incidents.

Relationship Between SDP and ZTNA

1. **Integration of Concepts**:
    - SDP and ZTNA complement each other by combining SDP's dynamic, context-aware access controls with the core principles of Zero Trust that underpin ZTNA. Together, they create a comprehensive security architecture suited to the realities of modern cloud environments.
2. **Unified Security Framework**:
    - By leveraging both SDP and ZTNA, organizations can provide secure, remote access to applications while also protecting sensitive data and resources from unauthorized access.

This exemplifies a robust security posture in an increasingly complex threat landscape.

Software-defined perimeter (SDP) and Zero Trust Network Access (ZTNA) redefine how organizations secure cloud environments. Enforcing identity-based access controls ensures that only verified users can interact with sensitive systems and data. This proactive approach strengthens security while simplifying user access. As threats grow more sophisticated, adopting SDP and ZTNA helps businesses stay resilient, safeguarding critical resources without compromising efficiency or trust in their operations.

7.6 Secure Access Service Edge (SASE)

Secure Access Service Edge (SASE) combines networking and security tools to help businesses adapt to cloud-based apps and remote work. By integrating these functions, SASE ensures faster connections, stronger protection, and simplified management for modern organizations. Whether supporting a hybrid workforce or safeguarding sensitive data, this solution keeps teams connected and secure without compromising performance or flexibility.

Here's an in-depth look at what SASE entails:

Definition of SASE

1. **Overview**:
    - SASE (pronounced "sassy") is an architectural framework introduced by Gartner that converges networking and security into a unified cloud service delivery model. It provides secure networking services that extend beyond traditional perimeter-based security to address modern security challenges.
2. **Components**:
    - SASE integrates security and networking functions, including secure web gateways, firewall as a service, secure access, and WAN optimization into a single cloud-native service. This convergence allows organizations to manage and secure access to resources from anywhere.

Key Features of SASE

1. **Cloud-Native Architecture**:
    - SASE is designed to be delivered from the cloud, ensuring scalability, flexibility, and efficient resource utilization. This cloud-native approach allows for rapid deployment and updates, aligning with the dynamic needs of modern enterprises.
2. **Zero Trust Network Access (ZTNA)**:
    - Central to SASE is the application of Zero Trust principles. Every user, device, and application is verified through identity-based access controls, ensuring access is granted based only on genuine need and legitimate identity.

3. **Secure Web Gateway (SWG)**:
    - These gateways are essential components of SASE, providing protection against malicious web traffic and helping to enforce security policies. SWGs monitor user activity in real-time to block potential threats.
4. **Firewall as a Service (FWaaS)**:
    - SASE includes cloud-delivered firewall capabilities that offer robust protection against internal and external threats, enabling organizations to manage firewall policies efficiently from a cloud service.
5. **SD-WAN Integration**:
    - SASE utilizes Software-Defined Wide Area Networking (SD-WAN) technology to optimize the performance and reliability of network connections across distributed and remote locations. By intelligently routing traffic based on real-time conditions, SD-WAN enhances user experiences and application performance.
6. **Data Loss Prevention (DLP)**:
    - SASE incorporates DLP capabilities to prevent unauthorized access to sensitive data and ensure compliance with regulatory requirements. Policies can be enacted to monitor and control data transfers to protect against data exfiltration.

Advantages of SASE

1. **Unified Security and Networking**:
    - By combining networking and security capabilities in a single cloud-based service, SASE simplifies management and reduces the complexity of deploying multiple-point solutions. This unified approach leads to improved operational efficiencies.
2. **Scalability and Flexibility**:
    - As organizations grow and adapt to changing demands, SASE services can scale seamlessly without requiring extensive hardware upgrades or infrastructure changes.
3. **Enhanced Security Posture**:

- Integrating Zero Trust principles ensures consistent security policies are applied regardless of the user's location or device type. This greatly reduces the risk of data breaches and cyberattacks.

4. **Improved User Experience**:
    - SASE optimizes traffic flow and reduces latency through SD-WAN technology, leading to better performance for cloud-based applications, critical for user satisfaction in remote work environments.

5. **Contextual Network Access**:
    - SASE provides real-time contextual insights based on user behavior and location, allowing organizations to apply adaptive security measures that respond to the current security landscape.

Implementation Considerations

1. **Vendor Selection**:
    - Organizations must carefully evaluate SASE vendors and assess their capabilities, including their approach to data security, bandwidth management, and support for specific cloud environments.

2. **Integration with Existing Infrastructure**:
    - Transitioning to a SASE model may require integrating with existing IT infrastructure while ensuring that legacy systems do not pose security risks or inhibit performance.

3. **Policy Management**:
    - Effective policies must be defined and continuously updated to reflect the evolving threat landscape and business requirements. This involves training IT personnel to understand and manage these new policies effectively.

4. **User Education**:
    - Organizations need to invest in educating their users about updated access methods and security practices, especially as they adapt to new cloud services and remote work

paradigms.

5. **Compliance Considerations**:
    - Organizations must ensure that their SASE implementation complies with relevant regulatory standards, such as GDPR or HIPAA, particularly as data is accessed and processed in a cloud environment.

SASE redefines how businesses handle networking and security by merging them into a cloud-based solution. Designed for today's remote workforce, it boosts agility, strengthens protection with Zero Trust principles, and scales effortlessly to meet cloud-driven demands. Companies embracing SASE gain stronger security and streamlined operations, reducing risks in an increasingly connected world.

Chapter Eleven

Domain 8: Cloud Workload Security

Introduction

Protecting cloud workloads means securing the software and data powering your business. Each comes with unique challenges, from virtual machines to containers and serverless functions. Prioritizing robust security measures ensures your applications and sensitive information stay safe from threats. By addressing specific needs—like safeguarding AI workloads—you can confidently operate in a cloud-driven world while keeping risks at bay. Strong defenses today lead to fewer worries tomorrow.

Learning Objectives

Learn how to secure cloud workloads with confidence. Master key areas like virtual machine protection, container best practices, serverless security, and safeguarding AI systems. Gain practical skills to address challenges, manage risks, and strengthen defenses in cloud environments. By focusing on real-world strategies, you'll be prepared to protect sensitive data and ensure robust security across diverse platforms.

8.1 Introduction to Cloud Workload Security

Securing cloud workloads demands a clear focus on protecting virtual machines, containers, and serverless applications. As businesses shift to cloud environments, tailoring security measures to each workload's unique needs becomes critical. Strong defenses help safeguard applications and data from threats, ensuring a safer operating environment. Organizations can confidently manage risks by prioritizing this understanding while maintaining trust in their cloud operations.

8.1.1 Types of Cloud Workloads

Understanding cloud workload types helps you apply security measures tailored to their unique needs. Each workload has specific risks and requirements, so aligning protections ensures better performance and safety. Whether you're managing applications, storage, or databases, knowing what you're working with makes all the difference in safeguarding your systems effectively.

The main types of cloud workloads include:

1. **Virtual Machines (VMs)**:
    - VMs are emulated hardware environments that allow multiple operating systems to run on a single physical server. Each VM operates as an independent unit, offering deployment and resource management flexibility. Security concerns for VMs include isolation, patch management, and securing data at rest and in transit.
2. **Containers**:
    - Containers provide lightweight virtualization that packages applications and their dependencies together, allowing them to run consistently across multiple environments. While containers are efficient for development and deployment, they introduce unique security challenges, such as managing container images, ensuring secure networking, and addressing vulnerabilities in the container runtime environment.
3. **Function as a Service (FaaS)**:
    - FaaS is a serverless computing model where applications are divided into smaller, event-driven functions. These functions automatically scale in response to triggers, reducing operational overhead. However, security for FaaS involves managing access controls, securing API endpoints, and considering the transient nature of functions, which can impact logging and monitoring.
4. **Bare Metal**:
    - Bare metal workloads involve deploying applications directly on physical hardware without a virtualization layer. This model provides high performance and control but

requires robust security measures to prevent unauthorized access and ensure the integrity of the physical server.

5. **Artificial Intelligence (AI) Workloads**:
    - AI workloads typically involve complex computations and large datasets for training algorithms. These workloads require specific security considerations, including securing sensitive data, managing access to AI models and resources, and addressing privacy concerns.

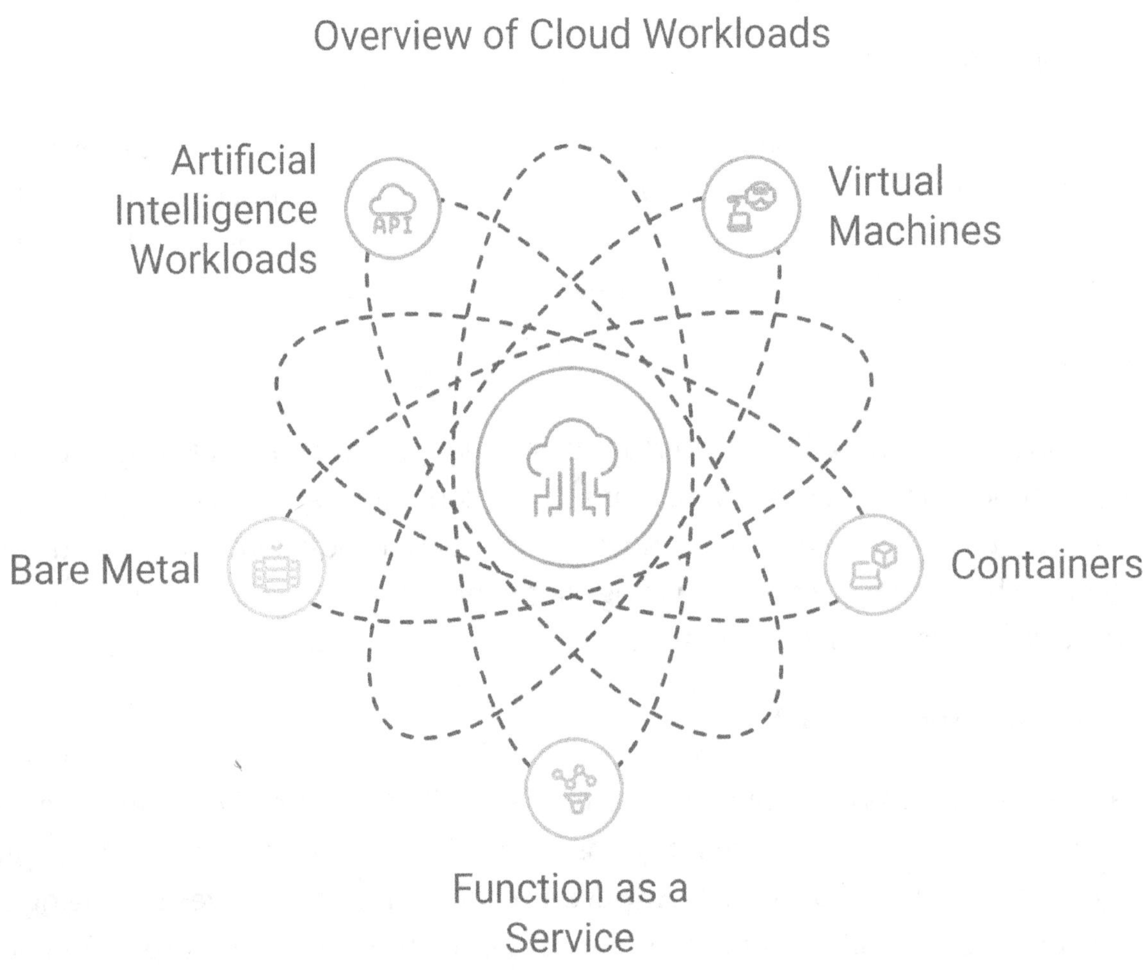

Categorizing cloud workloads helps organizations pinpoint specific security needs and challenges for each type. This clarity empowers teams to design tailored controls and risk strategies, ensuring stronger protection across all deployments. By understanding these distinctions, businesses can stay proactive and safeguard their operations effectively.

8.1.2 Impact on Workload Security Controls

Cloud workloads each demand tailored security measures. Their unique characteristics shape how protections are applied, ensuring vulnerabilities are addressed effectively. By understanding these nuances, businesses can craft strategies that safeguard data and operations without unnecessary complexity. Prioritizing workload-specific controls strengthens defenses and builds trust in your systems.

Key considerations include:

1. **Resource Isolation and Segmentation**:
    - Different workloads require varying degrees of isolation to ensure that malicious activity in one workload does not affect others. For instance, virtual machines benefit from strong hypervisor isolation, while containers may require network segmentation to restrict communication between containerized applications.
2. **Access Control Mechanisms**:
    - Workload types dictate how access controls are implemented. For VMs, traditional identity and access management (IAM) policies may suffice, but for serverless functions, fine-grained permissions are needed to control access to specific functions and trigger events. Based on workload needs, Role-Based Access Control (RBAC) or Attribute-Based Access Control (ABAC) approaches may be utilized.
3. **Data Security and Compliance**:
    - Different workloads process and store data in diverse ways. Virtual machines may store data locally on the host, while containerized applications might use external storage solutions. This difference impacts encryption requirements, data loss prevention (DLP) strategies, and compliance with regulations like GDPR or HIPAA. Organizations must assess where data is stored, how it is accessed, and implement controls accordingly.
4. **Monitoring and Incident Response**:
    - The ephemeral nature of certain workloads, especially serverless functions and containers, complicates traditional monitoring and logging practices. Security controls

must accommodate automated and continuous monitoring to detect anomalies and facilitate swift incident response, regardless of workload duration or state.

5. **Patch Management and Vulnerability Management**:
   - Each workload type has specific patching requirements. For example, VMs may require complete OS updates, while containers often need updates to both the container runtime and images. An effective vulnerability management program must account for these differences to ensure timely remediation and risk minimization.
6. **Performance and Security Trade-offs**:
   - Implementing robust security controls may impact workload performance. Extensive logging may provide better security visibility but also consume additional resources. Organizations must balance security measures with performance considerations, ensuring security does not hinder application functionality.

Tailoring security strategies to match each workload's unique needs helps reduce risks and keeps operations running smoothly. By understanding specific attributes and requirements, organizations can create smarter, more effective protections that truly work for them.

8.2 Securing Virtual Machines

Cloud virtual machines (VMs) are software-based computers hosted in a cloud environment. They mimic physical hardware, allowing users to run operating systems and applications without owning or managing physical servers.

8.2.1 Virtual Machine Challenges & Mitigations

Managing virtual machines in cloud environments has unique security risks, but you can tackle them effectively. Focus on strong access controls, regular updates, and robust monitoring to reduce vulnerabilities. Educate your team about potential threats and enforce strict policies to safeguard data. By staying proactive and prioritizing these strategies, organizations can maintain a secure infrastructure while maximizing the value of their virtual machine investments.

Here's a detailed explanation:

Challenges

1. **Attack Surface Expansion**:
    - Each VM instance represents an additional point of entry for potential attacks. As organizations scale up their infrastructure, the potential surface area for attacks increases, which can lead to more vulnerabilities if not properly managed.
2. **Isolation Vulnerabilities**:
    - While VMs are designed to provide isolation from one another, vulnerabilities in the hypervisor or misconfigurations can lead to cross-VM attacks, in which one compromised VM could affect others on the same host.
3. **Configuration Drift**:
    - Over time, VMs' configurations may deviate from defined security baselines due to changes in deployment practices, manual adjustments, or updates. This drift can lead to inconsistent security policies and vulnerabilities.
4. **Resource Overcommitment**:
    - Cloud environments often allow resource overcommitment, meaning that VMs are allocated more virtual resources than the physical infrastructure can handle. This can lead to performance degradation or unintended vulnerability exposure.
5. **Patch Management Complexity**:
    - Keeping VMs updated with the latest security patches can be challenging, especially in large environments with numerous VMs running different operating systems and applications. Neglecting patches increases the risk of exploitation.
6. **Access Management**:
    - Managing access to VMs can be complex, particularly in environments where multiple users have administrative privileges. Poor access controls can lead to unauthorized access and malicious activities.

Cloud Workload Security Challenges

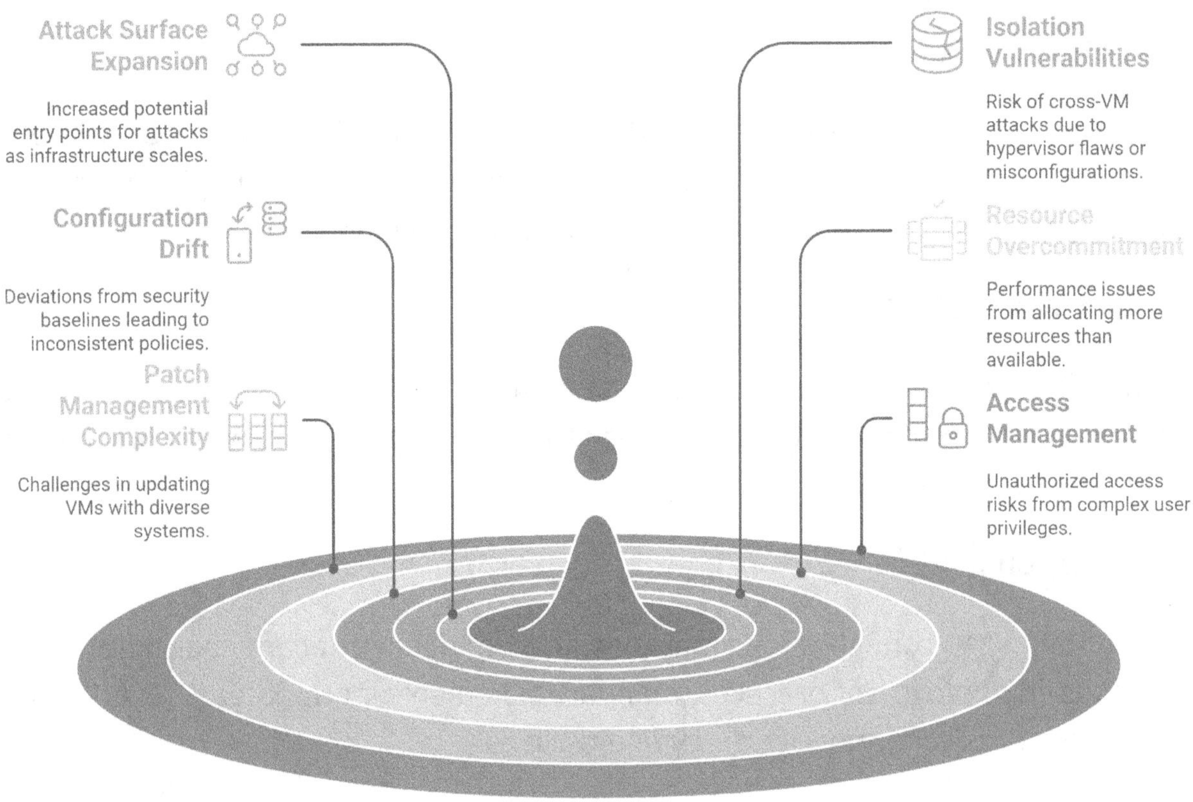

Mitigations

1. **Strong Access Controls**:
    - Implement robust identity and access management (IAM) policies, including multi-factor authentication (MFA) and least privilege access principles. This limits who can manage and access VMs, reducing the likelihood of unauthorized actions.
2. **Regular Audits and Monitoring**:
    - Conduct regular audits of VM configurations and monitor their activities. Continuous monitoring helps detect anomalies and ensures VMs comply with security policies and standards.
3. **Patch Management Policies**:
    - Develop and enforce a patch management strategy that includes routine vulnerability

assessments and timely patch application. Automated patch management tools simplify the process and ensure compliance.

4. **Configuration Management Tools**:
   - Utilize configuration management tools that automate the enforcement of security baselines and help prevent configuration drift. These tools can be configured to alert administrators of any unauthorized changes.
5. **Network Segmentation**:
   - Apply network segmentation to isolate VMs from one another based on their roles and security requirements. This reduces the risk of lateral movement attacks and limits the potential impact of a compromised VM.
6. **Training and Awareness**:
   - Ensure that staff responsible for VM management receive training on security best practices and potential risks. This can help foster a culture of security and promote proactive risk management.
7. **Backup and Recovery Solutions**:
   - Implement robust backup policies that ensure VMs and their data are regularly backed up. Up-to-date backups allow for quick recovery and minimize data loss in the event of a breach or failure.

Strengthening virtual machine security in cloud environments reduces risks and boosts resilience against threats. Organizations can protect sensitive data and maintain trust by addressing challenges with smart strategies. Proactive measures like regular updates, strong access controls, and monitoring ensure a safer infrastructure. Prioritizing these steps safeguards operations and builds confidence in your system's reliability. Stay prepared, stay secure—because peace of mind starts with robust protection.

8.2.2 Creating Secure VM Images with Factories

Building secure VM images doesn't have to feel overwhelming. Using image factories, you can create and manage templates tailored to your needs while prioritizing security. These templates ensure consistent configurations for deploying applications safely in cloud environments. Start by integrating best practices like automated updates, vulnerability scans, and access controls. A secure foundation leads to smoother deployments and greater peace of mind for your infrastructure.

Overview of VM Images

VM images are snapshots of virtual machines containing the operating system, application software, configurations, and any other elements required to run a service or application. Secure VM images are essential because they create a baseline standard that can be consistently deployed to multiple instances, reducing the potential for vulnerabilities introduced through manual configuration.

Challenges in VM Image Creation

1. **Inconsistent Configurations**:
    - Without a standardized process, manually creating VM images can lead to inconsistencies. Different configurations can introduce vulnerabilities and management difficulties.
2. **Software Vulnerabilities**:
    - Applications and operating systems may contain vulnerabilities, which can be inherited by the VM images if not adequately updated or patched before creating the image.
3. **Sensitive Data Exposure**:
    - Improper handling of sensitive data, such as credentials or personal data, during the image creation process can lead to exposure once the image is deployed.
4. **Malware Risks**:
    - If a VM is compromised and an image is created, any malware present can propagate across all new instances launched from that image.

Benefits of Using Image Factories

1. **Standardization**:
    - Image factories allow organizations to automate and standardize the VM image creation process. By utilizing predefined templates, they help ensure that all images meet security and compliance requirements.

2. **Automation**:
   - Automation can significantly reduce human error in the image creation, ensuring uniform security practices across all images.
3. **Continuous Updates**:
   - Organizations can ensure that new images are always built with the latest security enhancements by incorporating regular updates and patches into the image factory process.
4. **Version Control**:
   - Image factories can maintain version control for VM images, allowing organizations to roll back to previous versions if a new image introduces issues or vulnerabilities.

Best Practices for Creating Secure VM Images with Factories

1. **Define Security Baselines**:
   - Establish and document security baselines that specify the required configurations, applications, and security tools to be included in the VM images.
2. **Use Minimal Base Images**:
   - Start with minimal or "bare-bones" base images that contain only the essential components. This reduces the attack surface and potential vulnerabilities from unnecessary software.
3. **Automate Image Building**:
   - Implement automation tools to create images consistently and reproducibly. Use Infrastructure as Code (IaC) tools to script the image creation process, ensuring that images are built from the same set of code and configurations.
4. **Integrate Security Tools**:
   - Include security tools and agents in the VM image to monitor and protect the VM once deployed. This includes endpoint detection and response (EDR) software, vulnerability scanners, and logging agents.

5. **Regular Testing and Validation**:
    - Regularly test and validate the security and functionality of VM images before releasing them for production use. This can include automated security scans and penetration testing.
6. **Remove Sensitive Data**:
    - Ensure that sensitive data, such as credentials and specific configurations, is removed from images before deployment. Consider using secure vaults for sensitive information instead.
7. **Monitor and Update Images**:
    - Continuously monitor the current images for vulnerabilities and incorporate new patches and updates as needed. Implement a process for rebuilding and redeploying images on a regular schedule.
8. **Documentation and Change Management**:
    - Maintain thorough documentation of the image creation process and any changes made. Use a change management system to track image revisions and ensure proper approval processes are followed.

Creating secure VM images with factories strengthens cloud infrastructure by reducing initial vulnerabilities. Automating and standardizing processes ensures every deployed instance remains protected while streamlining resource management. This approach boosts security and simplifies operations, saving teams time and effort. Organizations can confidently maintain a safer, more efficient environment for their workloads by prioritizing consistency and best practices.

8.2.3 Snapshots & Public Exposures/Exfiltration

Snapshots in cloud environments can unintentionally expose sensitive data or enable unauthorized access. To reduce risks, restrict public access, enforce encryption, and regularly review permissions. Always monitor for unusual activity to prevent data exfiltration. By staying proactive and prioritizing security measures, you'll protect your information while controlling who can view or download it.

Understanding Snapshots

A **snapshot** is a point-in-time copy of a virtual machine (VM) that captures its state, data, and configuration. Snapshots are commonly used for backup, recovery, and testing purposes in cloud environments. They allow administrators to revert to a previous state of the VM or to create new instances based on an existing configuration.

Benefits of Snapshots

1. **Data Protection**:
   - Snapshots quickly back up VM data, enabling recovery from data loss due to corruption, accidental deletion, or failures.
2. **Testing and Development**:
   - Snapshots allow developers to create a stable environment without affecting the production system, facilitating the testing of new configurations or applications.
3. **Disaster Recovery**:
   - They can be integral to disaster recovery plans, efficiently restoring systems to a known good state.

Risks Associated with Snapshots

1. **Public Exposure**:
   - Snapshots can accidentally be configured to be publicly accessible or improperly secured. This can lead to unauthorized access to sensitive data stored within the snapshot.
2. **Data Exfiltration**:
   - If malicious actors gain access to snapshots, they can exfiltrate sensitive information, such as passwords, API keys, or other critical data. This threat is exacerbated if snapshots contain complete images of running VMs with sensitive applications.
3. **Inadvertent Sharing**:
   - Snapshots shared with external parties or left in a public storage class can lead to

unintended data breaches.

4. **Lack of Control**:
    - Organizations may not have enough visibility or control over how snapshots are used, leading to mistreatment or mismanagement of sensitive data.

Best Practices for Managing Snapshots

1. **Access Controls**:
    - Implement strict access controls and permissions for who can create, view, and manage snapshots. Ensure only authorized personnel can access snapshots and limit visibility to the minimum necessary.
2. **Use Encryption**:
    - Always encrypt snapshots, both in transit and at rest. This ensures that even if an unauthorized entity gains access to a snapshot, it cannot read the data without the proper decryption keys.
3. **Regularly Audit Snapshots**:
    - Conduct regular audits of snapshots to identify any publicly accessible snapshots, unused old snapshots, or snapshots that may contain sensitive data. Automated tools are used to detect and flag problematic configurations.
4. **Enforce Retention Policies**:
    - Establish and enforce retention policies to ensure that snapshots are kept only as long as necessary. Automatically deleting older snapshots is no longer needed to minimize exposure and reduce clutter.
5. **Tags and Metadata**:
    - Utilize tags or metadata to classify snapshots based on their sensitivity and usage. This can help streamline audits and provide context regarding each snapshot's intended use and access.
6. **Disable Public Access**:

- Ensure that public access is disabled for snapshot storage locations. Review cloud provider settings to prevent public exposure by default.

7. **Educate Employees**:
    - Train employees about the risks associated with snapshots, including proper procedures for creating, securing, and deleting snapshots. Awareness can significantly reduce accidental exposure.

8. **Implement Data Loss Prevention (DLP) Systems**:
    - Use DLP systems to monitor and protect data from unauthorized exfiltration. These systems can help identify sensitive data within snapshots and enforce policies governing sharing and storage.

9. **Clean Up Sensitive Data**:
    - Before creating a snapshot, assess and remove or anonymize sensitive data that does not need to be included in the snapshot. This reduces the risk of sensitive data exposure in a breach.

Snapshots play a key role in cloud data protection but can expose sensitive information if mishandled. To stay secure, focus on strong access controls, encryption, regular audits, and staff training. These steps reduce risks while keeping your operations efficient. You can confidently manage snapshots and safeguard critical data from potential threats by prioritizing security without sacrificing functionality.

8.3 Securing Containers

Securing containers means addressing unique challenges tied to containerized applications in cloud environments. Containers package apps with their dependencies, offering unmatched agility and scalability. However, they also introduce risks like misconfigurations or vulnerabilities. Prioritize robust security practices—like regular updates, access controls, and runtime monitoring—to protect workloads effectively. By staying proactive, you'll safeguard your operations while harnessing the full potential of container technology for efficient deployments.

8.3.1 Container Image Creation

Building secure container images keeps your applications safe and resilient. Start using trusted base images, removing unnecessary components, and regularly updating dependencies. Scan for vulnerabilities throughout the process to minimize risks. By prioritizing security at this stage, you create a strong foundation for reliable deployments in containerized environments. A proactive approach ensures smoother operations while protecting your data and users from threats.

Key Considerations for Container Image Creation

1. **Minimal Base Images**:
    - Use minimal or "distroless" base images that include only the essential libraries and dependencies needed for the application to run. This reduces the attack surface by limiting the number of potentially vulnerable components.
2. **Vulnerability Scanning**:
    - Regularly scan container images for known vulnerabilities using automated tools. This should include checking both the image layers and the included packages against vulnerability databases to identify and address security risks before deployment.
3. **Dependency Management**:
    - Update libraries and packages within the container regularly to keep dependencies up to date. Use dependency management tools to automate tracking and upgrading outdated components.
4. **Image Signing**:
    - Sign container images to verify their integrity and authenticity. This ensures that only trusted images are pulled and executed in production environments, mitigating the risk of running malicious or tampered images.
5. **Layer Management**:
    - Understand and manage the layers that comprise a container image. Each layer should ideally do one thing and be kept separate to improve modularity and enable quicker

updates without impacting the entire image.

6. **Environment Variables and Secrets**:
    - Avoid hardcoding sensitive information directly within the container image, such as passwords or API keys. Instead, use runtime configuration options or secret management tools to handle sensitive data, reducing the risk of exposing them.
7. **Immutable Images**:
    - Treat container images as immutable artifacts. They should not be modified after they are built and deployed. If changes are necessary, create a new image with a new version tag, ensuring that the previous versions remain unchanged and available.
8. **Multi-Stage Builds**:
    - Utilize multi-stage builds to create lean production images. This approach allows developers to compile and build applications in one stage and then copy only the necessary artifacts to a final image, minimizing its size and potential vulnerabilities.
9. **Configuration Management**:
    - Adopt configuration management best practices, such as configuration files and environment variables, to separate configuration data from the application binary. This allows for greater flexibility and security, as configurations can be managed without altering the image.

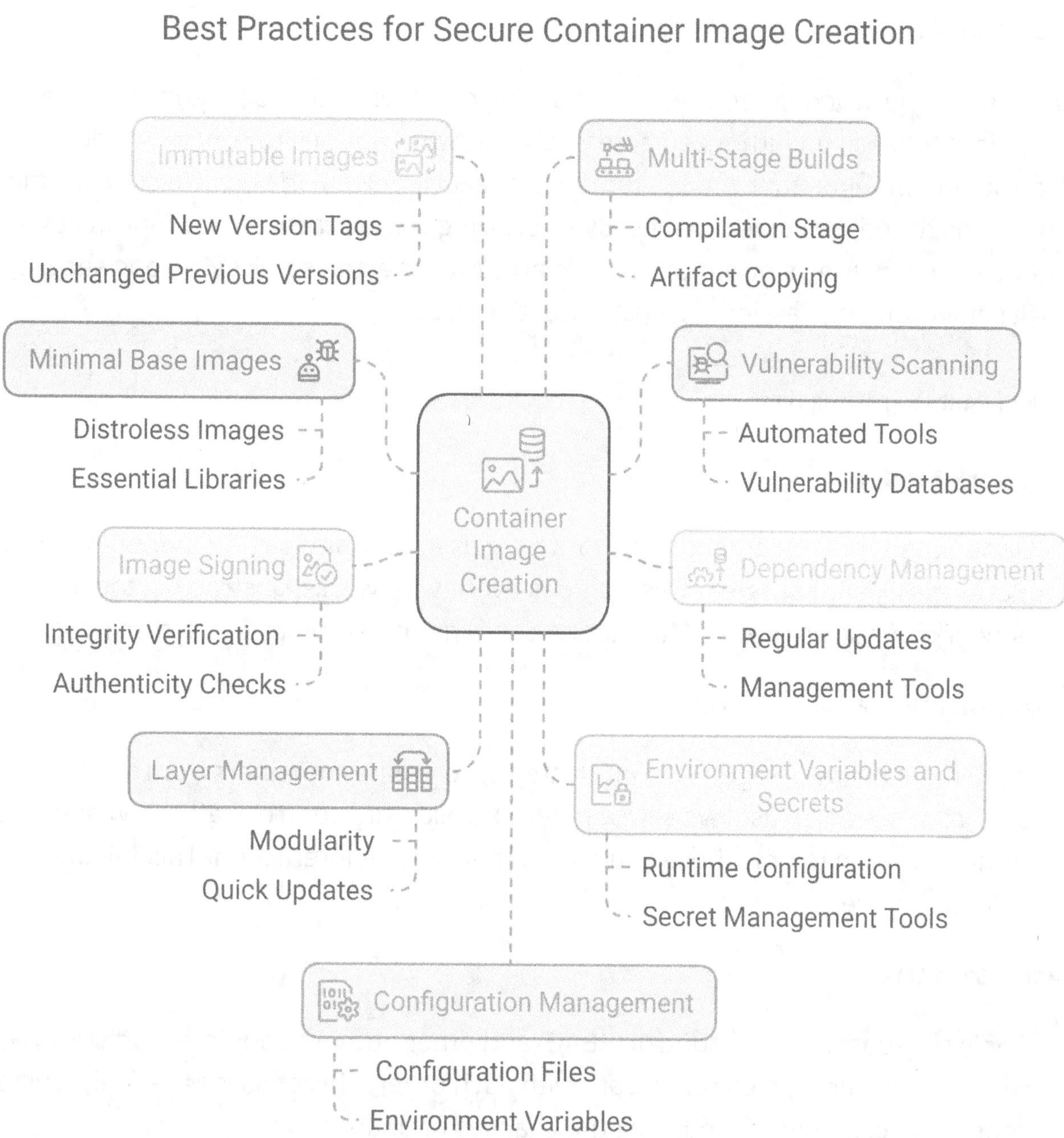

Securing container images strengthens application security. Use lightweight base images, scan for vulnerabilities often, manage dependencies wisely, and treat images as unchangeable assets. These steps reduce risks and build safer, more reliable cloud-native applications. By prioritizing these practices, teams create a stronger foundation for their containerized environments while staying ahead of potential threats. Keep your containers secure—it's an investment in long-term success and resilience.

8.3.2 Container Networking

Securing container networking requires safeguarding communication between containers and external services to block unauthorized access. Use network policies to control traffic, encrypt data in transit, and monitor connections for unusual activity. Regularly update configurations and limit permissions to reduce vulnerabilities. By prioritizing these practices, you'll protect your cloud environment while ensuring smooth operations across connected services. Strong security isn't optional—it's how you stay resilient against potential threats.

Key Aspects of Container Networking

1. **Network Models**:
   - Understand the fundamental network models applicable to container orchestration platforms like Kubernetes. This includes overlay networks, abstracting the underlying network infrastructure, and facilitating container communication across hosts.
2. **Segmentation and Isolation**:
   - Implement network segmentation strategies to isolate containers from one another based on their roles and trust levels. Use network policies to control traffic flow and limit communication to only those containers that require interaction. This minimizes the risk of lateral movement in the event of a compromise.
3. **Access Controls**:
   - Apply role-based access control (RBAC) and other authorization mechanisms to restrict which containers can communicate with each other. This ensures that only trusted containers can interact, reducing the chances of unauthorized access.
4. **Service Discovery and Load Balancing**:
   - Utilize service discovery mechanisms to facilitate container communication while ensuring that only authorized services can connect. Implement load balancers to manage traffic efficiently and securely, helping to protect backend services from direct exposure.
5. **Firewall Rules and Policies**:
   - Configure firewall rules and network policies at host and container levels to enforce secure

communication protocols. This may include whitelisting and blacklisting IP addresses or CIDR ranges and restricting unnecessary ports.

6. **Encrypted Communication**:
   - Ensure that communication between containers is encrypted to protect data in transit. Use protocols such as TLS (Transport Layer Security) to maintain the data's confidentiality and integrity.
7. **Monitoring and Logging**:
   - Implement monitoring and logging tools to track network traffic and detect suspicious interactions. Anomaly detection mechanisms can identify abnormal patterns or unauthorized access, enabling rapid incident response.
8. **Container Security Contexts**:
   - Use security contexts to define how a container interacts with the underlying host, including capabilities and network settings. Configuring these correctly can minimize the attack surface and reduce the risk of exploitation.
9. **Network Policies in Orchestrators**:
   - Leverage built-in network policy functionalities provided by container orchestration platforms (such as Kubernetes NetworkPolicies) to enforce rules about permitted traffic based on labels or namespaces, further enhancing security.

Securing container networks means protecting communication between containers and external services. To reduce risks, use strategies like network segmentation, access controls, encryption, and constant monitoring. These steps strengthen your containerized applications while fostering a safer cloud-native environment. By prioritizing security at every level, organizations can confidently safeguard their operations and maintain trust in their systems.

8.3.3 Container Orchestration & Management Systems

Container orchestration tools simplify how businesses deploy, manage, and scale containerized applications. These systems ensure smooth operations while prioritizing security and compliance. Automating repetitive tasks frees up teams to focus on innovation rather than maintenance. Whether you're managing a small app or a complex infrastructure, these platforms help keep everything running efficiently—saving time and reducing headaches for developers and IT professionals alike.

Key Concepts in Container Orchestration and Management

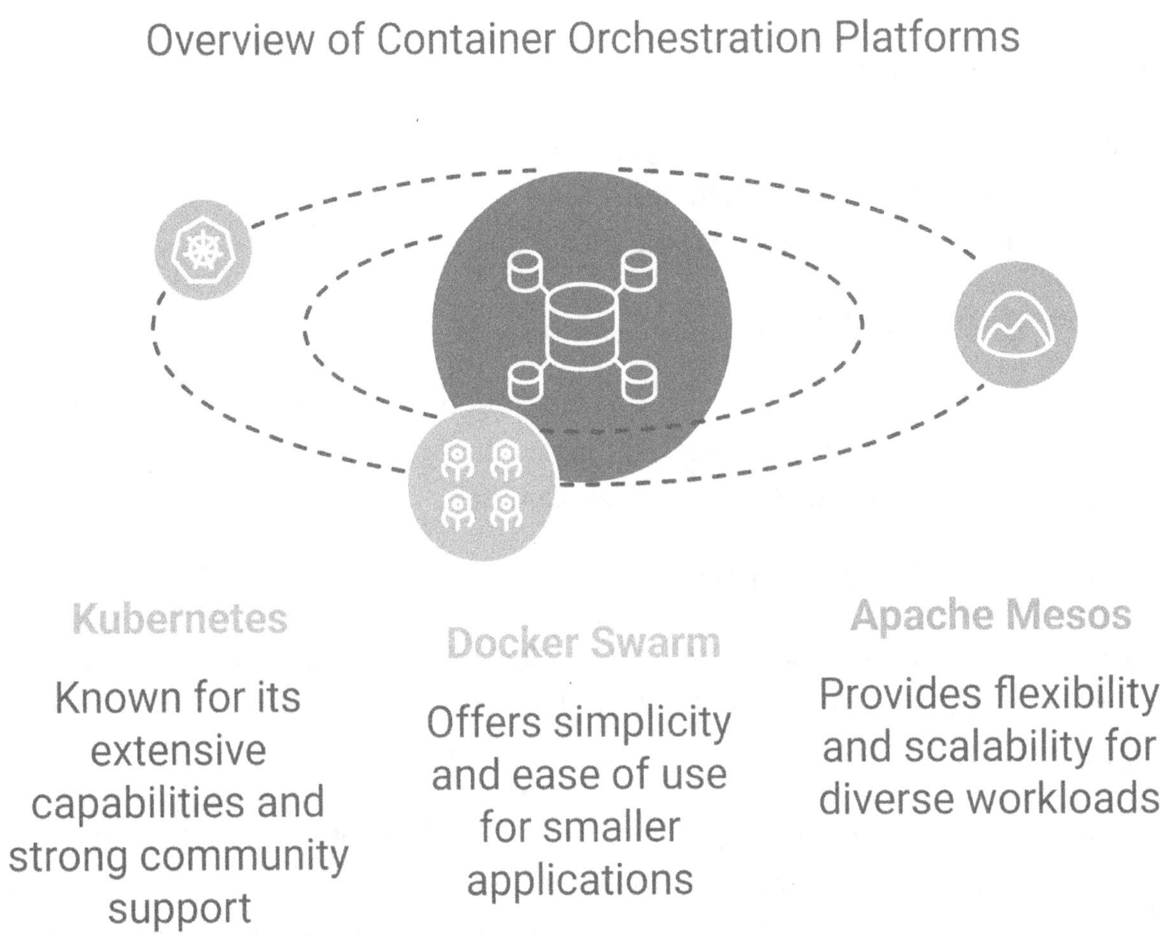

1. **Purpose of Orchestration**:
   - Container orchestration helps systematically manage the lifecycle of containers. It automates deployment, scaling, load balancing, and managing complex containerized applications.
2. **Popular Orchestration Platforms**:
   - Widely used container orchestration platforms include Kubernetes, Docker Swarm, and

Apache Mesos. Each platform provides features tailored to different use cases, with Kubernetes being the most popular due to its extensive capabilities and strong community support.

3. **Scaling and Load Balancing**:
    - Orchestration systems enable dynamic scaling of containerized applications based on demand. This can involve automatically adding or removing container instances in response to traffic patterns. Load balancing ensures that requests are distributed evenly across container instances, preventing any single instance from becoming a bottleneck.
4. **Service Discovery**:
    - Orchestration tools facilitate service discovery, allowing containers to locate and communicate with each other seamlessly. They typically provide internal DNS services that enable containers to connect using service names instead of IP addresses, which can change frequently.
5. **Configuration and Secrets Management**:
    - These systems offer mechanisms to securely manage application configuration and sensitive information, such as API keys and database passwords. This can include storing secrets in a secure store and injecting them into containers at runtime without hardcoding sensitive data into image files.
6. **Resource Management**:
    - Container orchestration platforms allocate and manage containers' resources (CPU, memory, etc.). They monitor resource usage and provide tools for optimizing resource allocation, ensuring efficient utilization of underlying infrastructure.
7. **Health Monitoring and Restart Policies**:
    - Orchestrators continuously monitor the health of running containers and automatically restart or replace unhealthy containers based on defined policies. This resiliency feature helps maintain application availability and stability.
8. **Network Security Policies**:
    - Orchestration systems permit the implementation of network security policies that govern the communication between different containers. This can include restrictions on which

services can talk to each other based on defined rules or labels.

9. **Centralized Monitoring and Logging**:
    - Most orchestration systems integrate with monitoring and logging tools to provide centralized visibility into the application's performance and security. This allows for easier troubleshooting and enhances the capability to respond to incidents effectively.
10. **Multi-Cloud and Hybrid Deployments**:
    - Container orchestration platforms can facilitate multi-cloud and hybrid cloud strategies by managing container workloads across various cloud environments. This flexibility can enhance business continuity and disaster recovery capabilities.

Container orchestration simplifies deploying and managing containerized apps, making them scalable, efficient, and secure. By automating tasks like resource allocation and monitoring, these systems save time while boosting performance. Strong security features ensure applications stay protected throughout their lifecycle. Adopting smart practices in orchestration empowers teams to build resilient cloud-native solutions that adapt quickly to changing needs. Ready for smoother operations? Start optimizing your containers.

8.3.4 Container Orchestration Security

Securing container orchestration platforms like Kubernetes demands proactive strategies to block threats and protect workloads. As businesses depend more on these systems, prioritizing security ensures smooth operations and data integrity. Focus on robust access controls, regular updates, and continuous monitoring to safeguard your environment. By staying vigilant, you'll reduce risks while maintaining trust in your infrastructure—a critical step for long-term success in today's tech-driven world.

Key Components of Container Orchestration Security

1. **Access Control**:
    - **Role-Based Access Control (RBAC)**: Implement RBAC to ensure that users and applications have permissions that align with the principle of least privilege. Roles should be defined based on specific responsibilities, limiting users to the minimum permissions necessary to perform their tasks.

- **Authentication and Authorization**: Use strong authentication methods for users and services accessing the orchestration platform. Ensure that every request to the orchestration API is authenticated and that robust authorization checks are performed.

2. **Network Security**:

    - **Network Policies**: Define and enforce network policies to control the communication between pods (containers in Kubernetes). This helps prevent unauthorized access and limits the blast radius of compromised components.
    - **Encryption of Traffic**: Secure communication between containers and between containers and external services by implementing TLS to encrypt data in transit. Ensure that sensitive data is protected from eavesdropping and man-in-the-middle attacks.

3. **Secrets Management**:

    - **Secure Storage of Secrets**: Use dedicated secrets management systems, such as Kubernetes Secrets or external tools like HashiCorp Vault, to store sensitive information (e.g., API keys and passwords) securely. Avoid hardcoding secrets in container images.
    - **Limited Exposure**: Use secrets only in the contexts where they are necessary and limit their exposure to specific containers or services.

4. **Image Security**:

    - **Vulnerability Scanning**: Regularly scan container images for vulnerabilities using automated tools. This ensures that known vulnerabilities are identified and mitigated before deployment.
    - **Trusted Image Registries**: Use trusted container image registries and maintain a whitelist of approved images. Implement image signing to ensure the integrity and authenticity of images.

5. **Runtime Security**:

    - **Monitoring and Logging**: Implement robust logging and monitoring to track container activity in real-time. Use tools that can alert to suspicious behavior or anomalies indicative of a security incident.
    - **Behavioral Analysis**: Employ runtime security tools that monitor container behavior to detect and block threats in real time, such as unauthorized file access or suspicious

process execution.

6. **Audit and Compliance**:
   - **Audit Logging**: Enable detailed audit logging on orchestration systems to capture significant actions, such as configuration changes, access requests, and deployment actions. Review logs regularly to detect potential security issues.
   - **Compliance Checks**: Conduct periodic compliance checks against established security benchmarks and standards (e.g., CIS Benchmarks for Kubernetes).
7. **Container Isolation**:
   - **Namespace and Cgroup Isolation**: Leverage the underlying features of container runtimes (like Linux namespaces) to ensure strong isolation of containers. This helps prevent unintended interference between containers and limits the impact of a security breach.
   - **Pod Security Standards**: Use pod security standards or policies to enforce security contexts at the pod level, such as running containers with non-root users and restricting privileged container capabilities.
8. **Patch Management**:
   - **Routine Updates**: Regularly update orchestration and container software to the latest versions. This minimizes exposure to known vulnerabilities, and leverages improved security features provided by new releases.
9. **Incident Response Preparedness**:
   - **Response Plans**: Develop and maintain incident response plans tailored for containerized environments. Conduct regular drills to test effectiveness and refine processes.
   - **Forensics**: Establish procedures for conducting forensics in case of a breach, allowing for investigating security incidents to identify root causes and strengthen defenses.

Securing container orchestration requires a layered approach. Focus on access control, network security, secrets management, image integrity, runtime monitoring, and compliance. By applying best practices and using built-in platform tools, you can reduce risks and protect your containerized apps. This proactive strategy safeguards sensitive data while maintaining system integrity in complex cloud setups. Stay vigilant to keep your applications secure and running smoothly in today's interconnected world.

8.3.5 Runtime Protection for Containers

Securing containerized applications during runtime protects your operations from threats lurking in production. Traditional security tools often fall short here, making runtime protection a must-have. You can safeguard workloads without disrupting performance by monitoring behavior, detecting anomalies, and blocking malicious activity. Think of it as locking the doors while keeping business running smoothly—because peace of mind matters when protecting what powers your success.

Key Aspects of Runtime Protection for Containers

1. **Behavioral Monitoring**:
    - **Anomaly Detection**: Implement systems that monitor containers' behavior in real-time to detect deviations from expected patterns. Anomalous behavior could indicate security breaches, such as unauthorized access or malware activity.
    - **Baseline Behavior Analysis**: Establish normal behavior baselines for containers and applications. Understanding typical behavior makes it easier to spot malicious actions.
2. **Intrusion Detection and Prevention Systems (IDPS)**:
    - **Container-Specific IDPS**: Utilize IDPS solutions specifically designed for container environments. These tools can identify and prevent common attacks, such as denial of service (DoS) attacks, privilege escalation, or suspicious networking activity.
    - **Integration with Orchestration Platforms**: Ensure that IDPS tools can integrate with container orchestration platforms (like Kubernetes) to provide visibility across all deployed containers and facilitate automated incident responses.
3. **Runtime Security Policies**:
    - **Policy Enforcement**: Define and enforce runtime security policies that govern how containers interact with each other, access resources, and handle sensitive data. This includes specifying which APIs can be accessed by which containers and under what conditions.

   - **Pod Security Policies**: In platforms like Kubernetes, pod security policies control container capabilities, user permissions, and privileged access settings. Limiting the privileges of containers reduces the risk of exploitation.

4. **Threat Intelligence Integration**:

   - **Real-Time Threat Intelligence**: Leverage intelligence feeds that provide information about emerging container threats and vulnerabilities. Integrating this intelligence can enhance decision-making regarding runtime security actions.

   - **Active Threat Mitigation**: Based on threat intelligence insights, perform proactive measures such as automated quarantining of potentially compromised containers or applying patches.

5. **Vulnerability Management**:

   - **Continuous Scanning**: Implement continuous vulnerability assessment tools that run scans against live containers to detect new vulnerabilities introduced post-deployment. This helps maintain an up-to-date security posture in dynamic environments.

   - **Automated Remediation**: Based on the results of vulnerability scans, establish processes for automatically remediating vulnerabilities, whether through patching or isolation.

6. **Isolation Techniques**:

   - **Process and Namespace Isolation**: Take advantage of the isolation features provided by the container runtime, such as Linux namespaces and groups, to limit the impact of any breaches. Ensure that processes within a container cannot affect processes in other containers or the host.

   - **Segmentation**: Implement network segmentation and micro-segmentation strategies to limit communication between containers only to those that require it, thus reducing the attack surface.

7. **Logging and Forensics**:

   - **Comprehensive Logging**: Enable detailed logging of container activities throughout their lifecycle. This includes access logs, error logs, and application-specific logs. Logs are vital for forensic analysis in the event of a security incident.

   - **Forensic Analysis Tools**: Utilize tools that allow for the analysis of logs and container states (including resource usage and configuration changes) to understand incidents after they occur and to improve security measures.

8. **Automated Incident Response**:
    - **Real-Time Alerts and Notifications**: Build systems that send real-time alerts based on detected anomalies or policy violations, allowing rapid response to security incidents.
    - **Automated Containment and Remediation**: Develop automated workflows for isolating compromised containers, rolling back changes, or initiating alternatives, all designed to mitigate damage.

Protecting containers during runtime means staying alert to threats while applications are active. By monitoring behavior, detecting intrusions, enforcing policies, using threat intelligence, and analyzing logs, organizations can guard against attacks from inside or outside. This continuous approach strengthens security for containerized apps in cloud-native environments. Staying proactive ensures your applications remain resilient and ready to handle modern cyber challenges confidently.

8.4 Securing Serverless and Function as a Service

Serverless computing, or Function-as-a-Service (FaaS), allows developers to run code without worrying about servers. The cloud provider provides, scales, and maintains the infrastructure so developers can focus entirely on writing and deploying their applications.

8.4.1 FaaS Security Issues

Serverless computing, especially FaaS, introduces unique security challenges. Functions run in isolated environments but often lack robust data flow and permissions control. Misconfigurations or insecure code can expose vulnerabilities. Regular audits, strong authentication, and encryption practices help mitigate risks. Developers must prioritize secure coding and stay updated on threats to protect sensitive information effectively. A proactive approach ensures safer deployments without compromising performance or scalability.

Here's a detailed explanation of the key security issues facing FaaS:

Key Security Issues in FaaS

1. **Ephemeral Execution Environment**:
    - **Short-lived Functions**: FaaS functions are often executed in short-lived, ephemeral environments that can be spun up and down quickly. This transient nature can complicate security measures such as logging and monitoring, making conducting thorough forensics after an incident harder.
    - **State Management**: As FaaS functions do not maintain a state between executions, developers must manage the state externally. This externalization of the state introduces additional security risks, particularly concerning data integrity and confidentiality when

data is shared among different function invocations.

2. **Access Control and Identity Management**:
    - **Granular Permissions**: Implementing granular access control becomes challenging because functions need permissions to interact with various cloud resources (like databases, storage, and services). Overly broad permissions can create vulnerabilities and increase the attack surface.
    - **Identity Federation**: Functions often need to authenticate and communicate with other services. Ensuring a secure identity federation, including managing tokens and credentials, is crucial to prevent unauthorized access.
3. **Cold Start Vulnerabilities**:
    - **Cold Starts**: FaaS functions may experience latency during "cold starts" (initial executions after idle). Attackers may exploit the delay or vulnerability during the startup process to perform unauthorized actions or reconnaissance.
    - **Timing Attacks**: The time taken for cold starts can be leveraged to perform timing attacks, where attackers measure the responses to infer the internal workings or bottlenecks in a system.
4. **Third-Party Dependencies**:
    - **Library and Package Vulnerabilities**: FaaS functions often utilize third-party libraries and packages. If these dependencies have known vulnerabilities, they can expose functions to risks such as code injection, data breaches, or service disruptions.
    - **Supply Chain Risks**: Using package managers and external repositories may lead to supply chain risks, where compromised third-party code can introduce malicious components into serverless applications.
5. **Denial of Service (DoS) Attacks**:
    - **Resource Limits**: FaaS providers typically impose resource limits (e.g., execution time, RAM usage) to mitigate abuse. Attackers may deliberately invoke functions repeatedly to exhaust these resources, leading to service unavailability.
    - **Event Storms**: A sudden surge in events triggering functions can lead to unmanageable load, risking application performance and availability. This storm can result from

legitimate heavy usage or malicious traffic.

6. **Data Security and Privacy**:
   - **Data Exposure**: Functions may handle sensitive data, and if proper encryption and access controls are not in place, this data could be exposed during processing or transmission.
   - **Data in Transit and at Rest**: Ensuring proper data encryption in transit to cloud services and at rest is vital to prevent interception or unauthorized access.
7. **Environment Isolation**:
   - **Shared Resources**: FaaS functions may execute in a shared environment where multiple functions from different users or customers run on the same hardware. This raises concerns regarding isolation and potential leakage of sensitive data or access tokens between functions.
   - **Container Vulnerabilities**: FaaS frameworks often use containerization for function execution. Any vulnerabilities in the container runtime or orchestration layer could lead to broader security issues affecting multiple users.
8. **Monitoring and Logging Challenges**:
   - **Limited Visibility**: The ephemeral nature of functions can make it difficult to implement comprehensive monitoring and logging, hampering the ability to detect and respond to security incidents effectively.
   - **Log Management**: Since logs may span multiple functions and services, correlating and analyzing these logs can be complex, complicating incident response efforts.

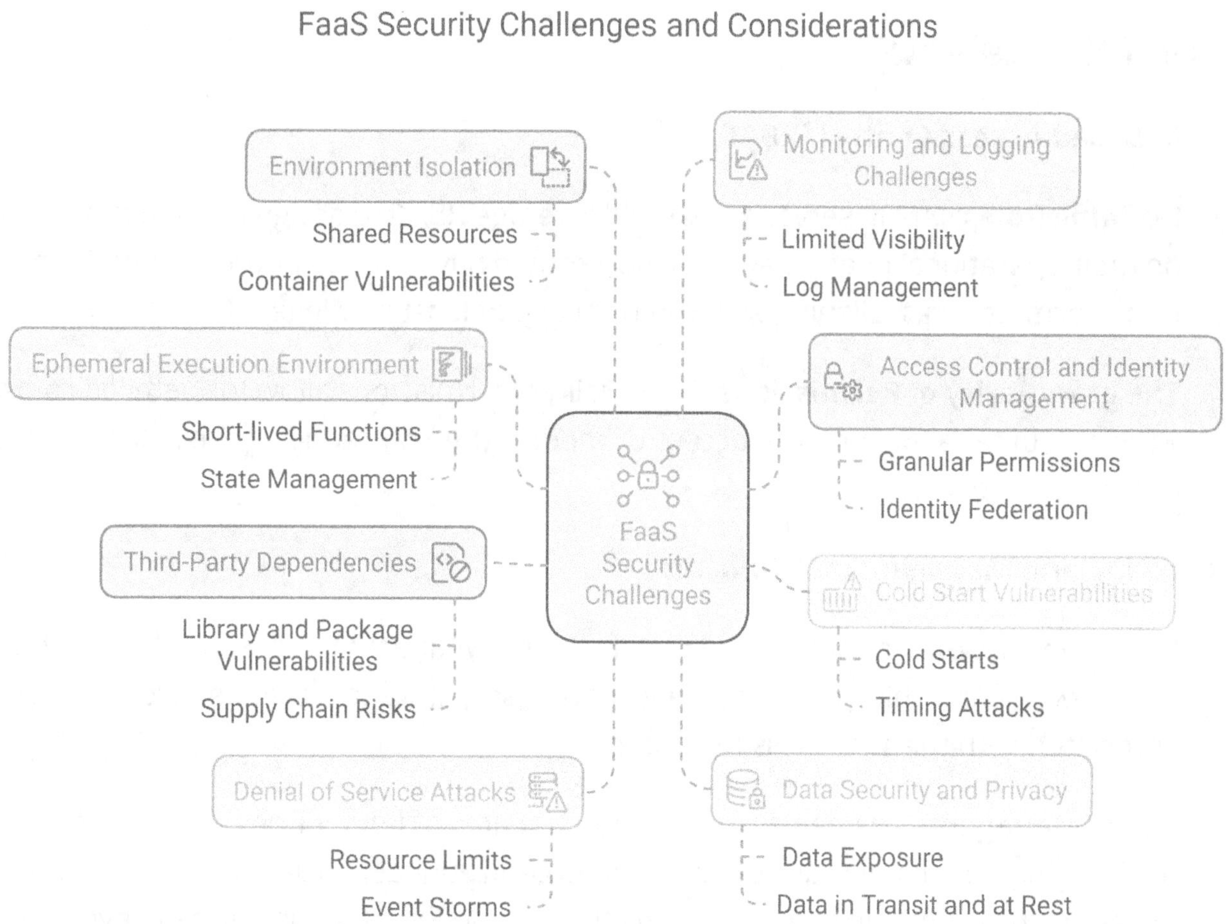

Serverless computing offers developers unmatched agility but comes with unique security challenges. Short-lived execution environments, access control gaps, and dependency risks demand proactive measures. Strengthen defenses with clear security policies, real-time monitoring, and strict identity management. By addressing these concerns head-on, organizations can safely harness the power of serverless technology while protecting sensitive data and ensuring reliable performance.

8.4.2 IAM for Serverless

Securing serverless applications starts with strong IAM practices. When deploying Function as a Service (FaaS) solutions, focus on assigning precise permissions to limit access and reduce risks. Avoid granting overly broad roles, and regularly review policies to ensure they align with current needs. By prioritizing security at every step, you'll protect sensitive data while running your serverless functions smoothly and safely.

Here's a detailed explanation of how IAM is applied within the context of serverless architectures:

Key Elements of IAM for Serverless

1. **Role-Based Access Control (RBAC)**:
    - **Defining Roles**: IAM in serverless should leverage RBAC to assign roles to functions based on their operational needs. Each function should have the minimum permissions required to perform its tasks, aligning with the principle of least privilege.
    - **The granularity of Permissions**: Fine-grained permissions allow for detailed control over what resources a function can access or modify, thereby reducing the risk associated with overly broad permissions.
2. **Creating and Managing IAM Policies**:
    - **Policy Definition**: Policies should clearly define what actions (e.g., read, write, delete) are allowable on which resources (e.g., databases, storage, other services) for each role associated with the serverless functions.
    - **Policy Management**: Regular reviews and updates of IAM policies are necessary to adapt to changing functional requirements and organizational policies. This includes removing or restricting permissions for functions that are no longer in use or have evolved.
3. **Function Principles and Authentication**:
    - **Authentication for Functions**: Serverless functions often need to authenticate with other services (like databases or APIs) to perform their tasks. A well-defined authentication strategy ensures that functions receive valid tokens and that these tokens are securely managed.
    - **Token Management**: To prevent unauthorized service impersonation, it is critical to use secured mechanisms for generating, rotating, and storing tokens (such as AWS IAM Roles for Service Accounts).
4. **Cross-Service Permissions**:
    - **Service Integration**: When serverless functions need to interact with other cloud services, careful configuration of cross-service permissions is required. This includes using service authorization scopes to limit what a function can do with external services.

   - **Implicit Trust Concerns**: In a serverless architecture, functions may implicitly trust other services based on shared environments. To prevent privilege escalation, it's vital to implement IAM policies that ensure robust qualifications of these trusts.

5. **Regular Auditing and Monitoring**:

   - **Audit Trails**: Employ detailed logging of IAM events related to serverless functions. Audit logs should record which functions were invoked, what resources were accessed, and changes to permissions or roles.

   - **Monitoring for Anomalies**: Continuous monitoring of IAM policies and events helps identify anomalous behaviors that may indicate security misconfigurations or attempted unauthorized access.

6. **IAM for Third-Party Integrations**:

   - **External Dependencies**: In many scenarios, serverless functions interact with third-party services (e.g., APIs from other providers). To mitigate risks, IAM mechanisms must ensure that any integrations are securely authenticated and authorized.

   - **Credential Management**: Establish secure methods for handling credentials, such as using secret management services to store API keys or sensitive information rather than hard-coding them into function code.

7. **Development and Deployment Practices**:

   - **Automating IAM Configuration**: Tools for Infrastructure as Code (IaC) should be used to automate the deployment of IAM roles and policies, ensuring consistent and repeatable configurations across environments.

   - **Environment Segregation**: Separate IAM roles and policies should be applied in development, testing, staging, and production environments to minimize risk exposure during the application lifecycle.

8. **Scalability Challenges**:

   - **Handling Growth**: As serverless applications scale, managing IAM roles and permissions can become increasingly complex. Templated IAM role configurations and delegating permissions to smaller roles or groups can simplify management.

   - **Dynamic Permission Adjustment**: Systems should support dynamic adjustments to IAM policies in response to changes in resource access patterns as serverless applications evolve.

To secure serverless architectures, focus on strong Identity and Access Management (IAM). Regularly review permissions, enforce least privilege, and separate duties to prevent unauthorized access. This will protect sensitive resources while meeting compliance standards. Strong IAM practices safeguard your serverless functions and ensure smooth operations in cloud environments.

8.4.3 Environment Variables & Secrets

Managing environment variables and secrets in serverless applications keeps sensitive data secure while simplifying configuration. Since serverless functions run in temporary environments, protecting credentials like API keys or database connections becomes critical. By securely storing this information, developers can prevent unauthorized access and ensure smooth application performance. Prioritize security by using encrypted storage solutions and limiting access to only what's needed for each function.

Here's a detailed explanation of the role of environment variables and secrets in serverless applications:

Key Concepts

1. **Environment Variables**:
    - **Definition**: Environment variables are key/value pairs that provide configuration settings to serverless functions. They allow functions to access settings such as database connection strings, API keys, and other configuration data without hard-coding them into the function code.
    - **Benefits**: Using environment variables helps achieve better code separation from configuration, making it easier to manage deployments across different environments (development, testing, production) without changing the codebase.
2. **Secrets Management**:
    - **Definition**: Secrets are sensitive data, such as passwords, API keys, or encryption keys, that must be kept confidential to protect them from unauthorized access.
    - **Secret Management Solutions**: Cloud providers often offer dedicated services for secret

management, such as AWS Secrets Manager, Azure Key Vault, and Google Cloud Secret Manager. These services provide secure storage, automatic rotation, and secret access control.

Best Practices for Environment Variables and Secrets

1. **Secure Storage**:
    - **Use Secret Management Services**: Instead of using plaintext environment variables for secrets, leverage cloud provider secret management services. These services encrypt secrets at rest and provide fine-grained access controls.
    - **Encryption in Transit**: Ensure that any secrets loaded into environment variables are encrypted in transit to prevent exposure during transfer.
2. **Configuration Overriding**:
    - **Environment-Specific Variables**: Use separate environment variables for deployment stages (e.g., development, testing, production). This way, configuration changes can be made without altering the function code.
    - **Dynamic Environment Variables**: Some serverless frameworks allow functions to dynamically set environment variables during deployment, adapting to different environments or runtime conditions.
3. **Limit Exposure**:
    - **Minimize Scope of Environment Variables**: Only load the environment variables necessary for the function's operation. This reduces the risk of exposing sensitive data unnecessarily.
    - **Access Controls**: Apply strict access controls to environment variables and secrets. Ensure only the necessary roles or users can access specific secrets required by functions.
4. **Regular Rotation and Expiration**:
    - **Automated Secret Rotation**: Implement policies to rotate secrets regularly, reducing the risk of long-term exposure. Secret management services often provide automated rotation features.
    - **Expiration Policies**: Set expiration dates for secrets and environment variables. This

ensures that they are reviewed and updated periodically.

5. **Audit and Monitoring**:
   - **Logging Access to Secrets**: Use audit logs to track access to secret management services. This helps identify suspicious activity or unauthorized attempts to access sensitive information.
   - **Monitoring Usage**: Monitor the usage of environment variables and secrets. Alerts can be set up to notify administrators of any unusual access patterns or usage spikes.
6. **Environment Variables in Code**:
   - **Avoid Hard-Coding**: Never hard-code sensitive information or secrets directly into the function code. This practice exposes secrets to anyone with access to the codebase.
   - **Use Environment Variable Loaders**: Utilize libraries that load environment variables securely during the function execution, ensuring that sensitive data is not exposed in logs or error messages.
7. **Emergency Access and Incident Response**:
   - **Emergency Secrets Access**: Ensure a secure and defined process for accessing secrets in case of emergencies or troubleshooting issues.
   - **Incident Response Planning**: Develop a response plan for scenarios where secrets may be compromised. This should include procedures for rotating secrets quickly and communicating changes to the affected teams.

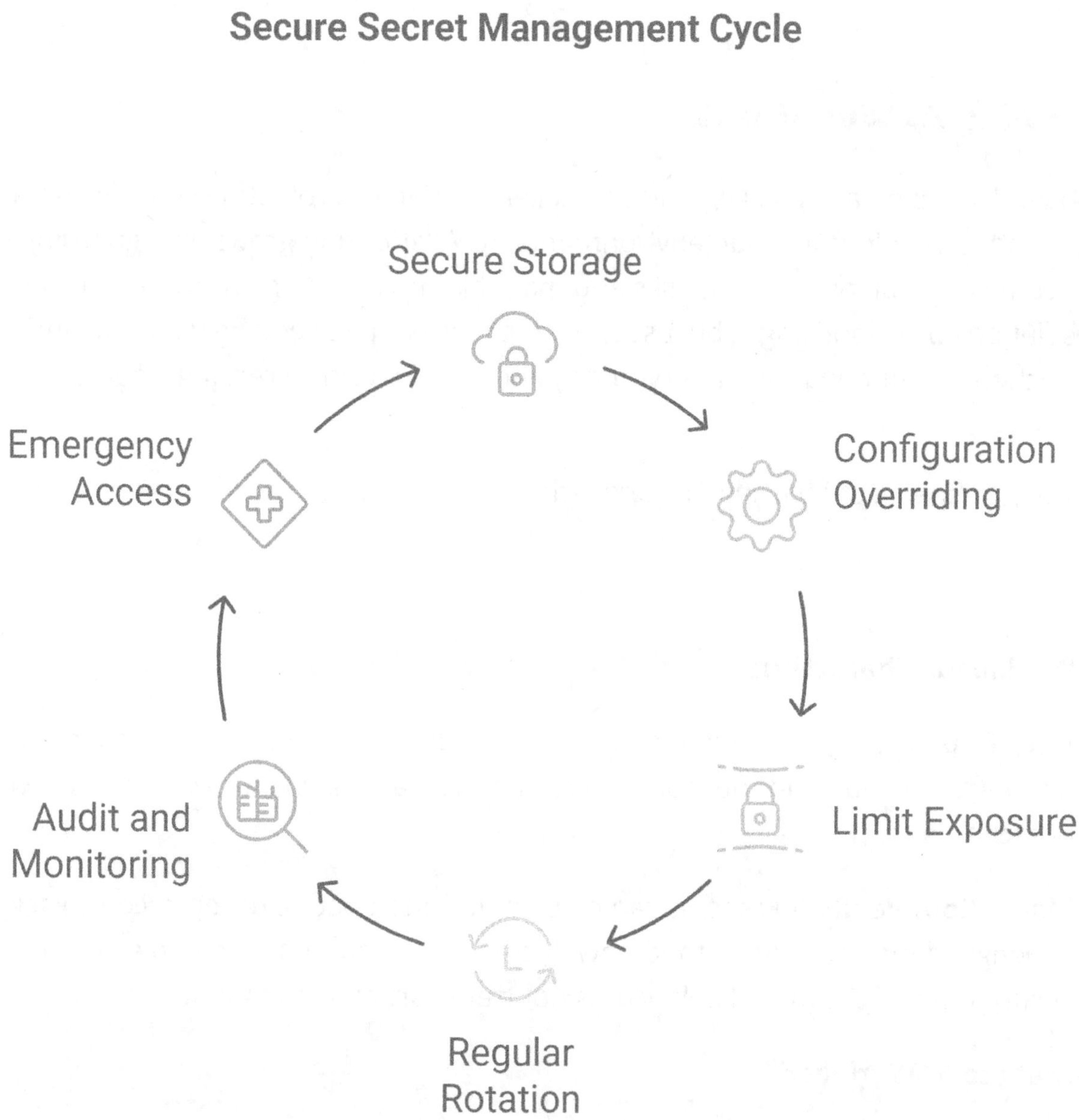

Managing environment variables and secrets in serverless apps keeps sensitive data safe and operations smooth. To stay secure, use cloud-based secret management tools, enforce strict access controls, and monitor for risks. This approach protects your app and simplifies configuration across environments, boosting reliability. Prioritize security practices to safeguard your applications while maintaining flexibility and peace of mind in today's cloud-first world.

8.5 Securing AI Workloads

Securing AI workloads means tackling unique challenges tied to protecting sensitive data and ensuring smooth operations in cloud environments. As AI adoption grows, safeguarding these systems becomes critical for reducing risks and maintaining trust. Organizations can confidently deploy AI solutions by prioritizing robust security measures while keeping vulnerabilities at bay. Strong protection isn't optional—it's how you stay ahead in a world increasingly powered by artificial intelligence.

Here are the key aspects of securing AI workloads:

Key Concepts

1. **AI Workloads Characteristics**:
    - **Data Dependency**: AI workloads are typically data-intensive, relying on large volumes of training data and real-time inputs. Securing this data against unauthorized access and breaches is crucial.
    - **Model Complexity**: AI models can be complex and opaque (often called "black boxes"), making it difficult to understand how decisions are made. This complexity can introduce security risks if the model behavior is not transparent and testable.
2. **Threats to AI Workloads**:
    - **Data Poisoning**: Attackers may attempt to manipulate the training data to influence the model's behavior, leading to biased or incorrect predictions.
    - **Model Inversion**: This technique can allow adversaries to infer sensitive information about the training data by querying the AI model.
    - **Adversarial Attacks** involve crafting inputs specifically designed to deceive the AI model, leading to incorrect outcomes or system failures.

Best Practices for Securing AI Workloads

1. **Data Security**:
    - **Data Encryption**: Always encrypt sensitive data at rest and in transit. This is crucial for protecting training data and ensuring confidentiality throughout processing.
    - **Access Controls**: Implement strict access controls to limit who can access training datasets and AI models. Use role-based access control (RBAC) to manage permissions.
2. **Model Protection**:
    - **Model Versioning**: Maintain version control for AI models to track changes and ensure only authorized versions are deployed.
    - **Protect Against Model Theft**: Use techniques such as watermarking or obfuscation to prevent unauthorized copying or use of AI models.
3. **Monitoring and Logging**:
    - **Audit Logging**: Maintain comprehensive logs of all actions taken on AI workloads, including data access, model training, and inference requests. This aids in tracking potential breaches and understanding model behavior.
    - **Real-Time Monitoring**: Implement monitoring tools to detect anomalies in data access patterns or model predictions, which may indicate possible security incidents.
4. **Input Validation and Sanitization**:
    - **Sanitize Inputs**: Validate and sanitize all inputs to AI models to protect against adversarial attacks that may exploit vulnerabilities in the input process.
    - **Rate Limiting**: Set rate limits on how often models can be queried to mitigate abusive access patterns that could lead to model inversion attacks.
5. **Model Training Security**:
    - **Secure Training Environments**: Ensure the environments used for training AI models are secured and isolated. This reduces the risk of unauthorized access during the training phase.

- **Data Source Verification**: Validate all data sources to ensure the integrity and credibility of the data being used for training, mitigating the risk of data poisoning.

6. **Robustness Against Attacks**:

   - **Adversarial Training**: Incorporate adversarial examples into the training dataset to help the AI model learn to identify and defend against potential adversarial attacks.

   - **Resilience Testing**: Regularly test AI models for vulnerabilities using penetration testing and red team exercises to identify weaknesses.

7. **Compliance and Governance**:

   - **Regulatory Compliance**: Ensure that AI workloads comply with relevant regulations and standards pertaining to data protection and AI ethics, such as GDPR or HIPAA.

   - **Ethical AI Practices**: Establish governance frameworks to ensure that AI models are developed and deployed ethically, proactively addressing biases and ensuring transparency.

8. **Incident Response Planning**:

   - **AI-Specific Incident Response**: Develop tailored response plans for AI workloads that address potential security breaches, data leaks, or adversarial attacks.

   - **Continuous Improvement**: Continuously refine security measures based on post-incident reviews and emerging threats in the AI landscape.

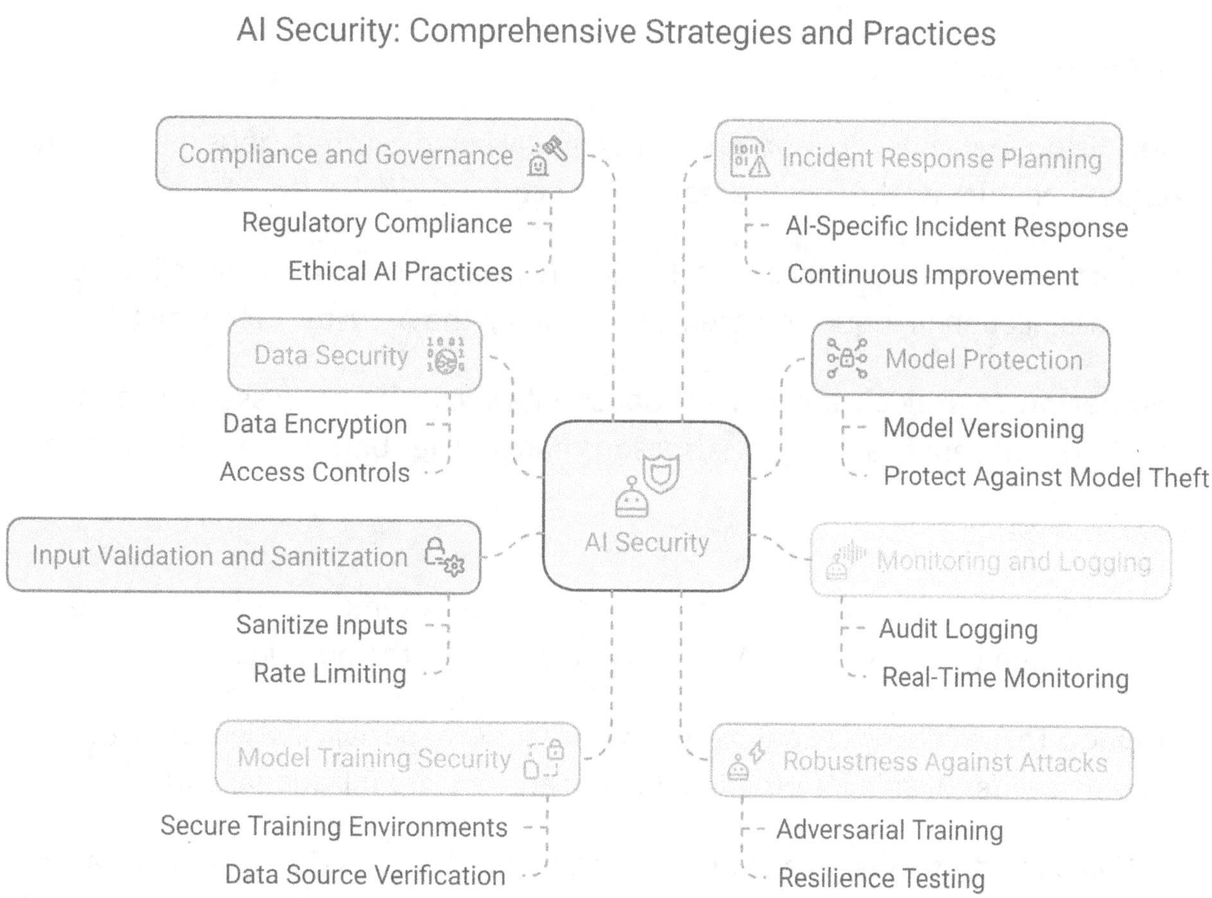

To secure AI workloads, focus on safeguarding data integrity, protecting models, and promoting ethical use. Stay alert to both traditional risks and AI-specific threats. You can reduce vulnerabilities by adopting strong data protections, active monitoring, and effective incident response plans. This approach builds trust in your AI systems while keeping them resilient against emerging challenges. Protecting your AI investments ensures they remain reliable and secure for long-term success.

8.5.1 AI-System Threats

AI systems face unique security threats, from data manipulation to adversarial attacks. As these technologies shape critical decisions, safeguarding them becomes crucial. Malicious actors can exploit vulnerabilities, compromising trust and outcomes. Organizations must prioritize robust defenses like encryption, regular audits, and bias detection to maintain reliability. Staying proactive ensures AI remains a trusted tool for innovation while protecting sensitive information and decision-making processes from potential harm.

Here's a detailed overview of the primary threats faced by AI systems:

Key AI-System Threats

1. **Data Poisoning**:
    - **Definition**: Data poisoning occurs when an attacker injects malicious data into the training dataset, corrupting the model's learning process.
    - **Impact**: This can lead to incorrect predictions, biased outcomes, or deliberate misclassification of inputs, severely undermining the AI system's reliability.
    - **Mitigation Strategies**: Implement robust data validation processes and anomaly detection to identify and reject suspicious data entries before they influence the model.
2. **Model Inversion**:
    - **Definition**: In model inversion attacks, adversaries attempt to reconstruct sensitive training data by querying the AI model and analyzing the outputs.
    - **Impact**: This can expose confidential information, especially if the training data includes personally identifiable information (PII) or sensitive organizational data.
    - **Mitigation Strategies**: Use differential privacy techniques during model training to obscure the influence of any single data point and reduce the risk of reconstructing sensitive information.
3. **Adversarial Attacks**:
    - **Definition**: Adversarial attacks involve crafting specific input data samples to deceive the AI model into making incorrect predictions or classifications.
    - **Impact**: Such attacks can compromise the AI system's integrity, leading to security vulnerabilities or manipulating outputs for malicious purposes (e.g., fraud, misinformation).
    - **Mitigation Strategies**: Employ adversarial training and robustness testing to strengthen the model against such attacks and make it more resistant to manipulated inputs.
4. **Model Stealing**:
    - **Definition**: In model stealing attacks, an adversary aims to create a copy of an AI model by querying it extensively and utilizing the outputs to approximate the original model.

- **Impact**: This can lead to intellectual property theft, unauthorized model use, and losing a competitive edge.
- **Mitigation Strategies**: To complicate the theft process, implement rate limiting on API usage, use model watermarking techniques, and obfuscate model outputs.

5. **Information Leakage**:
    - **Definition**: Information leakage occurs when AI models unintentionally reveal sensitive data about the training data during inference.
    - **Impact**: Attackers can exploit such leaks to gain insights into the underlying data and potentially access confidential information.
    - **Mitigation Strategies**: Conduct thorough testing to evaluate potential information leaks and apply techniques like output masking to hide sensitive information.
6. **Backdoor Attacks**:
    - **Definition**: Backdoor attacks involve embedding a hidden vulnerability into the model during its training phase, which specific inputs can trigger.
    - **Impact**: Attackers can exploit this vulnerability to manipulate model behavior selectively, leading to harmful outcomes.
    - **Mitigation Strategies**: Use rigorous testing and validation techniques to identify unexpected model behaviors and check for anomalies in the model's response to various inputs.
7. **Supply Chain Attacks**:
    - **Definition**: Supply chain attacks target the dependencies and components in developing AI systems, such as datasets, libraries, and frameworks.
    - **Impact**: Malicious alterations can compromise the integrity of the AI model and introduce vulnerabilities.
    - **Mitigation Strategies**: Establish secure coding practices, validate third-party libraries, and regularly audit supply chain components for security compliance.
8. **Overfitting**:

- **Definition**: Overfitting occurs when a model learns the training data too well, including its noise and outliers, making it perform poorly on unseen data.
- **Impact**: This reduces the model's generalization ability and can lead to unexpected behavior in real-world scenarios.
- **Mitigation Strategies**: To enhance model robustness, use techniques like cross-validation, regularization, and ensuring a diverse training dataset.

Understanding AI-specific threats helps organizations protect their systems and build trust. Risks like data poisoning, adversarial attacks, and model inversion can compromise security if left unchecked. By adopting proactive measures, companies safeguard sensitive information while ensuring ethical AI use. Strong defenses lead to safer, more reliable systems that deliver meaningful results without unnecessary risks. Stay prepared, stay secure—because resilient AI isn't optional; it's smart.

8.5.2 AI Risk Mitigation and Shared Responsibilities

AI risk mitigation thrives on teamwork. Organizations, developers, and service providers must share responsibilities to safeguard systems from threats. They can identify vulnerabilities, implement safeguards, and ensure accountability by working together. Collaboration not only strengthens security but also builds trust in AI technologies. Clear communication and defined roles make managing risks more effective, creating a safer environment for innovation while protecting users and stakeholders.

AI Risk Mitigation

1. **Comprehensive Risk Assessment**:
   - **Definition**: Conducting thorough assessments to identify potential risks associated with AI implementations, including security vulnerabilities, ethical concerns, and operational impacts.
   - **Implementation**: Utilize frameworks and guidelines to systematically identify risks, assess their likelihood and impact, and prioritize them based on organizational context.
2. **Data Governance**:
   - **Definition**: Establishing clear policies for data management, including data collection, storage, and processing to ensure data integrity and security.

  - **Implementation**: Develop policies encompassing data classification, access controls, and usage rights, along with strategies for ensuring compliance with regulations such as GDPR or CCPA.

3. **Model Validation and Testing**:
   - **Definition**: Thoroughly validate and test AI models to ensure their accuracy, reliability, and robustness before deployment.
   - **Implementation**: Employ various testing methodologies, such as cross-validation, stress, and adversarial testing, to evaluate model performance under different scenarios and potential attack vectors.
4. **Monitoring and Logging**:
   - **Definition**: Implementing ongoing monitoring and logging of AI system performance and behavior to detect anomalies or deviations.
   - **Implementation**: Use advanced monitoring tools to track usage patterns, system inputs and outputs, and trigger alerts for unusual behaviors that could indicate security incidents.
5. **Incident Response Planning**:
   - **Definition**: Developing a well-defined incident response plan tailored to AI systems and potential security breaches.
   - **Implementation**: Create procedures for identifying, responding to, and recovering from AI-related incidents, including clear roles and responsibilities for the incident response team.
6. **Security Controls Implementation**:
   - **Definition**: Applying appropriate security controls such as encryption, authentication, and access management to protect AI workloads.
   - **Implementation**: Implement multi-layered security measures, including network security, application security, and endpoint protection, to safeguard AI systems from various threats.

Shared Responsibilities

1. **Collaboration Among Stakeholders**:

- **Definition**: Acknowledging that AI security is a collective responsibility shared among multiple parties, including organizations, service providers, developers, and users.
- **Implementation**: Engage in open communication and partnership among stakeholders to share knowledge, insights, and best practices for AI security.

2. **Clear Role Definition**:
    - **Definition**: Clearly define the roles and responsibilities of each stakeholder in the AI ecosystem to ensure accountability and effective risk management.
    - **Implementation**: Establish detailed agreements outlining who is responsible for which aspects of AI security, including data management, model development, and operational security.
3. **Training and Awareness**:
    - **Definition**: Providing ongoing training and awareness programs for all stakeholders involved in developing and deploying AI systems.
    - **Implementation**: Regularly conduct workshops, seminars, and training sessions to educate stakeholders about AI risks, security practices, and ethical considerations.
4. **Regulatory Compliance**:
    - **Definition**: Ensuring all parties adhere to relevant laws, regulations, and industry standards concerning AI technologies.
    - **Implementation**: Regularly review and update compliance protocols to align with emerging legal and regulatory frameworks governing AI systems.
5. **Feedback Loops**:
    - **Definition**: Establishing feedback mechanisms among stakeholders to gather information about the performance and security of AI systems.
    - **Implementation**: Encourage the reporting of incidents, vulnerabilities, and lessons learned to improve AI security practices and continuously adapt to evolving threats.

Managing AI risks takes teamwork and clear strategies. Organizations can strengthen AI systems while protecting sensitive data by collaborating, defining roles, and prioritizing ongoing training. This shared effort builds trust and encourages ethical practices, ensuring AI remains reliable and secure.

Proactive planning reduces vulnerabilities and helps businesses confidently embrace AI's potential without compromising safety or integrity.

Chapter Twelve

Domain 9: Data Security

Introduction

Protecting data in the cloud requires smart strategies and reliable tools. Encryption should shield information during transfers and storage, and strict access controls should limit exposure. Security protocols should also be regularly reviewed to stay compliant with industry standards. Whether managing a business or overseeing IT operations, prioritizing cloud security safeguards sensitive information while building trust with clients and stakeholders. Stay proactive—your data's safety depends on it.

Learning Objectives

Protecting cloud data can feel overwhelming, but it doesn't have to be. Start by understanding storage types like block, object, and database storage. Strengthen security using IAM, encryption, access policies, and data loss prevention tools. Prioritize encryption at rest with strong key management practices. Don't overlook unique challenges like securing AI workloads or object storage environments. Safeguarding your cloud-stored information becomes a manageable and rewarding process with the right strategies.

9.1 Primer on Cloud Storage

Cloud storage has three forms: volume/block, object, and database. Each serves a distinct purpose and presents unique security challenges. By understanding these options, you'll confidently safeguard data in transit and at rest. This knowledge helps professionals protect sensitive information while tailoring cloud solutions to their needs. Make informed choices to enhance security and efficiency in your storage strategy.

9.1.1 Volume/Block Storage

Block storage stores data in fixed-size chunks, making it ideal for applications needing fast, reliable access. Perfect for databases and file systems, it handles high-performance workloads with ease. In cloud setups, block storage acts like a virtual hard drive you can attach to virtual machines, offering flexibility and speed. Whether running critical apps or managing large datasets, this storage solution ensures efficiency without compromising performance.

Key features of volume/block storage include:

1. **Performance**: Block storage offers high input/output operations per second (IOPS), making it ideal for workloads that demand fast read and write capabilities.

2. **Scalability**: It allows users to provision and scale storage volumes according to application needs, enabling flexibility as requirements change.

3. **Data Management**: Users can create snapshots, backups, and clones, which are crucial for data recovery and efficiency.

4. **Protocol Support**: Block storage commonly utilizes protocols such as iSCSI and Fibre Channel, allowing seamless integration with existing systems.

Understanding volume and block storage helps security professionals safeguard sensitive data while boosting cloud application performance. Mastering these storage types strengthens protection strategies and ensures smoother operations. This knowledge empowers teams to handle challenges confidently, keeping information secure and accessible when needed. Whether managing workloads or preventing breaches, knowing how storage impacts security makes all the difference in today's fast-paced tech environment.

9.1.2 Object Storage

Object storage treats data as self-contained "objects," combining the content, a unique key, and descriptive metadata. This flat structure scales effortlessly, making it perfect for managing massive amounts of unstructured data like photos, videos, or backups. By simplifying access and organization, object storage ensures businesses handle growing data demands with ease and efficiency.

Key features of object storage include:

1. **Scalability**: Object storage systems can easily accommodate growing amounts of data by adding more storage nodes, allowing for nearly limitless storage capacity. This is especially beneficial for organizations dealing with massive datasets.

2. **Metadata Richness**: Each object can have extensive metadata, which provides context and makes it easier to organize, search, and retrieve data. This feature enhances data management capabilities, allowing for advanced tagging and categorization.

3. **Access via API**: Objects are accessed through RESTful APIs, typically over HTTP, making them highly accessible for web applications and distributed systems. This simplifies the process of integrating storage with cloud services.

4. **Durability and Redundancy**: Object storage systems often incorporate built-in data redundancy and redundancy mechanisms, such as replication and erasure coding, enhancing data durability and reducing the risk of data loss.

5. **Cost-effectiveness**: Because it efficiently uses resources and can store large amounts of data at a lower cost, object storage is often more economical than traditional block storage, especially for infrequently accessed data.

6. **Data Lifecycle Management**: Object storage allows for easy implementation of data lifecycle policies, enabling automatic data transition between different storage classes based on access patterns, which optimizes costs.

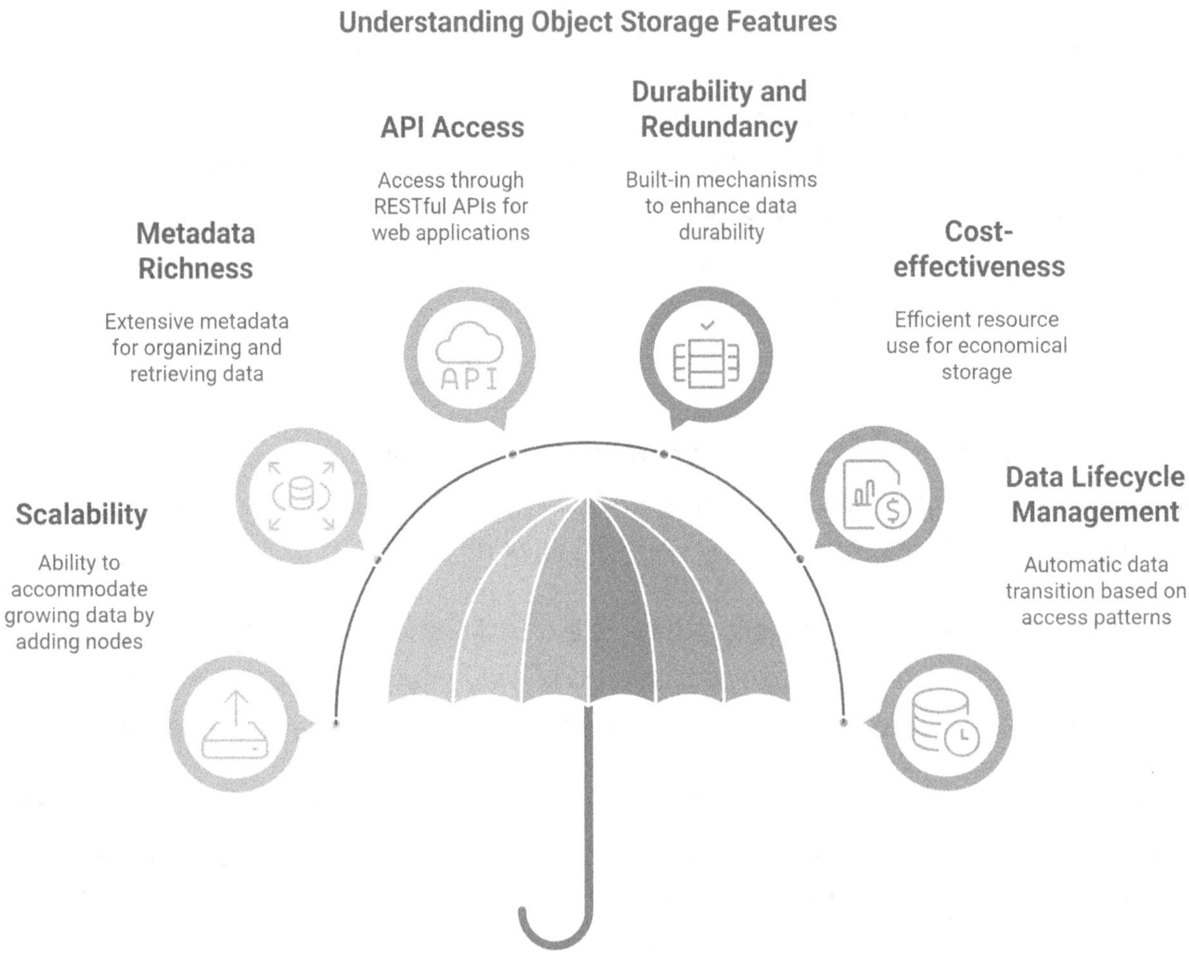

Understanding object storage matters for security professionals. It demands attention to access controls, encryption, and protecting sensitive data. With its modular design and scalability, this storage type introduces unique challenges that require thoughtful strategies. By prioritizing secure configurations and staying proactive, you can safeguard critical information while maintaining flexibility. Security isn't static—it's about adapting to evolving threats while ensuring your data remains protected and accessible only to those who need it.

9.1.3 Database Storage

Managing cloud-based database storage means keeping data secure and accessible while addressing unique challenges. Protecting sensitive information becomes a top priority as businesses rely more on cloud solutions. Strong security measures, regular updates, and proper access controls ensure your data stays safe. By staying proactive and informed, you can confidently handle the demands of modern database management without compromising security or performance.

Key considerations related to database storage in the CCSK framework include:

1. **Data Security and Protection**: Database storage often contains sensitive information, such as personal data and proprietary business information. Security professionals must implement strong encryption mechanisms for data at rest and in transit to protect against unauthorized access and breaches. Compliance with relevant regulations, such as GDPR or HIPAA, is also emphasized to protect user data.

2. **Access Control and User Management**: Access control is vital to maintaining database security. This includes enforcing the principle of least privilege, using role-based access controls (RBAC), and regularly reviewing user permissions to ensure only authorized individuals can access or manipulate data.

3. **Database Configuration and Hardening**: Proper configuration and hardening of database systems are essential in reducing vulnerabilities. This involves disabling unnecessary features, changing default settings, and applying security patches to mitigate risks associated with known vulnerabilities.

4. **Monitoring and Logging**: Continuous monitoring and logging of database activity help detect suspicious behavior and potential security incidents. Implementing alerting mechanisms based on abnormal patterns can lead to early detection of unauthorized access attempts or data breaches.

5. **Backup and Recovery**: Database storage solutions must include robust backup and recovery strategies to ensure data can be restored in the event of loss due to malicious attacks, accidental deletions, or system failures.

6. **Performance and Scalability Considerations**: Understanding the performance implications of database security measures is crucial, as overly stringent security controls can affect application response times. The CCSK encourages organizations to balance security with performance and scalability needs according to business requirements.

7. **Shared Responsibility Model**: Acknowledging the shared responsibility model for cloud security is essential. Service providers and customers must clearly define their respective roles in securing database storage, including understanding which aspects of security, such as data encryption and patch management, are each party's responsibility.

Securing database storage demands a strong grasp of cloud security, compliance, and risk management. By adopting smart protection strategies, you can shield sensitive data while fully embracing cloud computing's potential. Prioritize encryption, access controls, and regular audits to stay ahead of threats. A proactive approach safeguards information and builds trust in your cloud solutions, making security a cornerstone of success.

9.1.4 Other Types of Storage

"Other Types of Storage" in CCSK v5 covers cloud solutions that address unique data needs beyond object and database storage. These include specialized options like block storage or file systems, each requiring tailored security measures. Protecting sensitive information demands a clear understanding of these alternatives and their vulnerabilities. By adopting robust practices, organizations can ensure their data remains secure while effectively meeting diverse operational requirements.

Key considerations for "Other Types of Storage" in the CCSK framework include:

1. **Block Storage** is a storage type typically used for applications requiring low-latency access and high performance, such as databases and virtual machines. It treats data as blocks that can be accessed independently and is often used with traditional enterprise applications. Ensuring security involves implementing encryption, access controls, and regular audits to prevent unauthorized access to data blocks.

2. **File storage** allows for a hierarchical organization of data in directories and files, making it suitable for use cases such as shared file systems or media libraries. File storage security measures include user authentication, permissions management, and data encryption. Maintaining versioning and data integrity is also essential.

3. **Backup and Archival Storage**: Backup solutions are critical for disaster recovery strategies, while archival storage is used for long-term retention of infrequently accessed data. Security measures should include strong encryption for data at rest and in transit, access controls to limit who can restore or access backups, and regular testing of backup integrity and restorability.

4. **Content Delivery Networks (CDNs)**: CDNs efficiently deliver content, such as images and videos, to end-users. They distribute copies of data across various geographically distributed servers. Security in CDNs involves implementing HTTPS for secure data transfer, using access controls to restrict who can upload or modify content, and employing DDoS protection

measures.

5. **Unstructured and Semi-Structured Data Storage**: Other storage solutions may cater to unstructured data (like documents, videos, and images) and semi-structured data (e.g., JSON or XML files). The security focus here should include classification and tagging to facilitate data management, application of encryption, and deployment of data loss prevention (DLP) mechanisms to protect sensitive information.

6. **Considerations for Data Privacy and Governance**: Different types of storage often come with distinct regulatory requirements. Organizations should understand the legal and compliance obligations related to the stored data types (e.g., personal data, financial data) and implement governance frameworks accordingly.

7. **Shared Responsibility Model**: Similar to database and object storage, the shared responsibility model applies to all other types of cloud storage. Organizations must delineate responsibilities between themselves and the cloud service provider regarding data security, including data protection measures, incident response responsibilities, and compliance with data protection laws.

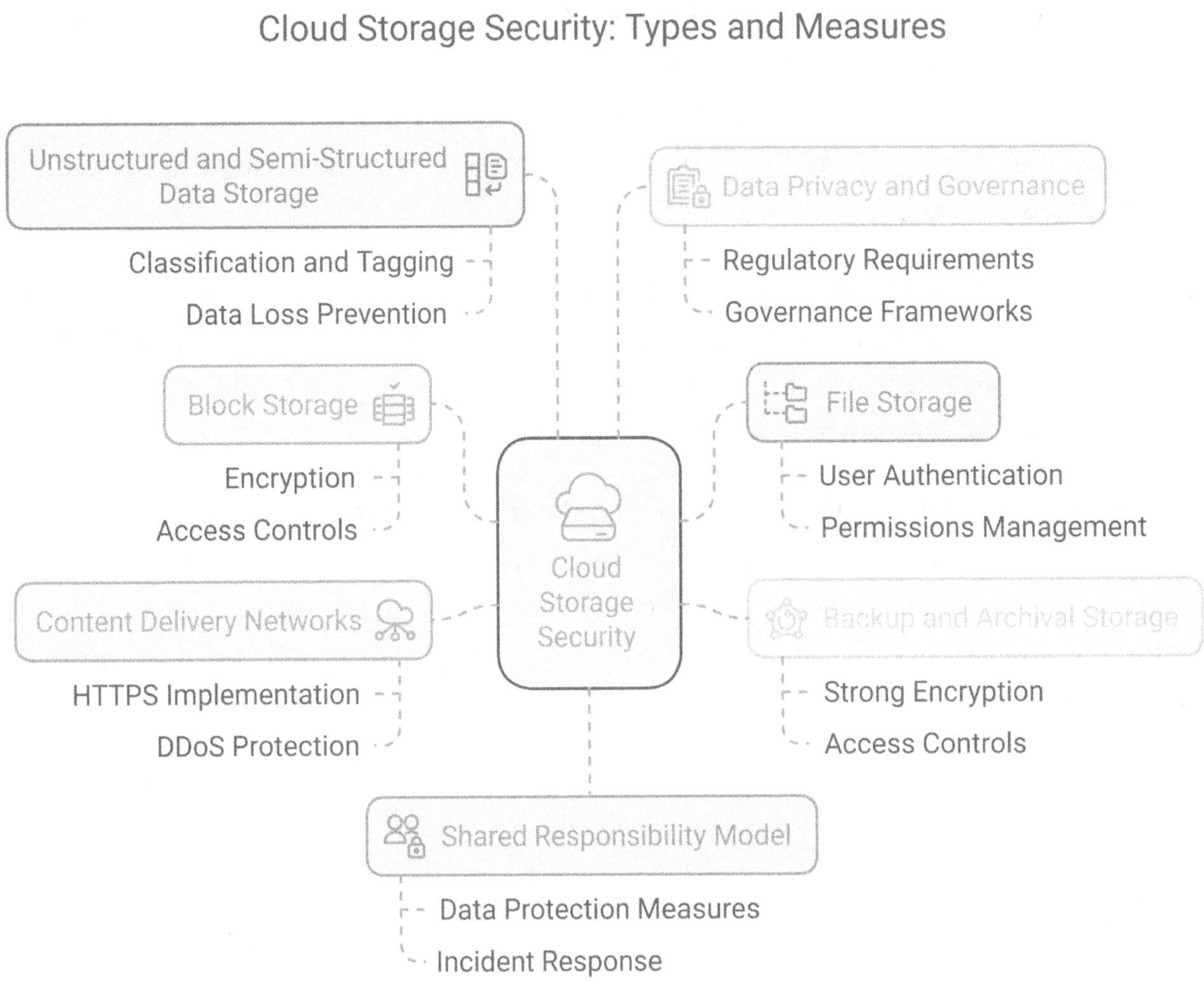

Understanding "Other Types of Storage" in CCSK v5 highlights the need to secure diverse cloud storage solutions. Each type has unique risks, so applying tailored protections ensures data stays safe while maximizing cloud advantages. By addressing these differences head-on, organizations can build trust and confidence in their security strategies, protecting sensitive information without compromising efficiency or innovation.

9.2 Data Security Tools and Techniques

Protecting data in cloud environments demands smart strategies and tools. Start with data classification to prioritize security needs, then enforce strong identity and access management (IAM) to limit exposure. Encryption and data loss prevention (DLP) systems safeguard information at rest and in transit. Real-time monitoring helps catch threats early, reducing risks. By adopting these practices, organizations strengthen their defenses while staying compliant with regulations keeping sensitive information safe from breaches or unauthorized access.

9.2.1 Data Classification

Data classification organizes information by sensitivity, importance, and regulations, helping businesses protect it effectively. Within the CCSK v5 framework, this process ensures secure management of cloud-based data assets while meeting compliance standards. By categorizing data thoughtfully, organizations can prioritize security measures where they're needed most, reducing risks and safeguarding trust. It's a practical step toward smarter data handling in today's increasingly cloud-reliant world.

Key Objectives of Data Classification:

1. **Understanding Data Sensitivity**: By categorizing data, organizations can understand which data is sensitive, confidential, or regulated, enabling them to apply the appropriate security measures. For example, personal identifiable information (PII) or financial data may require higher protection than less sensitive information such as internal documents.
2. **Risk Management**: Classification helps identify the risks associated with different types of data. By comprehending the potential impact of a data breach, organizations can prioritize their resources and efforts to safeguard the most critical assets.
3. **Compliance and Governance**: Many regulations, such as GDPR, HIPAA, and PCI DSS, dictate specific requirements for handling sensitive data. Proper classification ensures that organizations comply with these regulations and maintain data governance standards.

Classification Levels:

Data classification typically involves creating levels or tiers of classification, such as:

- **Public**: Data that can be freely shared without any adverse consequences. Examples include marketing materials or publicly available information.

- **Internal**: Information that is intended for internal use only and not meant for public disclosure. This category may include employee handbooks or internal reports.
- **Confidential**: Sensitive information that requires protection against unauthorized access. This can involve proprietary information, trade secrets, or personal data.
- **Restricted**: Highly sensitive data with strict access controls due to its potential impact on the organization if compromised. Examples include financial records or customer PII.

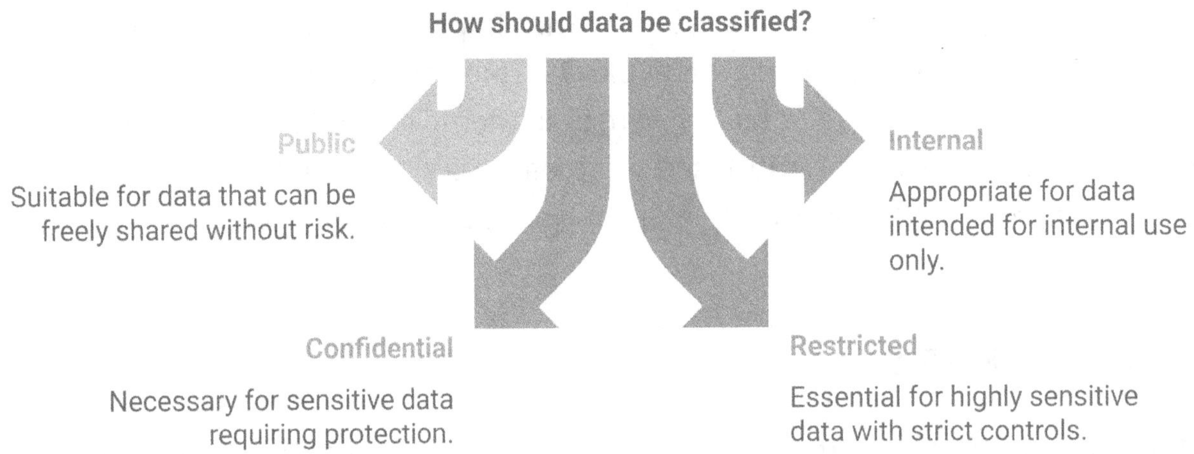

Classification Process:

1. **Asset Identification**: Organizations start by identifying all data assets that require classification, including databases, files, documents, and applications.
2. **Data Inventory**: Creating an inventory of identified data assets allows organizations to assess the amount and type of data they possess.
3. **Defining Criteria**: Establishing criteria for classification is vital. This may include factors such as sensitivity, value to the organization, legal requirements, and potential impact of loss or breach.
4. **Classifying Data**: Based on the defined criteria, data is classified into the established levels. This process often involves collaboration among various stakeholders, including legal, compliance, and IT teams.

5. **Implementing Security Controls**: Once data is classified, organizations can apply tailored security controls based on the classification level. For example, confidential data may need encryption and access restrictions, while public data may have fewer controls.

6. **Ongoing Review and Maintenance**: Data classification is not a one-time task. Organizations should regularly review and update their classifications as data changes or new regulatory requirements emerge.

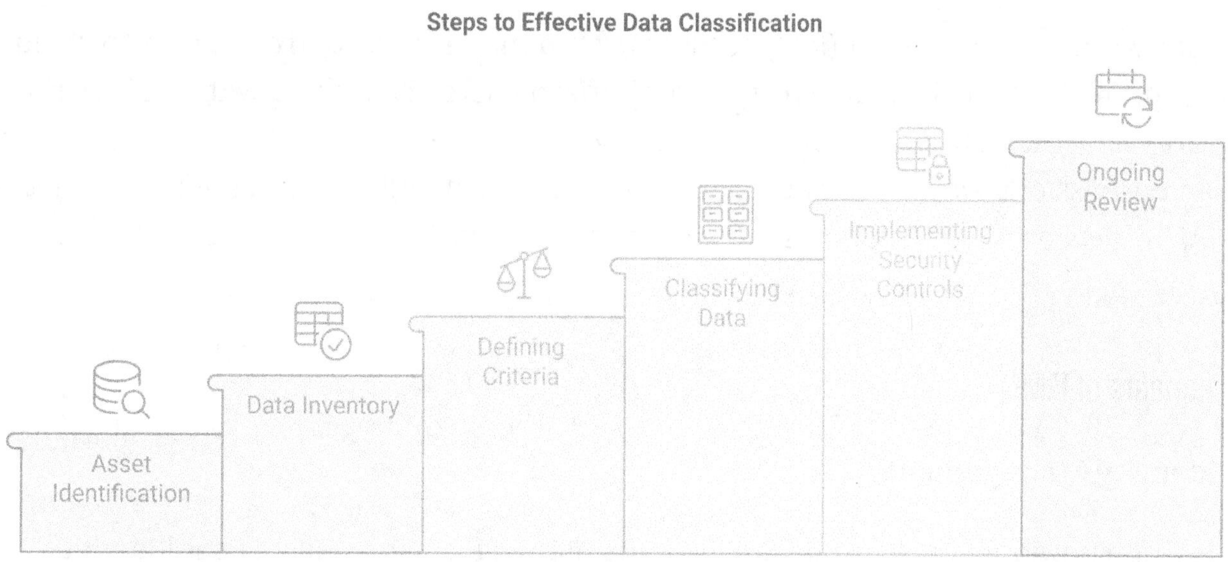

Benefits of Data Classification:

- **Improved Security Posture**: By identifying and applying appropriate security measures for sensitive data, organizations can minimize the risk of breaches.
- **Enhanced Operational Efficiency**: Clear categorization streamlines the process of data management and reduces redundancy, making it easier for teams to locate and utilize data.
- **Facilitated Compliance**: Data classification helps organizations adhere to regulatory requirements by ensuring that sensitive information is handled per prescribed standards.
- **Accountability and Responsibility**: Classifying data clarifies data ownership and accountability, making it easier to assign responsibilities for data protection across the organization.

Effective data classification strengthens cloud security by helping organizations manage and safeguard information while meeting legal and regulatory requirements. Within the CCSK framework, this approach simplifies compliance and reduces risks, ensuring sensitive data stays protected. By prioritizing clear categorization, businesses can build trust, enhance operational efficiency, and maintain control over their most valuable assets in a secure environment.

9.2.2 Identity and Access Management (IAM)

Identity and Access Management (IAM) secures user identities and controls access to cloud resources, protecting sensitive data from unauthorized users. By aligning with CCSK v5 principles, IAM ensures only the right people access critical systems. Strong policies and technologies simplify managing permissions while reducing risks. For businesses handling confidential information, robust IAM practices build trust and safeguard operations in today's connected world. Don't leave security to chance make IAM a priority!

Key Components of IAM:

1. **Identity Management**:
    - This component focuses on creating, maintaining, and managing user identities within an organization. It includes processes for registering new users, modifying existing user roles, and deactivating users no longer associated with the organization.
    - Each identity is associated with unique attributes, such as username, password, roles, and permissions, which determine the levels of access users have.
2. **Access Management**:
    - Access management involves defining and enforcing policies that dictate who can access what resources and under what conditions. This includes the implementation of authentication and authorization mechanisms.
    - **Authentication** is the process of verifying a user's identity, often through methods like usernames and passwords, biometrics, or multi-factor authentication (MFA).
    - **Authorization** follows authentication and determines what an authenticated user is permitted to do, such as viewing, editing, or deleting data.
3. **Role-Based Access Control (RBAC)**:

- RBAC is a widely used access control mechanism that assigns permissions based on user roles rather than individual identities. Roles are defined according to job functions or responsibilities within the organization, simplifying the management of permissions.
- For example, an employee in the finance department may have access to financial systems and data, while an IT staff member has access to systems management tools.

4. **Policy Management**:
    - IAM includes establishing and managing access policies that govern how identities and roles interact with resources. These policies define access rights, restrictions, and compliance requirements.
    - Organizations must regularly update and review policies to ensure they remain aligned with internal controls and regulatory obligations.
5. **Audit and Compliance**:
    - An essential aspect of IAM is the capability to track and audit user activity for compliance purposes. This involves monitoring logins, access attempts, and changes to permissions or roles.
    - Auditing helps organizations detect unauthorized access or policy violations and demonstrates adherence to regulatory requirements.

Benefits of Identity and Access Management:

1. **Enhanced Security**:
    - IAM systems help reduce the risk of unauthorized access and data breaches by enforcing strict controls over user identities and access rights.
    - Multi-factor authentication (MFA) enhances security by requiring additional verification methods beyond just passwords.
2. **Improved User Experience**:
    - IAM solutions streamline the authentication process for users, reducing friction with single sign-on (SSO) capabilities that allow access to multiple applications with a single set of credentials.

   - This enhances productivity by minimizing the time users spend managing passwords or logging into different systems.

3. **Operational Efficiency**:

   - Automating identity and access management reduces manual overhead associated with user onboarding, modifications, and offboarding, decreasing administrative burden on IT teams.

   - Organizations can quickly provision access for new hires or update permissions as job functions change.

4. **Regulatory Compliance**:

   - IAM helps organizations meet various regulatory requirements related to data privacy and protection by ensuring that sensitive data is accessible only to authorized personnel.

   - It facilitates reporting and audits, thereby demonstrating compliance with standards such as GDPR, HIPAA, or PCI DSS.

Challenges in IAM Implementation:

1. **Complexity**: Organizations with numerous applications and services may find it challenging to implement a unified IAM approach across diverse platforms.

2. **User Resistance**: Changes to authentication processes or user permissions may face resistance from employees accustomed to previous systems, requiring careful change management.

3. **Integration with Legacy Systems**: Integrating IAM solutions with existing legacy systems can pose technical challenges, often requiring additional resources and effort.

4. **Maintaining User Privacy**: Balancing security needs with user privacy concerns is vital. Organizations must ensure that IAM practices do not infringe on individual privacy rights.

Strong Identity and Access Management (IAM) is key to safeguarding sensitive data in cloud environments. By managing user identities and controlling access, organizations reduce security risks, boost compliance, and streamline operations. Effective IAM practices empower businesses to confidently embrace cloud technologies while keeping their data secure. Prioritizing IAM not only strengthens protection but also builds trust with stakeholders, ensuring a safer and more efficient approach to modern data management.

9.2.3 Access Policies

Access policies define how users gain permission to resources and data within an organization. They're a cornerstone of Identity and Access Management (IAM), especially in cloud environments where managing permissions across platforms can get tricky. Clear rules ensure security, prevent unauthorized access, and keep operations running smoothly. By implementing well-structured policies, organizations protect sensitive information while empowering teams to work efficiently and confidently in today's interconnected world.

Key Elements of Access Policies:

1. **Definition of Access Levels**:
    - Access policies clearly define various access levels and permissions assigned to users based on roles, responsibilities, or departments within the organization.
    - Common access levels include read-only, edit, delete, and administrative rights, each tailored to specific user needs.
2. **Role-Based Access Control (RBAC)**:
    - Access policies often utilize Role-Based Access Control (RBAC) to streamline permission management. In RBAC, users are assigned roles that encapsulate specific access rights, which aligns with their job functions.
    - By grouping permissions into roles, organizations can ensure that users receive only the access necessary for their duties, reducing the risk of unnecessary exposure.
3. **Access Request Process**:
    - Access policies establish procedures for requesting access to resources. This process may include formal requests through an access management system, approvals from supervisors or managers, and auditing mechanisms to review and log access requests.
    - Clear procedures help maintain accountability and ensure that access is granted based on legitimate business needs.

4. **Conditional Access**:

    - Access policies may include conditions that determine when and how access is granted. For example, conditional access policies might consider factors such as user location, time of access, or device security posture before allowing entry to sensitive systems.

    - This enhances security by implementing a more granular approach to access control.

5. **Periodic Review and Auditing**:

    - Access policies should require regular reviews of user access rights to ensure they are current and appropriate. This review process helps identify and revoke any unnecessary permissions as users change roles or depart from the organization.

    - Auditing capabilities also ensure compliance with internal policies and external regulations by tracking access logs and changes to permissions.

6. **Integration with Compliance Requirements**:

    - Access policies must align with relevant regulations and compliance frameworks that govern data protection, such as GDPR, HIPAA, or PCI DSS. Organizations need to ensure that access controls meet the stringent requirements set forth by these regulations.

    - Access policies should specify how access will be managed to comply with contractual and legal obligations regarding data privacy and security.

7. **User Training and Awareness**:

    - Effective access policies should incorporate training programs to educate users about their roles in maintaining data security. Users should understand the importance of access controls, how to request access appropriately, and the consequences of unauthorized access.

    - Creating awareness can reduce the risk of accidental violations and promote a security-focused culture.

Benefits of Access Policies:

1. **Enhanced Security**:

    - Well-defined access policies help minimize the risk of data breaches and unauthorized access by ensuring that only the right individuals can reach sensitive information or systems.

2. **Operational Efficiency**:
   - Automating policy enforcement simplifies access management processes, allowing for quicker provisioning and de-provisioning of access rights as needed.
3. **Accountability and Transparency**:
   - Access policies establish clear accountability for access decisions and actions taken, which supports organizational transparency and can aid in forensic investigations in case of security incidents.
4. **Regulatory Compliance**:
   - Adhering to strong access policies helps organizations meet compliance mandates, reducing legal and financial risks associated with data breaches.

Challenges in Access Policy Management:

1. **Policy Complexity**: As organizations grow and adopt new technologies, maintaining access policies can become increasingly complex, requiring ongoing review and adjustment to address technological and organizational changes.
2. **User Resistance**: Policies that are too restrictive may face pushback from users who find them cumbersome, necessitating a balance between security needs and user experience.
3. **Lack of Awareness**: If users are not adequately trained or informed about access policies, they may inadvertently violate them or fail to follow established procedures.
4. **Integration Issues**: Organizations may encounter difficulties integrating access policies across various platforms and applications, especially when using third-party services or legacy systems.

Access policies shape strong security practices by managing who gets access to what. Clear roles, streamlined request processes, and conditional safeguards protect sensitive data while meeting compliance standards. By prioritizing these measures, organizations reduce risks and simplify operations.

9.2.4 Encryption and Key Management

Protecting sensitive data in cloud environments starts with strong encryption and secure key management. Encrypt information both at rest and in transit to safeguard it from unauthorized access. Equally crucial, manage encryption keys responsibly store them securely and control who can access them. These practices not only shield your data but also build trust with users by demonstrating a commitment to security and privacy.

Key Concepts of Encryption and Key Management:

1. **Encryption**:
    - **Purpose**: The primary purpose of encryption is to safeguard data from unauthorized access. By converting readable data (plaintext) into an unreadable format (ciphertext), encryption ensures that only authorized users with the correct decryption key can access the original data.
    - **Types of Encryption**:
        - **Symmetric Encryption**: Uses the same key for both encryption and decryption. It's efficient for large data volumes but poses risks if the key is compromised.
        - **Asymmetric Encryption**: Utilizes a pair of keys (public and private). The public key encrypts the data, and the private key decrypts it. This method enhances security but can be slower than symmetric approaches.
2. **Encryption in Cloud**:
    - **Data at Rest**: Refers to encrypting data stored on physical storage devices in the cloud. This includes databases, file systems, and backups. It protects data against unauthorized access and breaches.
    - **Data in Transit**: Involves encrypting data being transmitted over networks. This is crucial to prevent eavesdropping and man-in-the-middle attacks during data transfer.
3. **Key Management**:
    - **Key Lifecycle Management**: The process of managing cryptographic keys through their lifecycle, from generation and distribution to retirement and destruction. Effective key management is crucial to maintaining the security of encrypted data.

- **Key Generation**: Utilizing strong cryptographic algorithms to generate keys that are difficult to guess or brute-force.
- **Key Storage**: Secure methods for storing keys, ensuring they are protected from unauthorized access. This could involve hardware security modules (HSMs) or cloud provider key management services.
- **Key Rotation**: Regularly updating keys to mitigate risks associated with long-term key use. This helps to limit potential exposure if a key becomes compromised.
- **Access Control**: Implementing strict controls over who can access encryption keys, typically following the principle of least privilege.

4. **Regulatory Compliance**:

    - Organizations must comply with relevant regulations and standards (e.g., GDPR, HIPAA) that mandate specific encryption practices and key management procedures. Compliance not only enhances security but also helps in avoiding legal and financial penalties.

5. **Data Loss Prevention (DLP)**: Encryption is often coupled with DLP strategies to safeguard sensitive data. It helps in ensuring that even if data is stolen or lost, it remains unreadable without the proper keys.
6. **Cloud Provider Tools**: Many cloud service providers offer built-in key management solutions that integrate with their cloud services. These tools allow organizations to manage encryption keys more easily while maintaining compliance with security practices.

Strong encryption and secure key management can drastically cut the risk of data breaches while safeguarding sensitive information. Organizations must prioritize efficient practices to stay compliant with regulations and strengthen cloud security. By doing so, they not only protect their data but also build trust with clients and stakeholders. Make encryption a cornerstone of your strategy it's a proactive step toward safer operations and long-term success.

9.2.5 Data Loss Prevention

Data Loss Prevention (DLP) protects sensitive information from being lost, misused, or accessed by unauthorized users. By combining strategies and tools, DLP safeguards confidential data while helping organizations meet regulatory requirements. Think of it as a shield for your most valuable information—keeping it secure and ensuring only the right people have access. Strong DLP practices build trust and protect both businesses and their customers.

Key Elements of Data Loss Prevention:

1. **Definition**:

    - Data Loss Prevention involves policies and tools that monitor, detect, and respond to data breaches or unauthorized data transmissions. It aims to safeguard sensitive data, whether it is stored in the cloud, in transit, or being used within applications.

2. **Types of Data**:

    - DLP solutions focus on various types of sensitive data, including personally identifiable information (PII), financial records, healthcare data, intellectual property, and other proprietary information.

3. **DLP Strategies**:

    - **Data Discovery**: Identifying and categorizing sensitive data across all storage locations, which may include cloud environments, on-premises systems, and endpoints. This process helps organizations understand where their sensitive data resides and ensure appropriate protection measures are in place.

    - **Data Classification**: Classifying data according to its sensitivity level (e.g., public, internal, confidential, restricted) enables organizations to apply tailored security measures based on the classification.

4. **DLP Technologies**:

    - **Endpoint DLP**: Monitors and controls data transfer to and from endpoints such as laptops, desktops, and mobile devices. It may include preventing unauthorized copying of sensitive data to USB drives or blocking email attachments containing sensitive information.

    - **Network DLP**: Protects data during transmission over networks by monitoring traffic and preventing the unauthorized transfer of sensitive information outside the organization. This can include inspecting email, web traffic, and other protocols.

    - **Storage DLP**: Focuses on securing data stored within cloud storage services or databases. It involves setting policies to encrypt, mask, or restrict access to sensitive data.

5. **Policy Enforcement**:

    - Organizations establish DLP policies that define acceptable use, data protection standards, and response measures for data breaches. DLP solutions automate the enforcement of these policies, such as blocking unauthorized data transfers or notifying security personnel of potential incidents.

6. **Incident Response**:
    - DLP tools provide alerts and reporting mechanisms when sensitive data breaches or policy violations occur. This allows organizations to initiate incident response procedures to mitigate damage and investigate the incident.
7. **Compliance**:
    - Effective DLP measures help organizations comply with various regulations, such as GDPR, HIPAA, and PCI-DSS, which require the protection of sensitive data. Compliance is enforced through proper data handling procedures and reporting capabilities provided by DLP solutions.
8. **User Training and Awareness**:
    - An important aspect of DLP is educating users about the importance of data security and the policies in place. Continuous training helps to promote a culture of security, empowering employees to identify and report potential data loss risks.
9. **Cloud Provider Integrated DLP Solutions**:
    - Many cloud service providers offer integrated DLP capabilities that allow organizations to apply data protection measures natively within their cloud environments. This helps streamline management and enforcement of DLP policies across cloud resources.

Data Loss Prevention plays a key role in cloud security, shielding sensitive information from breaches or unauthorized access. By adopting smart strategies and using the right tools, businesses can reduce risks, meet compliance standards, and build trust with their customers. Strengthening your approach to protecting data doesn't just safeguard information it reinforces confidence in how you handle it.

9.3 Cloud Data Encryption at Rest

Protecting cloud-stored data requires strong encryption and smart key management. By encrypting information when idle, you reduce risks of unauthorized access or breaches. Focus on secure encryption methods and managing keys effectively to maintain confidentiality and integrity. These strategies empower security professionals to safeguard sensitive information while building trust in cloud environments.

9.3.1 Cloud Data Key Management Strategies

Managing encryption keys effectively keeps your cloud data safe and secure. This process includes creating, storing, sharing, and retiring cryptographic keys used to protect sensitive information. Weak practices can leave gaps for attackers, so strong strategies tailored to your setup are a must. Prioritize clear policies, automation where possible, and regular audits to reduce risks and maintain trust in your security measures.

Key Management Strategies:

1. **Key Lifecycle Management**: Implement processes to manage the key lifecycle—from generation and distribution to expiration and destruction. Ensure that keys are rotated regularly and that old keys are securely retired to prevent unauthorized access.

2. **Use of Key Management Services (KMS)**: Leverage built-in key management services provided by cloud vendors (e.g., AWS KMS, Azure Key Vault, Google Cloud KMS). These services offer secure key storage, automated key rotation, and audit logging, reducing the complexity of managing keys manually.

3. **Separation of Duties**: Establish a separation of duties for key management processes. Limit access to key management functions to specific roles within the organization, reducing the risk of insider threats or unauthorized access.

4. **Access Controls**: Implement strict access controls to ensure that only authorized personnel have access to cryptographic keys. Use role-based access control (RBAC) and policies to manage and restrict access based on users' needs.

5. **Encryption Key Location**: Consider where keys are stored relative to the data they encrypt. Storing keys in a different location (e.g., a KMS) from the encrypted data may provide an additional layer of security.

6. **Audit and Monitoring**: Regularly audit key management practices and monitor access to keys. Ensure that all key usage is logged, and conduct periodic reviews to identify and rectify any security gaps.

7. **Compliance and Regulatory Needs**: Familiarize yourself with compliance requirements (e.g., GDPR, HIPAA) that may dictate how encryption keys should be managed. Tailor key management practices to meet these legal and regulatory standards.

8. **Training and Awareness**: Provide training for personnel involved in key management processes to ensure they understand best practices, potential risks, and the importance of their roles in maintaining data security.

9. **Backup and Recovery**: Establish backups for keys in secure locations, ensuring that keys can be recovered in case of loss. Develop a disaster recovery plan that includes procedures for key recovery.

10. **Hybrid and Multi-Cloud Strategies**: If utilizing multiple cloud providers or hybrid environments, implement a consistent key management strategy that accommodates all platforms. This helps maintain security and compliance across diverse systems.

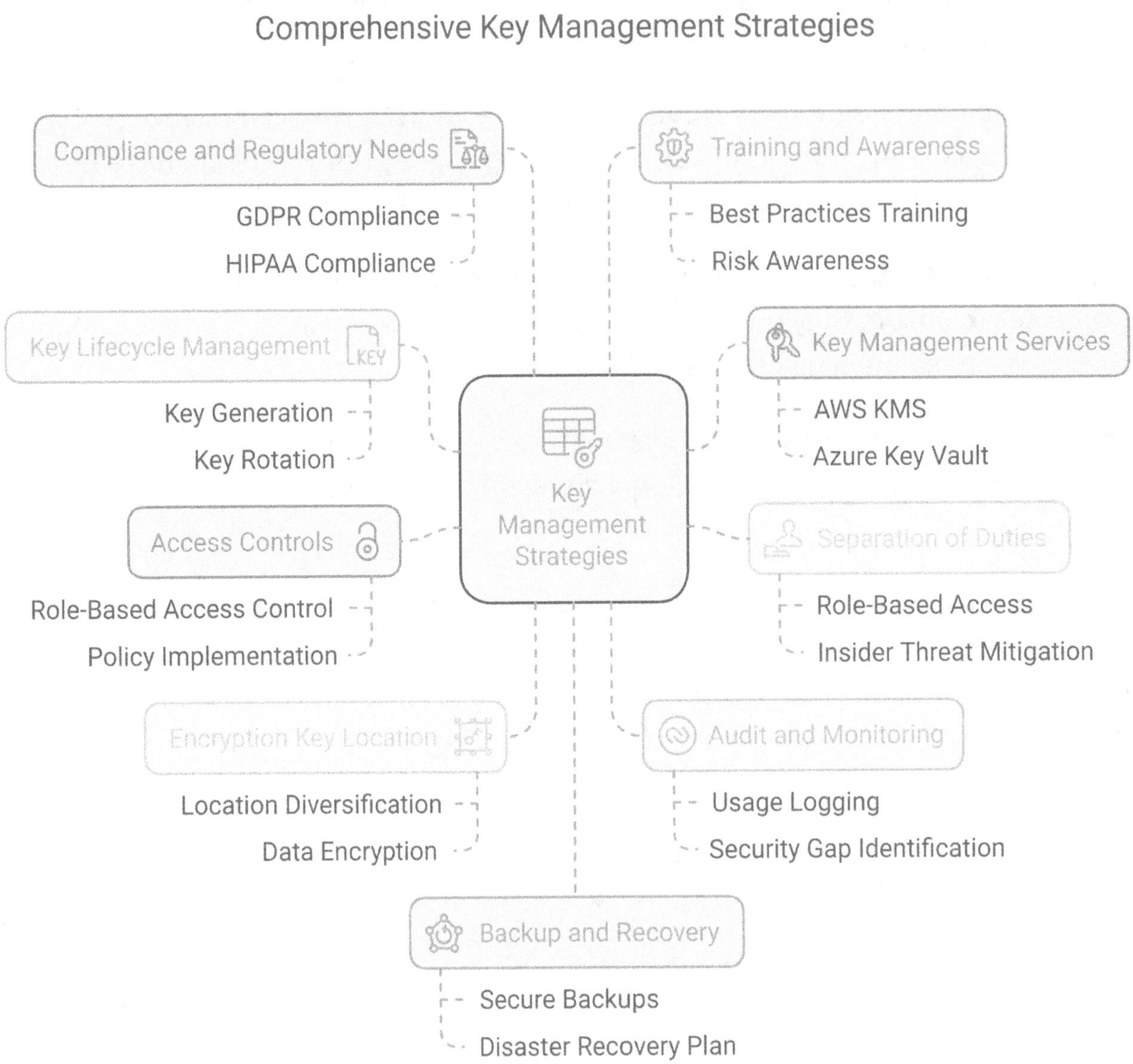

Tips and Best Practices:

- **Regularly Review Key Management Policies**: Conduct frequent reviews of key management policies and practices to adapt to changing threats and compliance requirements.
- **Test Key Recovery Procedures**: Periodically test key recovery processes to ensure that they work effectively in case of data loss or a disaster event.
- **Utilize Strong Encryption Algorithms**: Employ industry-standard, strong encryption

algorithms (e.g., AES-256) for data protection, ensuring that they are suitable for the data's sensitivity level.

- **Documentation**: Maintain thorough documentation of key management practices, including key generation, storage, access practices, and audit logs. This can assist in compliance audits and security reviews.

Adopting these strategies strengthens cloud data encryption key management, safeguarding sensitive information while reducing breach risks. By prioritizing robust practices, organizations build trust and ensure their data remains secure in cloud environments.

9.3.2 Data Encryption Recommendations

Encrypting data in the cloud keeps sensitive information safe, whether stored or moving. Strong encryption practices protect confidentiality, maintain integrity, and meet compliance standards. Use robust algorithms, secure key management, and encrypt both at rest and during transmission. By prioritizing these steps, you'll safeguard your data from unauthorized access while staying aligned with security regulations.

Encryption Recommendations:

1. **Use Strong Encryption Algorithms**:
    - **Recommendation**: Employ encryption algorithms that are widely recognized and trusted, such as AES (Advanced Encryption Standard) with a key size of at least 256 bits.
    - **Reason**: Strong encryption algorithms withstand brute force attacks and cryptographic analyses, ensuring robust protection against data breaches.
2. **Encrypt Sensitive Data at Rest and in Transit**:
    - **Recommendation**: Encrypt data both when stored (at rest) and during transmission (in transit).
    - **Reason**: Encrypting data at rest protects it from unauthorized access if storage infrastructure is compromised, while encrypting data in transit secures it against interception during transmission over networks.
3. **Implement End-to-End Encryption (E2EE)**:

- **Recommendation**: For highly sensitive data, use end-to-end encryption methods where data is encrypted on the sender's device and only decrypted by the recipient.
- **Reason**: E2EE ensures that no intermediaries can access unencrypted data, enhancing privacy and security.

4. **Utilize Key Management Practices**:
   - **Recommendation**: Implement robust key management practices to create, manage, and store encryption keys securely.
   - **Reason**: Keys must be protected to maintain data security; compromised keys can undermine the entire encryption scheme.
5. **Apply Encryption Based on Data Sensitivity**:
   - **Recommendation**: Conduct data classification to determine sensitivity levels and apply encryption accordingly.
   - **Reason**: Not all data requires the same level of encryption; focus resources on protecting the most sensitive information.
6. **Regularly Update Encryption Methods**:
   - **Recommendation**: Stay updated on the latest encryption technologies and best practices, and be willing to upgrade outdated or insecure encryption schemes.
   - **Reason**: As technology evolves, so do the methods used by attackers; regularly updating encryption techniques helps to keep data secure.
7. **Document Encryption Policies**:
   - **Recommendation**: Create comprehensive documentation outlining encryption policies, including algorithms used, key management processes, and roles and responsibilities.
   - **Reason**: Documentation ensures that all stakeholders understand encryption practices and assists with compliance audits.
8. **Use Hashing for Integrity Checks**:
   - **Recommendation**: Use cryptographic hashing functions (e.g., SHA-256) to create hashes for data integrity checks.

- **Reason**: Hashes can verify that data has not been altered or tampered with during storage or transmission.

9. **Be Compliant with Regulations**:

    - **Recommendation**: Familiarize yourself with applicable compliance regulations (e.g., GDPR, HIPAA) and ensure encryption practices meet these standards.
    - **Reason**: Regulatory compliance is crucial for avoiding fines and maintaining trust with customers and stakeholders.

10. **Conduct Regular Security Assessments**:

    - **Recommendation**: Periodically evaluate the effectiveness of encryption methods and related security practices through security assessments and penetration testing.
    - **Reason**: Regular assessments help identify vulnerabilities and areas for improvement, reinforcing overall security posture.

Tips for Implementation:

- **Implement Automated Encryption Solutions**: Utilize tools and services that provide automated encryption processes to reduce human error and ensure consistent application across all data.
- **Monitor for Anomalies**: Implement monitoring tools to detect any anomalous activities related to data access and encryption to quickly respond to potential security threats.
- **Educate Employees**: Conduct training sessions for employees about data encryption principles, the importance of data security, and how to handle sensitive information properly.
- **Back-Up Encrypted Data**: Ensure that backups of important data are also encrypted. This protects data from unauthorized access even if backup systems are compromised.

By encrypting data effectively, organizations strengthen cloud security and safeguard sensitive information from breaches or unauthorized access. Strong encryption practices not only protect critical assets but also build trust with users and stakeholders. Prioritizing robust encryption ensures a safer environment for operations while reducing risks. Start implementing these strategies today to secure your organization's future and maintain confidence in your ability to handle confidential information responsibly.

9.4 Data Security Posture Management

Data Security Posture Management (DSPM) strengthens cloud security by actively assessing and improving how organizations protect sensitive data. By identifying risks and ensuring compliance, DSPM safeguards against breaches while keeping your information secure. Think of it as a proactive shield for your cloud-stored data offering peace of mind in an increasingly connected world. Stay protected, stay compliant, and keep threats at bay with a robust DSPM strategy.

Key Components of Data Security Posture Management:

1. **Continuous Monitoring and Assessment**:
   - **Explanation**: DSPM involves continuous monitoring of cloud environments to assess the security of data at rest and in transit. This includes reviewing configurations, access controls, and encryption practices.
   - **Importance**: Regular assessments help detect misconfigurations, unauthorized access, or vulnerabilities before they can be exploited by attackers.
2. **Data Classification and Risk Assessment**:
   - **Explanation**: Organizations must categorize data based on sensitivity and value. Risk assessments identify potential threats and vulnerabilities associated with each category.
   - **Importance**: This prioritization helps implement appropriate security measures tailored to the level of risk posed to different data types.
3. **Policy and Compliance Management**:
   - **Explanation**: DSPM includes the development and enforcement of data security policies that govern data handling, access, and encryption. Compliance checks ensure adherence to legal and regulatory standards.
   - **Importance**: Establishing clear policies improves accountability and reduces the likelihood of data breaches, while compliance management helps avoid penalties and reputational damage.

4. **Incident Response Preparation**:
    - **Explanation**: Organizations should prepare for potential data breaches with an incident response plan that includes steps for containment, eradication, and recovery.
    - **Importance**: A well-defined incident response strategy minimizes the impact of security incidents on data and helps organizations recover quickly.
5. **Integration with Cloud Security Tools**:
    - **Explanation**: DSPM should integrate with cloud security tools such as Data Loss Prevention (DLP), Security Information and Event Management (SIEM), and Cloud Security Posture Management (CSPM).
    - **Importance**: Integrated tools provide real-time insights, alerting security teams to anomalies and potential threats related to data.
6. **Automated Reporting and Analytics**:
    - **Explanation**: Utilize automated reporting features and analytics to generate security insights related to data posture over time.
    - **Importance**: Automation reduces manual effort, provides real-time visibility, and helps data security teams make informed decisions quickly.

Tips for Implementing Data Security Posture Management:

1. **Establish a Data Governance Framework**: Create a comprehensive framework that outlines data ownership, classification, handling processes, and security responsibilities across the organization.
2. **Utilize Data Discovery Tools**: Implement tools to discover and classify data across cloud environments. Understanding where sensitive data resides helps in applying the appropriate security measures effectively.
3. **Set Up Baseline Security Configurations**: Define baseline security configurations for cloud services and data storage. Regularly review these configurations to ensure they comply with best practices and organizational policies.
4. **Conduct Regular Security Training**: Provide ongoing training for employees on data security best practices, new threats, and incident response protocols to foster a culture of

security awareness.

5. **Stay Updated on Compliance Requirements**: Regularly review and update security policies to stay compliant with evolving regulations and industry standards. Consider using compliance management tools for assistance.
6. **Implement Least Privilege Access Control**: Enforce the principle of least privilege by granting users and applications only the access needed to perform their functions. Regularly review access permissions to reduce potential risks.
7. **Review Third-Party Risk**: Assess the security practices of third-party vendors and partners with whom sensitive data is shared, ensuring they have strong data protection measures in place.
8. **Implement Incident Simulation Exercises**: Conduct incident response drills and simulations to evaluate the effectiveness of your response resources and processes, helping to prepare your organization for potential data breaches.
9. **Engage in Continuous Improvement**: Foster a culture of continuous improvement by regularly reviewing DSPM processes, identifying areas for enhancement, and adapting to the evolving threat landscape.
10. **Monitor Cloud Provider Security**: Continuously assess the security measures implemented by cloud service providers (CSPs) to ensure they meet your security requirements and standards.

Organizations can strengthen cloud data security by encrypting information during transfer and storage, regularly updating software, and patching vulnerabilities. Training employees on phishing scams and password safety reduces human error risks. Multi-factor authentication adds an extra layer of protection, while real-time network monitoring detects threats early. Partnering with reliable cloud providers ensures access to advanced tools. These steps build trust and safeguard sensitive information from potential breaches effectively.

9.5 Object Storage Security

Object storage security tackles the challenges of safeguarding data stored as objects in cloud environments. While this approach offers unmatched scalability and flexibility, it also brings unique risks like unauthorized access or data breaches. To stay secure, focus on encryption, strict access controls, and regular audits. By addressing these vulnerabilities head-on, businesses can confidently protect sensitive information while reaping the rewards of modern storage solutions.

Key Considerations for Object Storage Security

1. **Data Access Controls**:
    - Implement strict access policies to limit who can view or manipulate stored objects. Use Identity and Access Management (IAM) to define user permissions and roles.
2. **Encryption**:
    - Ensure data is encrypted both at rest and in transit. Utilize server-side encryption (SSE) for data stored in object storage and client-side encryption where applicable.
    - Consider managing encryption keys with a dedicated service or using a cloud provider's key management service (KMS) to enhance security.
3. **Data Integrity**:
    - Use checksums or similar methods to verify the integrity of data stored and ensure it has not been altered or corrupted.
    - Regularly audit and review the access logs to track who accessed data and when.
4. **Backup and Recovery**:
    - Implement a robust backup strategy to ensure that data can be restored in case of accidental deletion or corruption.
    - Test recovery procedures regularly to ensure that data can be effectively restored in an emergency.
5. **Versioning**:
    - Enable versioning features offered by many object storage solutions. This allows you to

preserve, retrieve, and restore every version of every object stored, which can help protect against data loss.

6. **Lifecycle Management**:
    - Implement data lifecycle policies to automate the movement of data to lower-cost storage classes or to delete data that is no longer needed.
    - This helps in managing storage costs while also ensuring compliance with data retention regulations.
7. **Network Security**:
    - Use Virtual Private Network (VPN) or private connections for accessing object storage to minimize exposure to the public internet.
    - Enable Network Access Control Lists (ACLs) to restrict access based on IP ranges or other criteria.
8. **Compliance and Governance**:
    - Ensure that the object storage solution complies with relevant regulations (e.g., GDPR, HIPAA). This may involve regular risk assessments and audits.
    - Use tags and metadata for better governance and management of compliance aspects.
9. **Monitoring and Alerts**:
    - Implement monitoring tools to track access patterns and detect anomalies that may indicate a security incident.
    - Set up alerts for suspicious activities, such as unauthorized access attempts or large data transfers.

Tips for Implementing Object Storage Security

- **Regular Updates**: Keep your object storage services and related software up to date to protect against known vulnerabilities.
- **Educate Users**: Provide training for users on the importance of security practices related to object storage.

- **Review Permissions**: Regularly review permissions and access controls to ensure that only authorized personnel have access to sensitive data.
- **Penetration Testing**: Perform regular penetration testing to identify and mitigate security weaknesses within your object storage configurations.

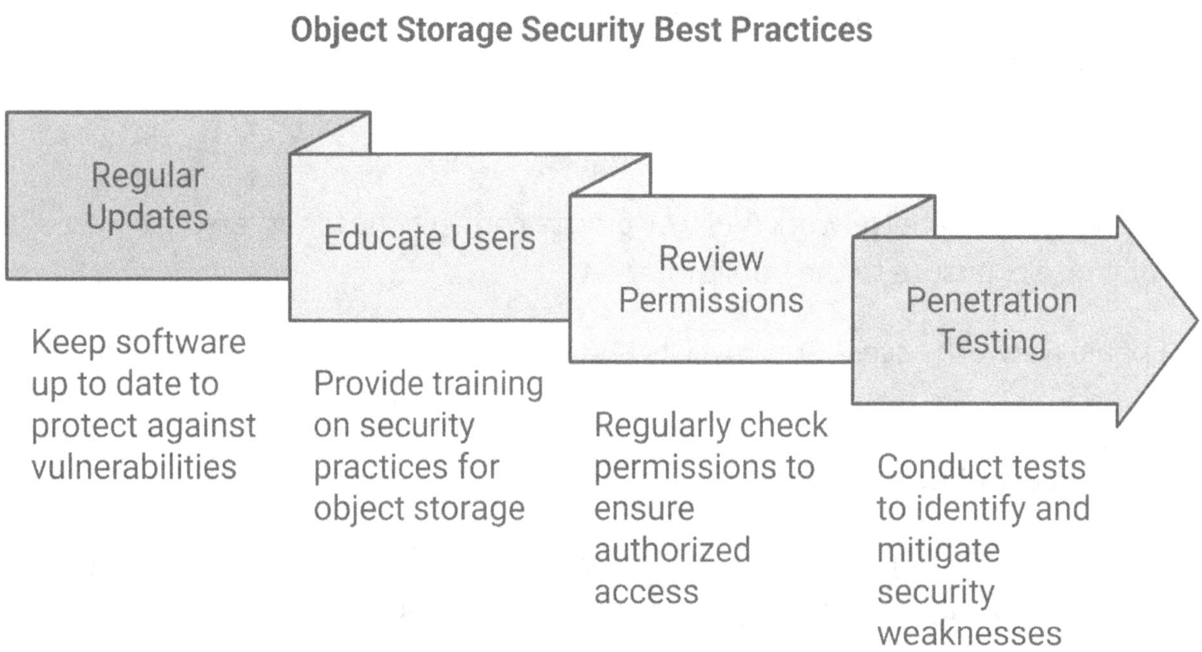

To protect object storage solutions and reduce risks like data breaches or unauthorized access, focus on strong security measures and best practices. Encrypt sensitive information, enforce strict access controls, and regularly monitor for vulnerabilities. By staying proactive, organizations can safeguard their data while building trust with users. A secure approach not only protects assets but also strengthens overall confidence in your storage systems.

9.6 Data Security for Artificial Intelligence

Securing data in AI systems means protecting both the datasets and algorithms that power them. With AI relying on vast amounts of information, safeguarding confidentiality, integrity, and availability becomes critical. Strong encryption, access controls, and robust monitoring can prevent breaches while ensuring trust in your AI models. Prioritizing security not only protects sensitive information but also strengthens confidence in how AI solutions perform and deliver value.

Key Considerations for Data Security in AI

1. **Data Classification**:
   - Understand the different types of data being used (e.g., sensitive, personal, confidential) and classify them accordingly. This helps in applying appropriate security measures based on the sensitivity level.
2. **Data Privacy**:
   - Implement privacy-enhancing technologies such as differential privacy or federated learning to protect individual data points while still enabling effective model training.
   - Ensure compliance with relevant privacy regulations (e.g., GDPR, CCPA) by anonymizing or pseudonymizing personal data.
3. **Data Integrity**:
   - Protect the integrity of data assets by implementing robust access controls and validation checks. This can prevent unauthorized modifications to the datasets used for training AI models.
   - Conduct regular audits to ensure data used is accurate and free from tampering.
4. **Access Controls**:
   - Enforce strict access controls to limit who can view and manipulate data used in AI. This includes employing IAM solutions to implement role-based access controls (RBAC).
   - Use logging and monitoring to track access and changes to sensitive data used in AI applications.
5. **Secure Data Storage**:
   - Store data used for AI in secure environments, utilizing encryption both at rest and in transit.
   - Tightly manage credentials and secrets required to access data and AI models, using secret management solutions.

6. **Model Security**:

    ◦ Protect machine learning models from adversarial attacks (e.g., data poisoning, model inversion) that aim to degrade model performance or extract sensitive information.

    ◦ Regularly update and retrain models to respond to new threats and changing data conditions.

7. **Training Data Ethics**:

    ◦ Ensure that the data used for training AI models is obtained ethically and legally. This involves obtaining necessary permissions and ensuring individuals' rights are respected.

    ◦ Assess the potential for bias within the datasets, as biased training data can lead to biased AI outcomes, impacting fairness and accountability.

8. **Incident Response**:

    ◦ Develop an incident response plan specifically for AI-related data breaches or attacks. This plan should outline procedures for containment, mitigation, and recovery.

    ◦ Include specific scenarios for dealing with compromised AI models or datasets.

Tips for Securing Data in AI Systems

- **Regular Security Training**: Educate data scientists and engineers about best security practices and the importance of data security in AI.
- **Data Minimization**: Limit the amount of personal data collected and used for training. Use synthetic data when possible to mitigate risks associated with real data.
- **Automated Security Tools**: Implement automated security solutions that can monitor data integrity and access in real-time, alerting teams to potential security incidents.
- **Conduct Risk Assessments**: Regularly assess the risks associated with the data and the AI models, adapting security measures as necessary.
- **Collaborate on Standards**: Engage with industry groups and standards bodies to stay updated on best practices and emerging threats for data security in AI.

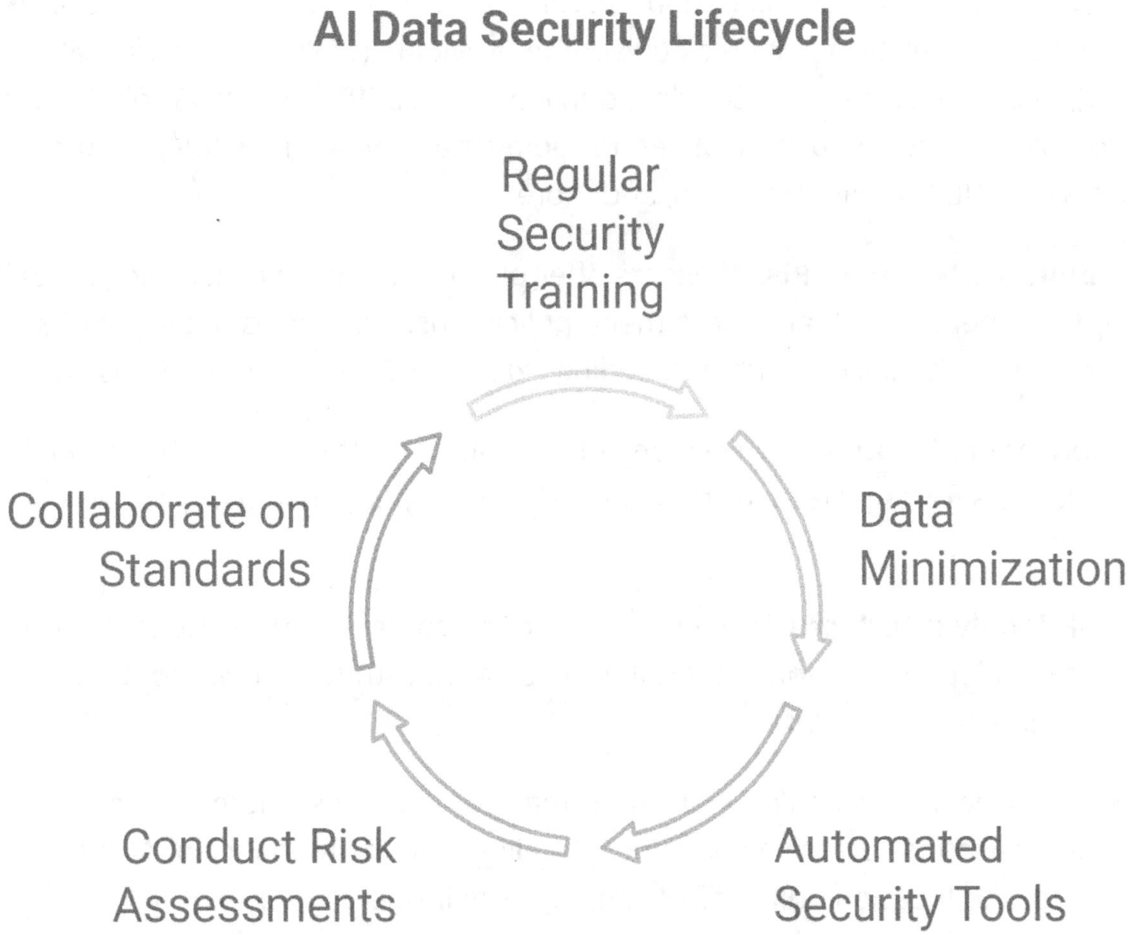

To safeguard sensitive data in AI systems, organizations should adopt strong security measures. Doing so builds trust and ensures their AI applications remain reliable. By prioritizing protection, businesses not only shield critical information but also enhance user confidence in their technology.

9.6.1 AI as a Service

AI as a Service (AIaaS) delivers artificial intelligence tools through cloud platforms, making advanced tech accessible without hefty upfront costs. Businesses can tap into AI solutions on demand, skipping the need for expensive hardware or specialized expertise. This flexible model empowers companies to innovate faster while focusing on their core goals. With AIaaS, you're free to scale smarter and stay competitive in today's fast-paced world.

Key Components of AIaaS

1. **Cloud-Based Platforms**: AIaaS solutions are typically hosted on cloud platforms, enabling scalability and flexibility. Major cloud service providers (CSPs) like Amazon Web Services (AWS), Microsoft Azure, and Google Cloud Platform (GCP) offer AIaaS solutions that encompass various AI functionalities, including machine learning (ML), natural language processing (NLP), computer vision, and more.

2. **Pre-built Models and APIs**: Providers offer pre-trained machine learning models or APIs that developers can integrate into their applications. This allows organizations to quickly implement AI capabilities without needing extensive data science expertise or resources.

3. **Customizable Solutions**: While many AIaaS solutions offer off-the-shelf models, they also provide tools for organizations to build, train, and deploy custom AI models tailored to their specific needs.

4. **User-Friendly Interfaces**: Many AIaaS platforms come with user-friendly interfaces that enable developers and non-technical users to work with AI tools without deep knowledge of the underlying algorithms.

5. **Managed Services**: AIaaS often includes managed services where the cloud provider handles the infrastructure management, scaling, and maintenance of AI resources, allowing businesses to focus on utilizing AI to enhance their operations.

Benefits of AI as a Service

1. **Cost-Effective**: Organizations can avoid significant capital expenditures on hardware and software. With AIaaS, costs are based on a pay-as-you-go model, which can lead to more predictable budgeting.

2. **Scalability**: AIaaS solutions can be scaled up or down according to the organization's needs, making it easier to manage resources effectively and respond to fluctuating workloads.

3. **Access to Expertise**: By leveraging AIaaS, businesses can access cutting-edge AI technologies developed by seasoned experts without needing in-house expertise. This democratizes access to advanced AI solutions.

4. **Faster Time to Market**: Organizations can implement AI solutions quicker, which can provide a competitive advantage in rapidly evolving markets.

5. **Continuous Updates**: CSPs typically provide regular updates and improvements to their AI tools, ensuring that organizations have access to the latest advancements without additional overhead.

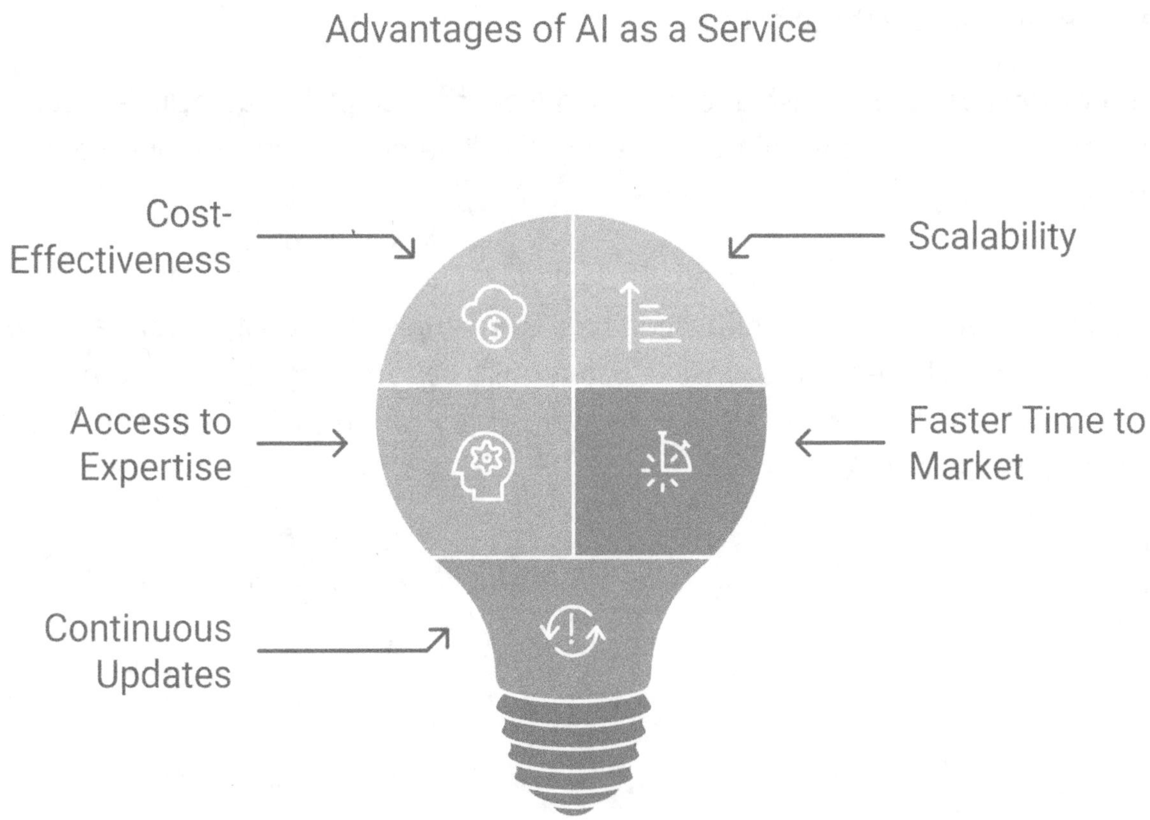

Security and Compliance Considerations for AIaaS

When using AIaaS, organizations must remain vigilant about data security and compliance. Here are some considerations:

1. **Data Security**: Ensuring that sensitive data used for training AI models is protected is paramount. Organizations should implement encryption, access controls, and monitoring for any data uploaded to AIaaS platforms.

2. **Data Privacy**: Adherence to privacy regulations (e.g., GDPR, CCPA) is crucial when dealing with personally identifiable information (PII). Organizations should anonymize data where possible and understand the data handling policies of their AIaaS provider.

3. **Vendor Management**: Organizations should conduct thorough due diligence on the AIaaS vendors they choose, assessing their security practices, compliance certifications, and reputation in the industry.

4. **Model Bias**: AI models can inadvertently learn biases present in training data. Organizations must actively monitor and evaluate the models for potential biases and take corrective measures to mitigate these risks.

5. **Incident Response**: Establish a robust incident response plan that includes scenarios for data breaches or AI model failures, ensuring quick detection and resolution of any security issues.

AI as a Service (AIaaS) offers businesses an efficient way to integrate artificial intelligence into daily operations. By tapping into cloud-based tools, companies can boost performance while keeping costs in check. However, responsible use requires addressing security, compliance, and ethical concerns upfront. Done right, AIaaS empowers organizations to innovate confidently without unnecessary complexity or risk.

Chapter Thirteen

Domain 10: Application Security

Introduction

Securing cloud applications starts with strong foundations. From designing with security in mind to ongoing maintenance, every step matters. Focus on threat modeling, testing, and integrating DevOps/DevSecOps practices to embed protection throughout development. Prioritize identity and access management tailored to application needs. By adopting these strategies, businesses safeguard sensitive data while building trust in their cloud-based solutions proving that robust security isn't optional; it's a commitment to excellence.

Learning Objectives

The learning objectives for Domain 10: Application Security include:

1. Understanding the Secure Development Lifecycle (SDLC) and its stages, including threat modeling and security testing both prior to and after deployment.

2. Recognizing the importance of architecture in securing cloud applications and how cloud-specific factors influence architectural security.

3. Exploring the relationship between identity and access management (IAM) and application security, focusing on effective secrets management.

4. Analyzing the integration of DevOps practices and the principles of DevSecOps to enhance security throughout the application lifecycle.

10.1 Secure Development Lifecycle (SDLC)

Building secure applications starts with embedding security into every stage of development. From gathering requirements to design, coding, testing, and maintenance, each phase offers opportunities to strengthen defenses. By prioritizing this approach, teams reduce risks, protect sensitive data, and ensure compliance. A secure SDLC isn't just a process it's a commitment to creating trustworthy software that meets both user needs and organizational goals while staying resilient against threats.

Special Note:

The terms **Software Development Lifecycle (SDLC)**, **Secure Software Development Lifecycle (SSDLC)**, and **Secure Development Lifecycle** refer to frameworks and methodologies used in the software development process, each with a distinct focus.

Software Development Lifecycle (SDLC)

The **Software Development Lifecycle (SDLC)** is a structured approach to software development that outlines the various stages involved in creating software applications. The typical phases include:

1. **Planning**: Identifying project goals and resource allocation.

2. **Requirements Gathering**: Collecting functional and non-functional requirements.

3. **Design**: Creating architectural and interface designs.

4. **Development**: Actual coding of the software.

5. **Testing**: Verifying that the software is free of defects and meets requirements.

6. **Deployment**: Releasing the software to users.

7. **Maintenance**: Ongoing support and updates post-deployment.

Software Development Lifecycle

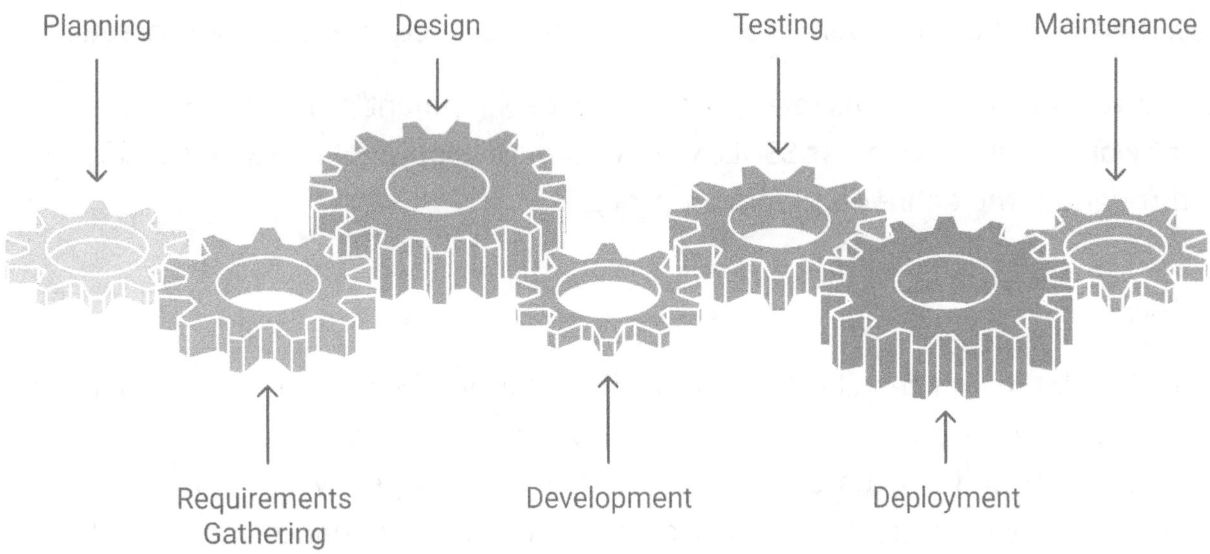

The primary goal of SDLC is to produce high-quality software efficiently while minimizing costs and risks.

Secure – Software Development Lifecycle (S-SDLC)

The **Secure Software Development Lifecycle (SSDLC)** incorporates security practices into each phase of the SDLC. Unlike traditional SDLC, which may address security concerns reactively, SSDLC emphasizes proactive security measures from the outset. Key features include:

Security Integration: Security considerations are embedded in the planning and design phases.

Continuous Testing: Security tests are performed throughout the development process rather than only at the end.

Risk Management: Identifying and addressing security risks early reduces potential costs associated with fixing vulnerabilities later in the lifecycle.

The SSDLC aims to ensure that software is not only functional but also secure against threats, making it essential for applications handling sensitive data or requiring high levels of trust.

Secure Development Lifecycle

The term **Secure Development Lifecycle** is often used interchangeably with SSDLC, emphasizing similar principles of integrating security into all phases of software development. This approach focuses on creating resilient applications by addressing security issues proactively rather than reactively, thereby enhancing overall software quality and safety against cyber threats.

In summary, while all three terms relate to software development processes, SDLC focuses on general software creation, whereas SSDLC and Secure Development Lifecycle specifically prioritize security throughout the entire development process.

10.1.1 SDLC Stages

The Secure Development Lifecycle (SDLC) for cloud security ensures protection is built into every phase of development. From planning and design to testing and deployment, each step strengthens application defenses and safeguards data. By prioritizing security early, teams reduce vulnerabilities while fostering trust with users. This proactive approach not only enhances resilience but also aligns with best practices for creating safer cloud-based solutions.

Below are the key stages and their significance in the context of cloud security:

1. **Requirements Gathering**: This initial phase involves collecting and defining the necessary security requirements for the application. Considerations include compliance with regulations (like GDPR, HIPAA), understanding user data protection needs, and defining the security controls needed for the cloud environment. Stakeholders collaborate to ensure all requirements are captured, providing a foundation for security considerations throughout the development process.

2. **Design**: In the design phase, architects and developers create a blueprint for the application, incorporating security features such as data encryption, access controls, and secure APIs. This phase also includes threat modeling, which helps identify potential security risks and vulnerabilities in the architecture. By proactively addressing these threats during the design, the application can better withstand attacks when deployed.

3. **Development**: During the development stage, coding practices are critical. Developers should follow secure coding standards and utilize tools that help identify vulnerabilities in real-time. Adopting programming languages and frameworks that are known for their security features is essential, as well as implementing security libraries and frameworks that can streamline the development of secure applications in the cloud.

4. **Testing**: This stage is crucial for validating the security of the application before deployment. Security testing methods such as static code analysis, dynamic application security testing (DAST), and penetration testing are employed to uncover vulnerabilities. Testing should be an ongoing process, not just a one-time event, to ensure that security is constantly verified against the evolving threat landscape.

5. **Deployment**: Once the application has passed all security testing, it is ready to be deployed to the cloud environment. This phase involves configuring the cloud infrastructure securely, including network configurations, access controls, and monitoring tools. Additionally, Secure Configuration Management practices should be applied to maintain the integrity of the deployed environment.

6. **Maintenance and Monitoring**: Post-deployment, the application requires ongoing maintenance to address security issues that may arise after launch. Regular updates, patch management, and continuous monitoring for anomalies are essential to ensure the application's security in the cloud. This includes using security information and event management (SIEM) solutions and embracing logging practices to detect, respond to, and mitigate threats effectively.

7. **Post-Deployment Review**: Finally, a post-deployment review is conducted to evaluate the application's performance against its security objectives. Lessons learned from any security incidents or testing outcomes are documented to improve future iterations of the SDLC, fostering a culture of continuous improvement in secure application development.

By following SDLC stages within cloud security frameworks, organizations strengthen application security, minimize vulnerabilities, and safeguard sensitive data from threats. This proactive approach not only protects valuable information but also ensures compliance and fosters user trust.

10.1.2 Threat Modeling

Threat modeling plays a key role in secure cloud development. By identifying and prioritizing risks early, teams can build stronger defenses into applications from the start. This proactive approach not only saves time but also reduces vulnerabilities, protecting sensitive data and ensuring user trust. Strong security begins with understanding potential threats and addressing them head-on during development.

Here's a comprehensive explanation of threat modeling in cloud security:

Key Aspects of Threat Modeling

1. **Understanding Assets**: The first step in threat modeling is to identify the assets that need protection. In a cloud environment, these assets may include sensitive data (such as personally identifiable information or payment information), application code, cloud infrastructure components, and user accounts. Understanding what needs protection helps prioritize security efforts.

2. **Identifying Threats**: This phase involves brainstorming and listing potential threats that could exploit vulnerabilities in the cloud application. Common threats may include:

    - **Data Breaches**: Unauthorized access to sensitive data due to vulnerabilities or misconfigurations.

    - **Denial-on-Service Attacks**: Attempts to make a service unavailable by overwhelming it with traffic.

    - **Insider Threats**: Malicious actions by employees or users with access to cloud resources.

    - **Malware**: Introduction of malicious software that can compromise the integrity of the application or steal data.

    - **Supply Chain Attacks**: Exploits that target third-party services integrated into the cloud application.

3. **Analyzing Attack Vectors**: Once the threats are identified, the next step is to analyze how these threats could be realized. This includes examining potential attack vectors such as:

    - **Network Vulnerabilities**: Weaknesses in network configurations or architecture that could be exploited.

    - **Application Vulnerabilities**: Flaws in application logic, code, or configurations that adversaries could exploit.

    - **User Behavior**: Risks posed by social engineering, credential theft, or poor security hygiene by users.

4. **Assessing Risks**: This phase involves evaluating the likelihood of each identified threat and its potential impact on the organization. Using a risk assessment framework, such as quantitative or qualitative analysis, teams can prioritize their security efforts based on the

severity of the threats. Factors to consider include:

- **Likelihood of Occurrence**: How probable is it that a specific threat will be realized?
- **Impact Assessment**: What would be the consequences for the organization if the threat were successfully executed?

5. **Defining Security Controls**: Based on the risk assessment, organizations can determine the appropriate security measures to mitigate identified threats. This can include:
    - **Access Controls**: Implementing strong authentication and authorization mechanisms to limit access to sensitive data.
    - **Encryption**: Encrypting data both at rest and in transit to protect it from unauthorized access.
    - **Network Security**: Utilizing firewalls, intrusion detection/prevention systems (IDS/IPS), and secure network architecture to protect the cloud environment.
    - **Regular Security Testing**: Conducting penetration testing and vulnerability assessments as part of the SDLC lifecycle to identify and remediate vulnerabilities continuously.
6. **Documentation and Review**: Documenting the threat modeling process is essential for ensuring ongoing awareness of potential threats and vulnerabilities. This documentation serves as a reference and should be regularly reviewed and updated as the application evolves, new threats emerge, and additional assets are introduced.
7. **Continuous Improvement**: Threat modeling is not a one-time activity; it should be revisited regularly, especially when significant changes are made to the application or its environment. Organizations should adapt their threat models based on feedback from incident responses, testing outcomes, and the evolving threat landscape.

Threat modeling empowers organizations to spot and tackle security risks during cloud application development. By identifying potential threats early, teams can strengthen defenses, allocate resources wisely, and enhance resilience. This proactive approach safeguards assets, ensures compliance with regulations, and builds trust with users and stakeholders. When you understand risks upfront, you're better equipped to protect what matters most your data and your reputation.

10.1.3 Testing: Pre-Deployment

Testing: Pre-Deployment is a crucial phase in the Secure Development Lifecycle (SDLC) specifically tailored for cloud security. This phase focuses on identifying and remediating vulnerabilities, ensuring that the application is robust and secure before it is made publicly available or deployed in a production environment. Below is a detailed examination of Pre-Deployment Testing in the context of cloud security:

Key Aspects of Pre-Deployment Testing

1. **Objectives of Pre-Deployment Testing**:
   - **Vulnerability Identification**: The primary goal is to identify and mitigate security vulnerabilities before the application goes live. This proactive approach helps reduce the attack surface and improve the application's overall security posture.
   - **Validation of Security Controls**: Testing aims to verify that the implemented security controls function properly and effectively mitigate identified risks.
   - **Compliance Verification**: Ensuring adherence to security policies, regulatory requirements, and industry standards is critical, especially for organizations handling sensitive data.
2. **Types of Testing**: Pre-deployment testing can include several testing methodologies and techniques, including:
   - **Static Application Security Testing (SAST)**:
     - SAST involves analyzing the application's source code or binaries without executing the program. This technique is used to uncover vulnerabilities such as SQL injection, cross-site scripting (XSS), and insecure code practices.
     - By integrating SAST early in the development phase, developers can identify and address coding flaws before deployment.
   - **Dynamic Application Security Testing (DAST)**:
     - DAST evaluates the application while it is running, simulating attacks to discover vulnerabilities that could be exploited. This includes testing for common web application vulnerabilities listed in the OWASP Top Ten.

        - DAST is particularly useful for identifying runtime issues, including configuration errors, authentication flaws, and session management vulnerabilities.

    - **Interactive Application Security Testing (IAST)**:
        - IAST combines elements of both SAST and DAST, providing real-time analysis of code execution during testing. This allows for more context-aware results and helps identify vulnerabilities in both the functionality and the security of an application.

    - **Penetration Testing**:
        - A method wherein ethical hackers simulate real-world attacks on the application to identify security weaknesses. Penetration testing typically mimics how an adversary might exploit vulnerabilities, providing an in-depth assessment of the application's security.
        - Results from penetration testing can guide further security enhancements and necessary remedial actions.

    - **Configuration Review**:
        - Conducting a thorough review of the cloud environment's configuration settings helps uncover security misconfigurations that can lead to vulnerabilities. This review should cover aspects like access control lists, identity and access management (IAM) policies, and network settings.

    - **Compliance Assessment**:
        - Ensuring that the application meets relevant compliance requirements (e.g., PCI DSS, HIPAA, GDPR) is a part of pre-deployment testing. This could involve checking security controls, data handling practices, and user consent mechanisms.

3. **Test Automation**:
    - Integrating automated security testing tools into the CI/CD pipeline accelerates vulnerability detection, enabling teams to identify issues faster and respond to them effectively. Automated security scans can be configured to run at various stages of development, providing continuous feedback.
    - Tools for automated testing include SAST and DAST tools, which can be triggered during build processes, providing developers immediate insights on security issues.

4. **Threat Modeling Validation**:
    - As part of pre-deployment testing, validating the threat model is essential. Teams should reexamine whether the identified threats have been adequately addressed and review any changes made to the application since the original threat model was created.
    - Updating threat models based on the testing outcomes enhances their relevance and accuracy.
5. **Remediation and Retesting**:
    - Once vulnerabilities are identified, teams should prioritize and remediate them based on severity and potential impact. Effective remediation may involve code changes, configuration updates, or implementing additional security controls.
    - After remediation, retesting is essential to ensure that vulnerabilities are effectively fixed and that no new vulnerabilities were introduced during the remediation process.
6. **Documentation**:
    - Maintaining thorough documentation of the pre-deployment testing process, results, and remediation actions is crucial for compliance, audit purposes, and knowledge sharing within the organization.
    - Documenting the testing results can also help inform future security initiatives and testing strategies.

Pre-deployment testing strengthens cloud application security by identifying and fixing vulnerabilities early. This proactive step boosts user trust, ensures compliance with regulations, and reinforces resilience. By prioritizing thorough testing, organizations create safer applications while fostering confidence among users and stakeholders.

10.1.4 Testing: Post Deployment

Post-deployment testing plays a crucial role in the Secure Development Lifecycle (SDLC), focusing on cloud security after an application goes live. This phase ensures applications stay secure, functional, and resilient while identifying vulnerabilities that may surface during production. By addressing these issues promptly, teams can strengthen security measures and enhance overall performance, fostering trust with users and maintaining operational stability in real-world environments.

Key Aspects of Post Deployment Testing

1. **Objectives of Post Deployment Testing**:
    - **Identify New Vulnerabilities**: After deployment, applications may face new risks that were not apparent during pre-deployment testing due to differing real-world usage patterns and environmental factors. The goal is to discover these vulnerabilities before they can be exploited.
    - **Verify Security Controls**: This phase assesses whether the implemented security controls are functioning as intended once the application is under actual usage conditions.
    - **Conduct Compliance Checks**: Ensuring that the application continually complies with applicable regulatory requirements and organizational security policies is paramount.
2. **Types of Testing**: Post-Deployment Testing encompasses several methodologies, including:
    - **Dynamic Application Security Testing (DAST)**:
        - Since DAST assesses applications while they are running, it remains relevant in the post-deployment phase. It simulates real-world attacks to uncover vulnerabilities that might emerge due to changes in configuration, usage patterns, or newly introduced features.
        - DAST can denote issues such as authentication flaws, permission escalations, and session management vulnerabilities that manifest during actual usage.
    - **Penetration Testing**:
        - Conducting penetration testing on a deployed application provides a comprehensive security assessment by simulating advanced attacks. This testing phase identifies vulnerabilities that could be exploited by malicious actors once the application is live.
        - The reports generated can guide the development team in making necessary adjustments to the application and reinforcing security measures.
    - **Vulnerability Scanning**:
        - A regular and automated vulnerability scanning process should be employed to search for known vulnerabilities in the deployed application and its underlying infrastructure.

    - These scans can be integrated into DevOps practices, ensuring ongoing vigilance and timely remediation of identified issues.

  - **Security Monitoring and Threat Detection**:

    - Implementing continuous security monitoring solutions is essential for identifying anomalous behavior, potential breaches, and threats in real-time. This includes monitoring logs, usage patterns, and traffic anomalies.

    - Employing tools for Security Information and Event Management (SIEM) provides insights into security incidents and can trigger alerts for any suspicious activities.

  - **Code Reviews and Application Audits**:

    - Regular code reviews and audits of the application should be performed post-deployment to ensure that security best practices are maintained. This practice helps identify any unintended changes that might have introduced security risks.

    - Systematic audits may also cover configurations, access controls, and data handling processes.

3. **Incident Response and Remediation**:

  - Establishing a rapid incident response plan is critical for addressing any vulnerabilities detected during post-deployment testing. The team should be prepared to take immediate remediation actions based on the testing outcomes.

  - This may involve patch management, configuration updates, or re-engineering features that facilitate vulnerabilities.

4. **User Feedback and Reporting**:

  - Post-deployment testing should include mechanisms for collecting user feedback regarding the application's functionality and security. This user-centric approach can help identify usability issues that may translate into security gaps.

  - Preparing detailed reports on the findings derived from post-deployment testing, including trends and patterns, is essential for informing stakeholders and guiding future development efforts.

5. **Continuous Integration and Continuous Deployment (CI/CD)**:

- Incorporating post-deployment testing practices within CI/CD pipelines promotes continuous assessment of security. Automated testing can ensure that changes made to the application do not introduce new vulnerabilities.
- Continuous security assessments facilitate more agile and responsive development processes, ensuring security remains a central focus throughout the application's lifecycle.

6. **Documentation and Knowledge Sharing**:
   - Maintaining comprehensive documentation of post-deployment testing, findings, and remediation actions is vital for compliance purposes and ongoing security assessments.
   - Knowledge sharing across the development and security teams helps build a culture of security awareness and fosters collaboration in mitigating risks.

Post-deployment testing keeps cloud applications secure and trustworthy by identifying and fixing vulnerabilities in real-world use. Regular testing ensures your app stays strong against new threats while meeting compliance standards. By integrating continuous security practices, you not only protect sensitive data but also build user confidence. Staying proactive with these tests helps safeguard both your application's performance and its reputation in an ever-changing environment.

10.2 Architecture's Role in Secure Cloud Applications

Crafting secure cloud applications starts with smart architecture. Thoughtful design—like choosing the right frameworks, embedding security early, and enforcing access controls—helps block vulnerabilities. By aligning scalability with strong safeguards, businesses can stay protected without sacrificing performance. A well-structured application doesn't just function; it defends against threats while delivering reliability users trust.

10.2.1 Cloud Impacts on Architecture-Level Security

Cloud computing reshapes how organizations design applications and protect them. Security strategies must adapt to handle unique challenges like shared resources and remote access. By prioritizing flexibility and proactive measures, businesses can safeguard sensitive data while staying agile in a fast-changing environment.

1. Shared Responsibility Model

One of the foundational principles of cloud security is the shared responsibility model. In this paradigm, both cloud service providers (CSPs) and customers bear responsibilities, but they differ significantly based on service models (IaaS, PaaS, SaaS). For example:

- **Infrastructure as a Service (IaaS)**: The customer is responsible for securing the operating system, applications, and data while the CSP secures the physical infrastructure.
- **Platform as a Service (PaaS)**: The provider takes on more responsibility, managing security for the underlying platform while customers focus on the application level.
- **Software as a Service (SaaS)**: The provider handles most security aspects, leaving customers primarily responsible for user access and data governance.

Understanding this division of labor impacts how organizations architect their applications in the cloud, necessitating security strategies that align with the responsibilities they assume.

2. Dynamic and On-Demand Resources

Cloud architectures are inherently dynamic, allowing for rapid scaling of resources. This agility, while beneficial for performance and cost-efficiency, introduces security challenges:

- **Ephemeral Instances**: Virtual machines and containers can be created and destroyed quickly, making it difficult to maintain a consistent security posture. Security measures must be automated and integrated into the deployment process to ensure all instances are appropriately secured upon creation.
- **Auto-Scaling**: As resources scale up or down in response to demand, security configurations must be adaptable to ensure that new instances inherit the correct policies and protections without manual intervention.

The architectural design must incorporate automated security measures such as configuration management tools, which ensure adherence to security standards and eliminate configuration drift.

3. Multi-Tenancy Implications

A key characteristic of cloud environments is multi-tenancy, where multiple customers share the same physical resources. This presents unique security challenges that must be carefully addressed in architecture:

- **Data Segregation**: Architectures must ensure clear demarcations between data belonging to different tenants to prevent unauthorized access or data leakage.
- **Access Controls**: Fine-grained access controls become essential, requiring robust identity and access management (IAM) practices to manage user permissions effectively across a shared environment.

Designing applications with a focus on isolation, both at the network and data layers, will enhance security in multi-tenant scenarios.

4. Distributed Architectures and APIs

Cloud applications often utilize distributed architectures, comprising microservices and APIs for communication. While this model offers flexibility and scalability, it raises security considerations:

- **API Security**: With increased reliance on APIs, safeguarding them from threats such as injection attacks, data exposure, and inadequate authentication is crucial. Architectural designs should implement API gateways, rate limiting, and proper authentication mechanisms to secure API interactions.
- **Service-to-Service Communication**: Security must be ingrained in inter-service communications. Utilizing secure protocols, mutual TLS (Transport Layer Security), and service mesh technologies can significantly enhance security for these interactions.

5. Resilience and Redundancy

Cloud architectures are often designed for high availability and redundancy, which also impacts security:

- **Failover Mechanisms**: As applications are designed for resilience, it's important to ensure that failover systems are equally secure. Architectures should include security measures in backup and restore processes to prevent exacerbating vulnerabilities during transitions.
- **Data Integrity and Availability**: Backup solutions must guarantee data integrity and accessibility, emphasizing the implementation of encryption in transit and at rest, as well as robust access controls.

6. Regulatory Compliance

Finally, the architecture must consider compliance with various regulatory frameworks that govern data security and privacy, such as GDPR, HIPAA, or PCI-DSS. This requirement necessitates:

- **Architectural Compliance Considerations**: Integrating compliance not as an afterthought but as a core component in the architectural design will streamline audits and regulatory adherence. This includes embedding encryption, logging, and monitoring capabilities into applications from the outset.

Cloud security reshapes how organizations approach architecture. Moving to the cloud means addressing shared responsibility, multi-tenancy, distributed systems, and compliance challenges. By embedding security into design from the start, businesses strengthen defenses, minimize risks, and build resilient applications. This proactive strategy ensures your cloud solutions remain secure while meeting modern business demands. Rethink your architecture today security isn't an afterthought; it's a foundation for success.

10.2.2 Architectural Resilience

Architectural resilience in cloud security means designing applications that can bounce back quickly from attacks, failures, or sudden changes. By building systems with strong recovery capabilities, businesses ensure operations stay on track, even during tough situations. This approach not only protects sensitive data but also builds trust with users by demonstrating reliability and preparedness for unexpected challenges.

Key Aspects of Architectural Resilience

1. **Redundancy**:
    - Implementing redundant components within the architecture can prevent single points of failure. This could involve using multiple servers, data storage systems, or network connections to ensure that if one component fails, others can take over without disruption.
2. **Scalability**:
    - Designing the architecture to scale up or down based on current demand can enhance resilience. This allows the application to handle varying loads effectively, which is crucial during peak times or in response to rapid increases in user demand.

3. **Failover Mechanisms**:
   - Architectural resilience includes coding for failover scenarios where backup systems can be activated automatically if the primary system fails, allowing for uninterrupted service.
4. **Load Balancing**:
   - Distributing traffic evenly across multiple servers prevents any single server from becoming a bottleneck. This also enhances resilience by ensuring that if one server goes down, others can manage the load.
5. **Monitoring and Alerts**:
   - Continuous monitoring of application performance and health can help identify potential issues before they escalate into failures. Implementing an alerting system enables rapid response to incidents.
6. **Regular Testing**:
   - Conducting regular disaster recovery drills and resilience testing ensures that the response strategies are effective and that the personnel involved are familiar with the processes needed in an incident.
7. **Data Backup and Recovery**:
   - Keeping consistent backups of data and having clear recovery plans in place ensures that, in the event of a data loss incident, restoration can occur with minimal downtime.
8. **Adaptive Techniques**:
   - Employing adaptive architectures that can adjust operations dynamically based on real-time conditions helps to maintain service levels during variable situations.
9. **Documentation and Training**:
   - Maintaining comprehensive documentation of the architecture's design and resilience strategies aids in understanding and managing the system. Additionally, training teams on these procedures ensures preparedness for incidents.

Architectural resilience keeps cloud services running smoothly, even when challenges arise. By designing with redundancy, monitoring systems effectively, and ensuring scalability, businesses can protect applications from disruptions. This approach not only boosts performance but also strengthens security and builds user trust. In a world where cloud resources constantly shift, staying adaptable ensures your organization remains reliable and prepared for whatever comes next.

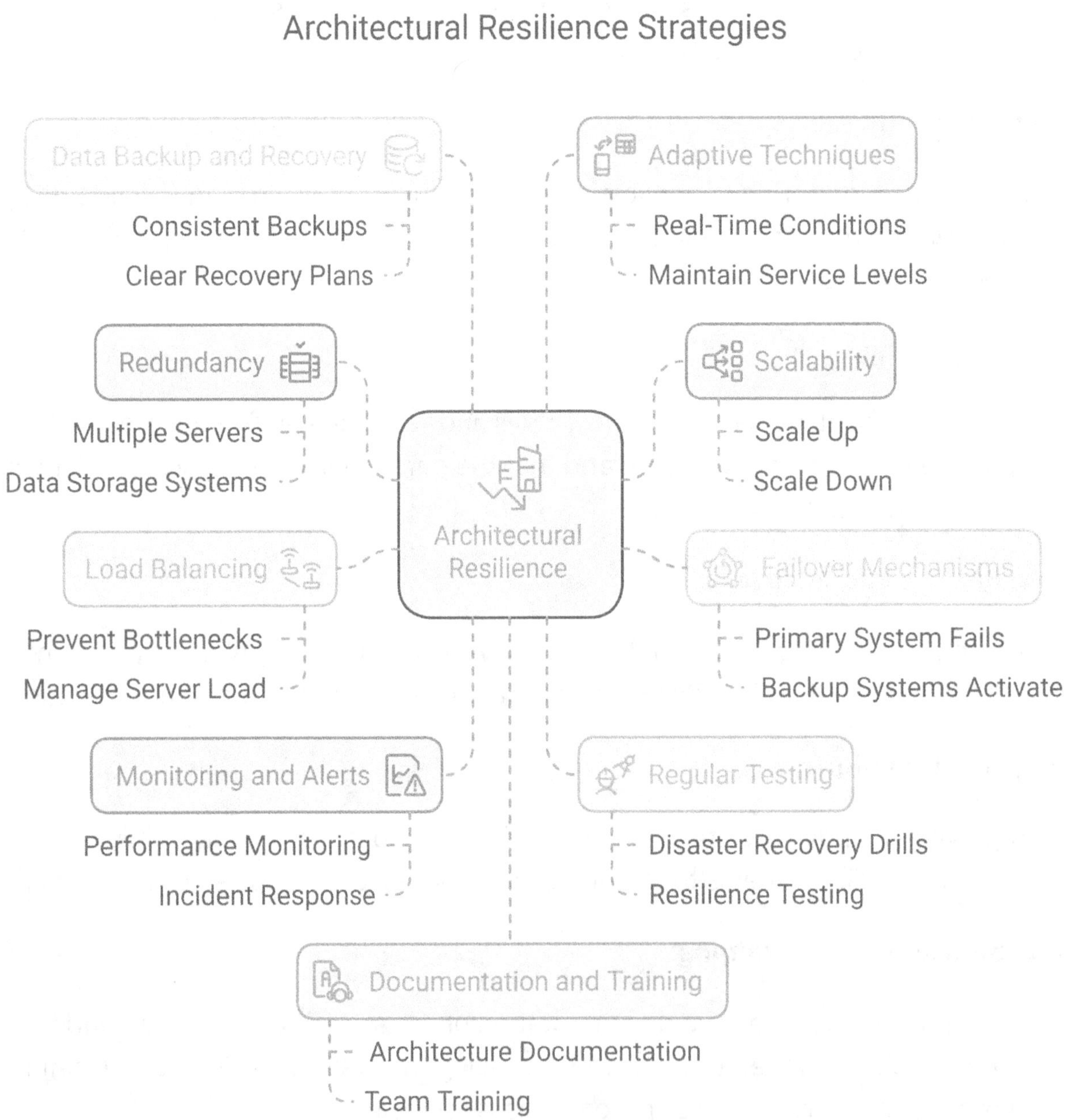

10.3 Identity & Access Management and Application Security

Identity and Access Management (IAM) works hand-in-hand with application security to safeguard sensitive data. By controlling who can access applications and their resources, organizations ensure only authorized users interact with critical systems. This proactive approach not only strengthens protection but also builds trust with users. Strong IAM practices combined with robust security measures create a safer environment for managing information while reducing risks tied to unauthorized access or breaches.

Below are the key components and concepts involved in this integration:

Key Components of Identity & Access Management (IAM)

1. **User Identity Management**:
    - Involves the creation, maintenance, and deletion of user identities in the organization. This includes managing user profiles, credentials, and associated attributes such as roles and responsibilities.
2. **Authentication**:
    - The process of verifying the identity of a user or system attempting to access resources. This may include various methods such as passwords, multi-factor authentication (MFA), biometric verification, and federated identity protocols.
3. **Authorization**:
    - Once authenticated, authorization determines what resources or actions a user is permitted to access or perform. This often involves role-based access control (RBAC), attribute-based access control (ABAC), or policies that govern access at specific levels.
4. **Access Control Policies**:
    - Organizations implement policies that define the rules based on which access is granted or denied. These policies can be fine-grained and tailored to meet specific security requirements and regulatory compliance.
5. **User Lifecycle Management**:
    - This refers to managing user identities throughout their lifecycle in the organization,

including onboarding, role changes, and offboarding. Maintaining proper access during each phase helps mitigate security risks.

6. **Audit and Monitoring**:
    - Continuous monitoring of access logs and activities around identity usage is crucial. Auditing can reveal unauthorized access attempts, help ensure compliance with regulations, and improve overall security by identifying anomalies.

Integration with Application Security

1. **Application-Level Security Controls**:
    - These are security measures embedded within applications that protect them from threats and vulnerabilities. IAM must be integrated closely with these controls to ensure that only authenticated and authorized users can interact with sensitive application features.
2. **Secure Development Practices**:
    - Incorporating IAM considerations during the software development lifecycle (SDLC) enhances application security. This involves conducting threat modeling, performing security testing, and ensuring that IAM policies are enforced in code.
3. **Secrets Management**:
    - Safeguarding sensitive information like API keys, tokens, and passwords is essential. Proper secrets management practices involve encrypting secrets and using secure storage solutions to prevent unauthorized access within applications.
4. **Identity Federation**:
    - Allows users to authenticate once and gain access to multiple applications across different domains without the need for separate credentials. This enhances user experience while maintaining security through robust authentication measures.
5. **Single Sign-On (SSO)**:
    - A user authentication process that allows a user to access multiple applications with a single set of credentials. SSO can streamline the user experience and reduce the risk of password fatigue, but it requires strong security practices to prevent single points of

failure.

6. **Compliance and Regulatory Considerations**:
    - Organizations must ensure IAM practices comply with standards and regulations that govern data protection, such as GDPR, HIPAA, or PCI DSS. Access controls should be implemented in accordance with these regulations to maintain legal compliance.

Combining Identity & Access Management (IAM) with application security strengthens data protection and builds trust. IAM ensures only authorized users gain access, while application security defends against threats. Together, they create a safer environment, protecting sensitive information from breaches. This integration not only enhances user confidence but also supports compliance efforts, making it easier for organizations to safeguard their operations effectively and responsibly.

10.3.1 Secrets Management

Secrets management safeguards sensitive information like API keys, passwords, tokens, and encryption keys. By storing and sharing these securely, you protect applications and data from breaches. Think of it as locking up your valuables—only trusted hands get access. Whether you're managing cloud services or internal systems, strong secrets management practices build trust and keep operations secure. Don't leave sensitive details exposed; treat them with care to maintain integrity.

Importance of Secrets Management

1. **Protection of Sensitive Information**:
    - Secrets often provide access to critical services or sensitive data. Managing them securely is essential to prevent unauthorized access and data breaches.
2. **Reducing Attack Surface**:
    - Poor management of secrets can lead to vulnerabilities that attackers can exploit. Effective secrets management minimizes the risk of inadvertent exposure.
3. **Regulatory Compliance**:
    - Many regulations require organizations to protect sensitive data, including secrets. Effective management helps in demonstrating compliance with these regulations.

4. **Facilitating DevOps Practices**:
    - In modern software development, especially within DevOps practices, applications are built and deployed rapidly. Secrets must be managed dynamically within these environments without hindering the deployment process.

Key Components of Secrets Management

1. **Storage Security**:
    - Secrets should be stored in secure vaults or repositories that provide encryption at rest and in transit. This prevents unauthorized reading or tampering with secrets.
2. **Access Control**:
    - Define strict access controls around who or what can retrieve secrets. Use identity and access management (IAM) concepts to ensure that only authorized principals (users, services, applications) have access to specific secrets.
3. **Encryption**:
    - Secrets should be encrypted both at rest and when in transit. This ensures that even if a secret is intercepted or accessed, it cannot be used without the decryption key.
4. **Versioning**:
    - Implement versioning of secrets to manage updates and changes over time. This enables rollback to previous versions in case a newly revoked secret is compromised.
5. **Audit and Monitoring**:
    - Continuously monitor and log access to secrets. This aids in recognizing unauthorized access attempts and helps organizations track the usage and interactions with their secrets.
6. **Dynamic Secrets**:
    - Instead of static secrets, consider using dynamic secrets that are generated on-the-fly and have a limited lifespan. For example, database access credentials can be granted temporarily and automatically revoked after use.

7. **Secret Rotation**:
   - Regularly rotate secrets to reduce the risk of compromise. Automating the rotation process helps organizations maintain a secure environment without significant disruption.
8. **Integration with CI/CD Pipelines**:
   - Ensure secrets management tools are integrated into continuous integration and continuous deployment (CI/CD) pipelines. This allows secrets to be automatically handled securely during software builds and releases.

Tools and Technologies for Secrets Management

1. **Secret Management Solutions**:
   - Tools such as HashiCorp Vault, AWS Secrets Manager, and Azure Key Vault are specifically designed to manage secrets securely. They provide features like secure storage, access controls, auditing, and automated secret rotation.
2. **Environment Variables**:
   - Some applications leverage environment variables to store secrets. However, caution is required here as environment variables may be exposed to processes that should not have access to them.
3. **Configuration Management Tools**:
   - Tools like Ansible, Chef, or Puppet can help manage configuration settings, including secrets, ensuring they are delivered securely to services during deployment.
4. **Identity Providers**:
   - Many cloud service providers and identity management solutions offer native support for secrets management, integrating seamlessly with the services for authentication and access management.

Best Practices in Secrets Management

1. **Least Privilege Principle**:
   - Only provide the minimum necessary access to secrets for users and services based on

their specific needs and roles.

2. **Keep Secrets Out of Codebases**:
    - Avoid hardcoding secrets in source code or configuration files. Instead, retrieve them from a secure secrets management tool at runtime.
3. **Educate and Train Staff**:
    - Regularly train staff on the importance of secrets management and the best practices for handling sensitive information.
4. **Regular Security Assessments**:
    - Continuously assess the security measures around secrets management, testing for vulnerabilities and compliance with organizational policies.

Protecting sensitive information in cloud environments hinges on strong secrets management. This practice involves securely storing, controlling access to, and auditing the use of confidential data. By adopting effective strategies, organizations reduce risks like unauthorized access or breaches. Safeguarding systems and sensitive data doesn't have to be complicated—thoughtful planning ensures security stays intact while keeping operations running smoothly in an increasingly connected world.

10.4 Dev Ops & DevSecOps

DevOps & DevSecOps bring security into every stage of software development and deployment. By encouraging collaboration between developers, operations, and security teams, this approach strengthens cloud application protection. It's about building trust, reducing risks, and creating a safer environment for users while keeping processes efficient. Security isn't an afterthought—it's part of the process from start to finish, ensuring stronger outcomes for everyone involved.

Understanding DevOps

DevOps is a methodology that integrates software development (Dev) and IT operations (Ops) to improve collaboration, increase efficiency, and reduce the time to market for software applications. Key characteristics of DevOps include:

1. **Collaboration**:
    - Breaking down silos between development and operations teams fosters collaboration, leading to improved communication and shared goals.
2. **Automation**:
    - Automating repetitive tasks, such as testing, deployment, and monitoring, streamlines processes and reduces human errors.
3. **Continuous Integration and Continuous Deployment (CI/CD)**:
    - Implementing CI/CD practices allows for frequent code integrations and automated deployments, enabling rapid delivery of features and updates.
4. **Monitoring and Feedback**:
    - Continuous monitoring of applications in production provides valuable feedback, allowing organizations to identify issues quickly and improve the development process iteratively.

Understanding DevSecOps

DevSecOps extends the DevOps philosophy by integrating security as a shared responsibility throughout the entire software development lifecycle. Instead of treating security as a separate phase or function, DevSecOps ensures that security practices are embedded at every stage, from design to deployment and beyond. Key aspects of DevSecOps include:

1. **Security as Code**:
    - Security controls and policies are defined and managed via code, just like application code. This allows for version control, auditing, and consistency across environments.
2. **Shift Left Approach**:
    - Emphasizing proactive security measures early in the development process helps identify and remediate vulnerabilities before they can be exploited in production.
3. **Collaboration and Training**:
    - Cross-functional teams involving developers, security professionals, and operations engineers collaborate throughout the lifecycle, fostering a culture of security awareness and continuous improvement.
4. **Automation of Security Practices**:
    - Automating security testing and compliance checks during the CI/CD pipeline ensures vulnerabilities are addressed continuously and efficiently.
5. **Compliance and Governance**:
    - Integrating compliance requirements into the DevSecOps process helps organizations adhere to regulatory standards and maintain a secure application environment.

Key Components of DevSecOps

1. **Threat Modeling**:
    - Conducting threat modeling sessions during design and development phases to identify potential security risks and how they can be mitigated.
2. **Automated Security Testing**:
    - Implementing security testing tools (SAST, DAST, IAST, and SCA) within the CI/CD pipeline to automatically scan code and dependencies for vulnerabilities.
3. **Static and Dynamic Analysis**:
    - Static Application Security Testing (SAST) analyzes the codebase for vulnerabilities without executing the application. Dynamic Application Security Testing (DAST) tests running

applications to identify vulnerabilities.

4. **Infrastructure as Code (IaC) Security**:
   - Ensuring that infrastructure configurations defined in code are secure. This involves scanning IaC configurations for misconfigurations and compliance.
5. **Continuous Monitoring**:
   - Implementing tools for continuous monitoring of applications and infrastructure for suspicious activities or compliance violations. This includes logging, threat detection systems, and response tools.
6. **Incident Response Planning**:
   - Establishing and practicing a clear incident response plan that integrates all teams, ensuring everyone knows their responsibilities when facing a security breach.

Benefits of DevSecOps in Cloud Security

1. **Enhanced Security Posture**:
   - Integrating security into the development lifecycle enhances overall security, reducing vulnerabilities in production workloads and improving resilience.
2. **Faster Time to Market**:
   - With automated security practices, teams can identify and fix vulnerabilities efficiently, minimizing delays in releases due to security concerns.
3. **Cost Savings**:
   - Addressing security issues early in development reduces the cost associated with late-stage vulnerability discoveries and remediations.
4. **Increased Compliance**:
   - Continuous integration of compliance checks ensures that applications adhere to regulatory standards, reducing the risk of non-compliance fines.
5. **Improved Collaboration and Culture**:

- A culture of shared responsibility in security fosters collaboration and enhances team cohesion, creating a more productive and security-conscious environment.

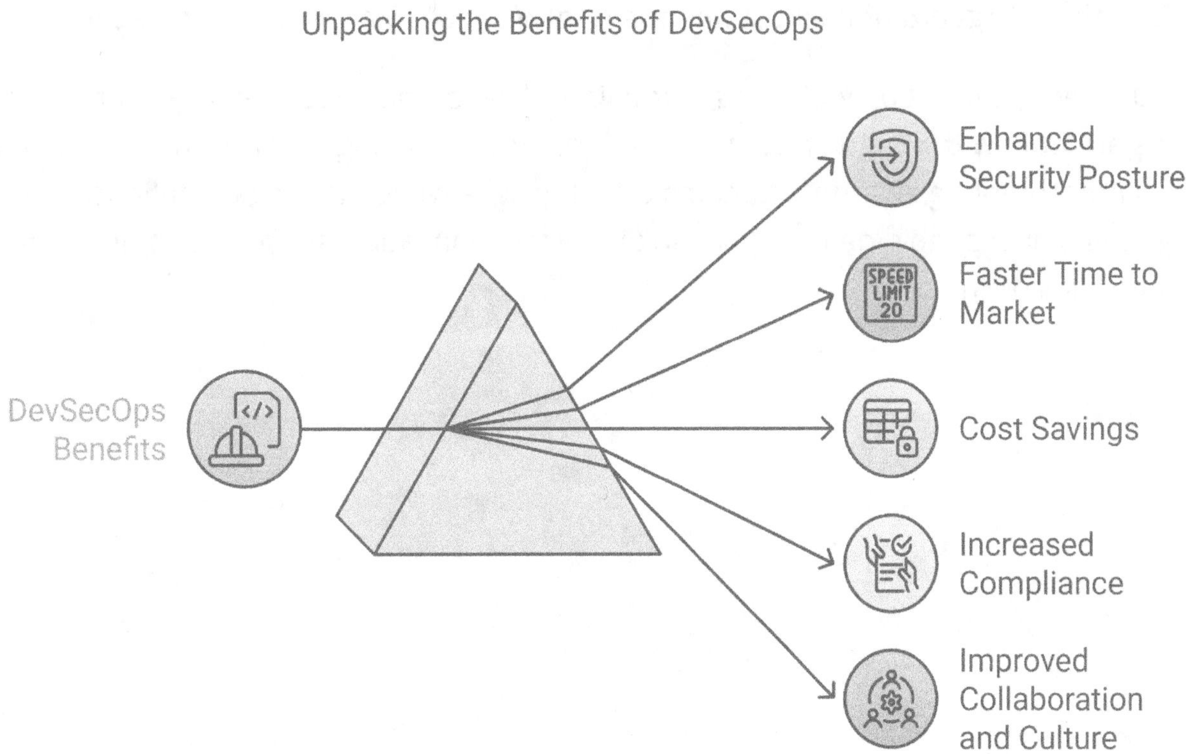

Challenges and Considerations

1. **Cultural Resistance**:
    - Transitioning to DevSecOps requires a cultural shift that may face resistance. Organizations must foster a mindset that emphasizes security as a collective responsibility.
2. **Toolchain Complexity**:
    - Integrating various tools for security, development, and operations can lead to complexity. Organizations need to carefully select tools that offer seamless integration.
3. **Skill Gaps**:
    - The demand for professionals skilled in both development and security may outpace the

supply. Continuous training and education are necessary to bridge this gap.

4. **Balancing Speed and Security**:

    - There is often a tension between rapid development cycles and thorough security practices. Organizations must find the right balance to ensure both objectives are met.

DevOps & DevSecOps focus on weaving security into development workflows, ensuring cloud applications are built with speed and safety in mind. By automating security checks, encouraging teamwork, and promoting awareness, teams can stay agile while meeting compliance needs. This approach balances rapid delivery with strong protection, addressing today's need for secure software without slowing progress.

Chapter Fourteen

Domain 11: Incident Response and Resilience

Introduction

Incident response equips security professionals with the skills to manage and contain threats in cloud environments. A well-structured plan covers preparation, detection, analysis, containment, eradication, and recovery—addressing unique cloud challenges. Strong training, effective detection tools, and forensic capabilities ensure quick action when needed. By building a solid strategy, organizations strengthen resilience and reduce disruption from security incidents. Prepared teams respond faster, minimizing damage and keeping operations running smoothly.

Learning Objectives

Incident response equips security professionals with a clear understanding of handling threats in cloud environments. Knowing each stage of the response process helps teams act fast, minimize damage, and strengthen defenses. Best practices ensure quick detection, containment, and recovery, reducing risks and downtime. Staying prepared means fewer surprises and better protection against cyber threats. Strong strategies keep data safe and businesses running smoothly.

Key objectives include:

1. **Incident Response Lifecycle**: Understand the stages of the incident response lifecycle, including preparation, detection, analysis, containment, eradication, recovery, and post-incident review.

2. **Preparation**: Learn how to effectively prepare for incidents, including the role of cloud service providers and the importance of training for cloud incident responders.

3. **Detection and Analysis**: Explore methods for detecting incidents and analyzing their impact,

specifically addressing the unique factors that influence incident response in cloud systems.

4. **Containment, Eradication, and Recovery**: Gain insights into strategies for containing security incidents, eradicating threats, and recovering from incidents to restore normal operations.

5. **Post Incident Analysis**: Understand the significance of conducting post-incident analyses to evaluate the response and improve future incident management practices.

Professionals need strong skills to build and run incident response plans designed for cloud security. A well-structured approach helps teams detect threats faster, minimize damage, and keep operations running smoothly. By mastering these strategies, experts stay prepared for unexpected challenges while protecting sensitive data. With the right knowledge, handling security incidents becomes more efficient, reducing risks and strengthening overall protection in an increasingly connected world.

11.1 Incident Response

Think of incident response like a fire drill—only for cybersecurity threats. When a data breach or cyberattack happens, having a solid plan keeps damage under control. Quick action, clear communication, and expert handling can mean the difference between chaos and recovery. Organizations need strong strategies to detect, contain, and eliminate threats while protecting sensitive information. A well-prepared team ensures faster recovery and stronger security moving forward.

11.1.1 Incident Response Lifecycle

The Incident Response Lifecycle refers to a structured process that organizations follow when responding to security incidents, such as data breaches or cyber attacks. It involves several key stages that help ensure a coordinated and effective response to minimize damage and recover from the incident.

In simple terms, here's what each part of the lifecycle generally entails:

1. **Preparation**: This is about getting ready for potential incidents. Organizations create plans,

set up tools, and train teams to effectively handle incidents when they occur.

2. **Detection and Analysis**: Here, the goal is to identify that an incident has occurred. This could involve monitoring systems for unusual activity and investigating alerts to understand what happened.

3. **Containment**: Once an incident is confirmed, the next step is to contain it, which means preventing it from spreading or causing more damage. This could involve isolating affected systems from the network.

4. **Eradication**: After containing the incident, organizations work to eliminate the root cause. This might involve removing malware, fixing vulnerabilities, or addressing any weaknesses that allowed the incident to happen.

5. **Recovery**: This stage focuses on restoring affected systems and services to normal operation. It often includes applying updates or patches to prevent future incidents.

6. **Post-Incident Analysis**: Finally, after the incident is resolved, organizations review what happened. They analyze the response to learn lessons, improve processes, and ensure better preparedness for future incidents.

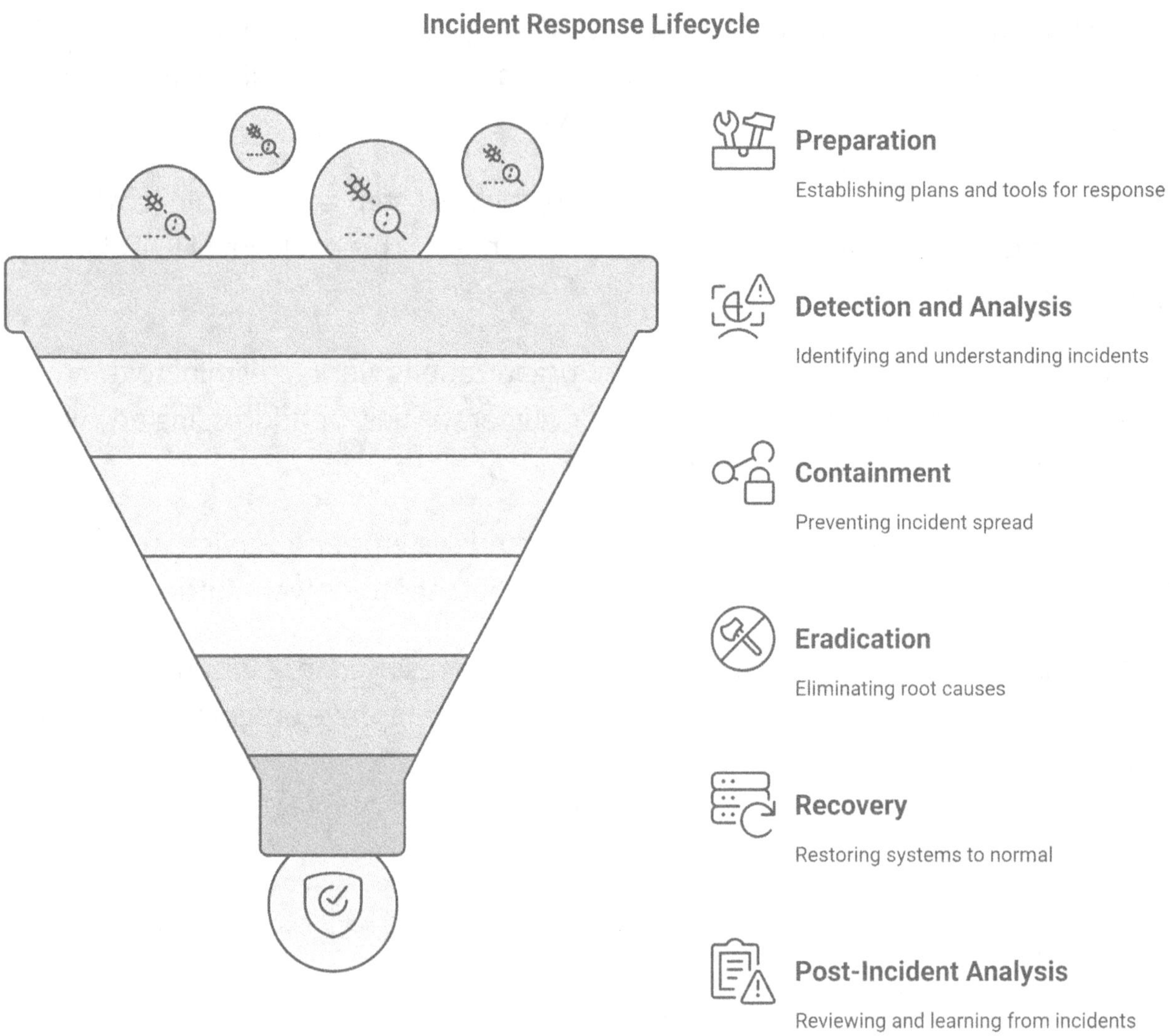

Overall, the Incident Response Lifecycle is about being proactive: preparing for incidents, responding effectively when they happen, and learning from them to enhance security.

11.2 Preparation

Preparation lays the groundwork for an effective incident response strategy. Organizations develop strong policies, procedures, and tools tailored to specific risks. Key steps include crafting a response plan, setting up communication protocols, training teams, and running regular simulations. A proactive approach strengthens detection and response capabilities, minimizing security threats. Readiness ensures swift action when needed, reducing potential damage and keeping operations secure. Strong preparation leads to a more coordinated and efficient response.

11.2.1 Incident Response Preparation & Cloud Service Providers

Preparing for security threats in cloud services like AWS or Microsoft Azure means having a solid response plan. Companies must act fast when facing cyber attacks or data breaches. Strong defenses, regular audits, and clear protocols help minimize risks. Training teams to handle incidents ensures quick recovery. Staying proactive keeps systems secure and business operations running smoothly. A well-prepared approach makes all the difference when challenges arise.

This includes:

1. **Creating a Response Plan**: Just like having a fire escape plan, businesses need a clear set of steps to follow if a security incident happens in the cloud.
2. **Knowing Your Cloud Provider's Role**: It's crucial to understand what responsibilities the cloud service provider has regarding security and what the company itself is responsible for.
3. **Training Team Members**: Employees should be trained on the incident response plan so everyone knows what to do if an issue arises.
4. **Regular Practice**: Just like practicing fire drills, companies should regularly simulate security incidents to ensure their team is prepared to act quickly.

Businesses protect data and services more effectively by preparing in advance. Strong security measures reduce risks and limit damage when threats arise. Regular updates, employee training, and secure access controls keep information safe. A proactive approach ensures smoother operations and fewer disruptions. Staying ahead of potential issues builds trust with customers and partners. Prioritizing security today prevents costly problems later, keeping everything running smoothly while maintaining confidence in cloud-based systems.

11.2.2 Training for Cloud Incident Responders

Incident responders act like first responders—but for cyber threats. Strong training prepares them to handle security breaches and data leaks with confidence. When attacks happen, quick action minimizes damage and protects sensitive information. Without proper preparation, chaos takes over, making recovery harder. By sharpening their skills, these professionals stay ready to tackle any challenge, keeping systems secure and businesses running smoothly. Effective response makes all the difference in cybersecurity defense.

Here's what this training usually includes:

1. **Understanding Cloud Technologies**: Responders need to know how cloud services work. This means learning about the different types of cloud setups, like IaaS (Infrastructure as a Service) or SaaS (Software as a Service).

2. **Recognizing Threats**: They should be trained to identify potential security issues or attacks, so they can react quickly when something goes wrong.

3. **Practicing Response Plans**: Just like fire drills help prepare people for emergencies, responders should practice responding to cloud security incidents to learn what to do step-by-step.

4. **Learning Communication**: It's important for responders to know how to communicate effectively both within their team and with other parts of the organization during a crisis.

5. **Staying Updated**: Security threats evolve over time, so training should include information on the latest threats and best practices to stay ahead of them.

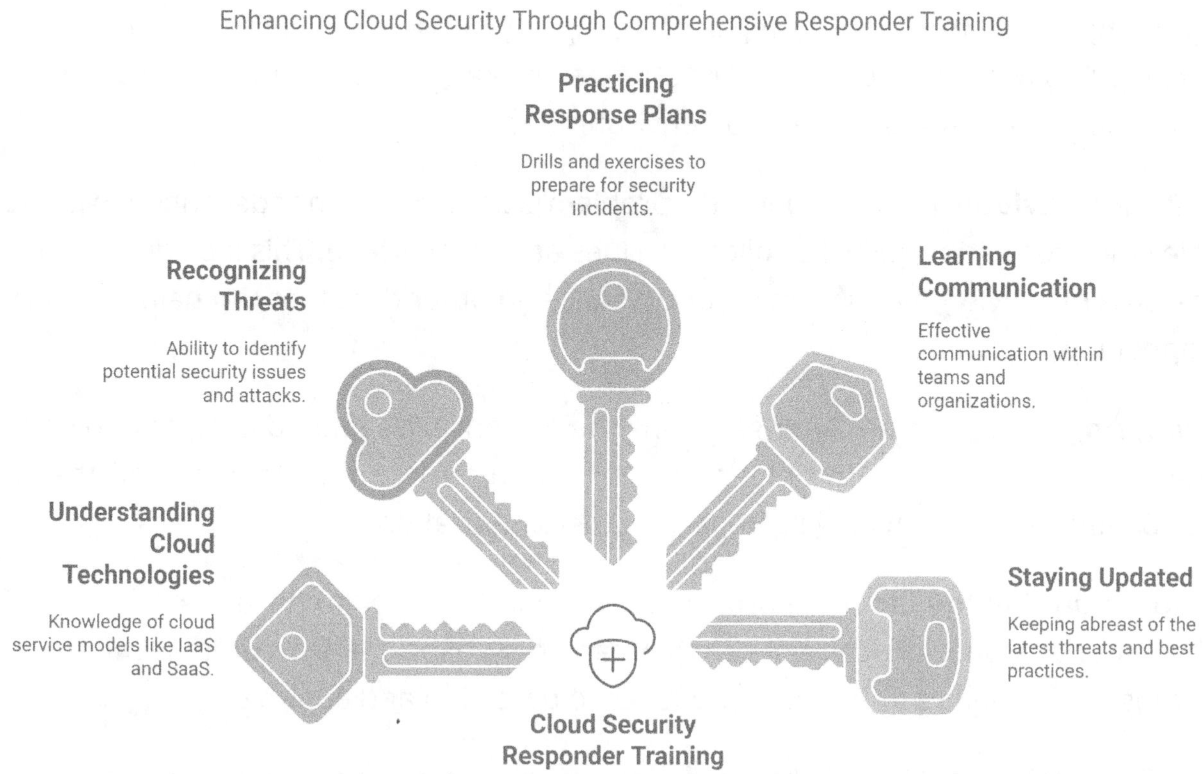

Training keeps incident responders ready to tackle cloud security threats, protecting sensitive data and maintaining trust. Well-prepared teams react faster, minimize damage, and strengthen defenses. Without proper preparation, breaches can escalate, putting valuable information at risk. Investing in knowledge builds confidence and ensures a swift response when challenges arise. Strong security starts with skilled professionals who know how to handle threats effectively—because staying ahead means staying secure.

11.3 Detection & Analysis

Spotting security issues in cloud services is like being a detective piecing together clues after a crime. Something suspicious might be happening—your job's to find out what and how. By tracking unusual activity, identifying weak spots, and understanding potential threats, you can stay ahead of risks. A sharp eye and quick action make all the difference in keeping data safe from cyber threats. Stay alert, stay secure.

Here's what this involves:

1. **Spotting Problems**: The first step is detecting any unusual activity or signs of a security breach. This might include things like strange login attempts, unauthorized access to data, or unexpected changes in the cloud environment.

2. **Gathering Evidence**: Once a potential problem is detected, responders need to gather all the relevant information, just like collecting clues at a crime scene. This includes looking at logs (records of activity), alerts from security tools, and other data that can help explain what's happening.

3. **Analyzing the Situation**: After gathering the evidence, it's time to analyze it to understand the nature of the threat. This means looking for patterns, understanding how the attack happened, and determining its impact on the organization.

4. **Understanding the Cloud Environment**: Responders need to have a good grasp of how their specific cloud services work so they can analyze incidents accurately. Different cloud setups might require different approaches to detection and analysis.

5. **Making Decisions**: After analyzing the information, the responders can decide on the best course of action to take—whether that's containing the issue, eradicating the threat, or notifying other parts of the organization.

Spotting issues fast in cloud security means catching problems early, figuring out what went wrong, and fixing them efficiently. This keeps data safe and systems running smoothly. A strong detection and response strategy helps organizations stay ahead of threats while protecting sensitive information. By acting quickly and understanding risks, teams can prevent bigger challenges down the road. Staying secure starts with knowing when something's off—and responding without delay.

11.3.1 Cloud Impact on Incident Response Analysis

Handling security incidents changes when working with cloud services. Traditional methods don't always apply, making quick response and adaptation key. Teams must rethink strategies, focusing on shared responsibility, real-time monitoring, and rapid mitigation. Understanding these shifts helps prevent breaches and minimize damage. Strong communication, clear protocols, and the right tools make all the difference in staying ahead of threats while keeping data safe.

Here's what it means:

1. **Different Environment**: When a company uses cloud services, their data and applications

are stored and managed online, rather than on their own physical servers. This means incident responders need to consider the cloud setup and the specific provider they're using, which can be different from traditional IT environments.

2. **Accessing Information**: In a cloud environment, data is often spread across different systems and locations, making it essential for responders to know how to access logs and information quickly. They need to be familiar with the cloud provider's tools and interfaces to gather the necessary details.

3. **Shared Responsibilities**: In the cloud, security is a shared responsibility between the cloud service provider and the user organization. So, incident response might involve coordinating with the cloud provider to understand what happened. This collaboration is important for gathering accurate data and addressing issues.

4. **Speed and Scalability**: Cloud systems can change rapidly, which means incident responders need to analyze and respond quickly to threats. The flexibility and scalability of cloud services mean that security incidents can also impact many more users or systems at once, which requires an agile response.

5. **Deployment Models**: Different types of cloud setups—like public, private, or hybrid clouds—can influence how incidents are managed. Responders need to tailor their analysis and response strategies based on the specific cloud model being used.

Cloud incidents demand a different approach than traditional security threats. Response strategies must adapt to cloud-specific challenges like shared responsibility, rapid scaling, and remote access. A well-prepared team ensures quick action, minimizing damage and maintaining security. Understanding these nuances helps organizations stay resilient, even in complex environments. Effective response isn't just about speed—it's about knowing how cloud technology shapes every step of the process.

11.3.2 Cloud System Forensics

Investigating security incidents in cloud environments works like detective work—gathering evidence, tracing actions, and uncovering what went wrong. Quick response and thorough analysis help pinpoint vulnerabilities and prevent future breaches. Understanding attack patterns strengthens defenses, keeping data safe. With expertise and the right tools, teams can track threats efficiently, ensuring a secure system. Every detail matters when protecting sensitive information from cyber risks.

Here's a breakdown of what this involves:

1. **Collecting Evidence**: Just like detectives gather clues, cloud forensics involves collecting data and logs from the cloud systems involved in an incident. This can include things like access logs, error messages, and security alerts that can help show what happened.

2. **Understanding the Cloud**: Since the data is stored online, investigators need to be familiar with how the cloud service works. This means understanding the specific provider's tools and configurations so they can effectively gather and analyze data.

3. **Analyzing Data**: Once they have the evidence, forensic experts analyze it to understand how an incident occurred. They look for patterns or unusual activities that could indicate breaches or unauthorized access.

4. **Examining the Attack**: Forensics also involves looking at how attackers might have gained access to the system. This could be through exploited vulnerabilities, phishing attacks, or other methods. Understanding these details is crucial for preventing future incidents.

5. **Documenting Findings**: The results of the investigation need to be carefully documented. This can be important for legal reasons, compliance, and improving security measures going forward. It's like writing a report that explains what happened and what needs to be done next.

6. **Improving Security**: Finally, the insights gained from forensics help organizations improve their security measures. By understanding how incidents occur, they can strengthen defenses and put new policies in place to safeguard against future threats.

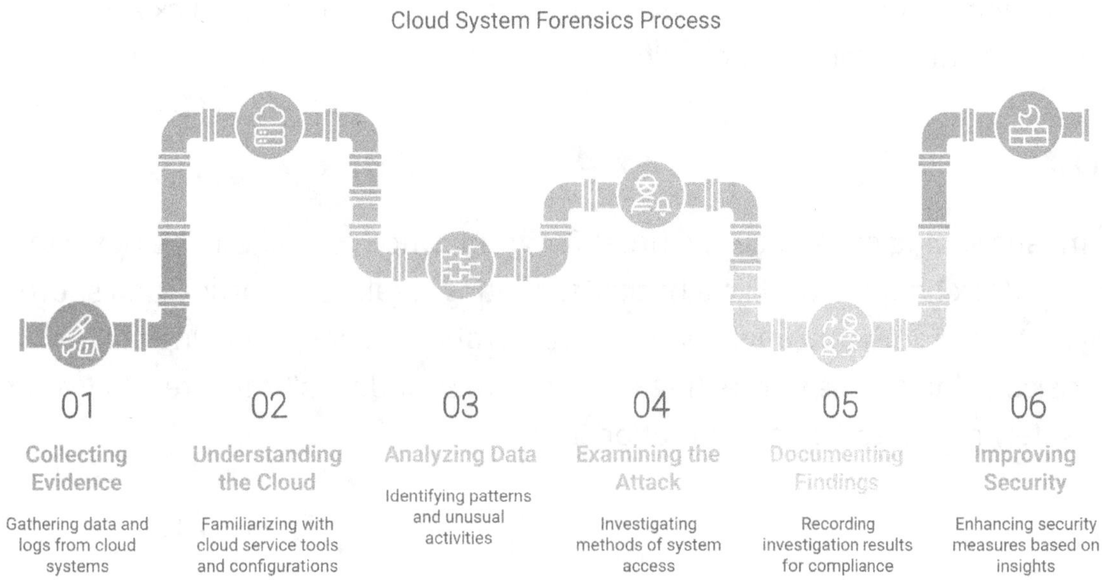

Cloud system forensics investigates security breaches, collects evidence, and uncovers how incidents happen. These insights strengthen defenses, helping organizations respond faster and smarter. By learning from past attacks, teams can close gaps and prevent future threats. A strong forensic approach ensures better protection and a more resilient infrastructure. Staying ahead of risks means understanding weaknesses and turning them into strengths—because security isn't just about defense; it's about staying prepared.

11.4 Containment, Eradication, & Recovery

Handling security incidents in cloud environments requires swift action. Containment stops threats from spreading, while eradication removes the root cause. Recovery focuses on restoring systems and fixing vulnerabilities to prevent future attacks. A well-executed response strengthens defenses and keeps operations running smoothly. Security teams must act decisively, ensuring minimal disruption while safeguarding data and infrastructure. Strong incident management builds trust and resilience in an increasingly connected world.

11.4.1 Containment

Containment means stopping a security breach from spreading. Think of it like putting out a fire—act fast, isolate affected systems, and cut off access to prevent further damage. If an attacker gets in, shutting them out quickly protects sensitive data. Strong containment measures keep threats from escalating, helping organizations stay secure and minimize harm. Quick action makes all the difference in protecting valuable information.

11.4.2 Eradication

Eradication means wiping out a security threat for good. Once contained, the next step involves finding how an attack happened—like a hacker exploiting weak passwords—and shutting that door permanently. Stronger authentication, patching vulnerabilities, and removing malicious files ensure no lingering risks. Think of it as fully extinguishing a fire so it doesn't reignite. Only after this step can systems safely return to normal operations.

11.4.3 Recovery

Think of recovery like cleaning up after a wild party. Once the chaos is contained and broken items are tossed, it's time to restore everything. In cybersecurity, this means bringing systems, data, and services back to normal. Backups help recover lost information, while checks ensure everything runs smoothly. The goal? A secure, fully operational environment where business continues without lingering issues from the incident.

11.5 Post Incident Analysis

After resolving a security incident, reviewing what happened helps teams improve. Think of it like a sports team watching game footage—spotting strengths, weaknesses, and areas for growth. Gathering those involved to discuss what worked and what didn't strengthens future responses. Asking "How did this happen?" and "What could be done differently?" builds stronger defenses, refining strategies to prevent similar issues. Learning from real experiences makes organizations more prepared.

Chapter Fifteen

Domain 12: Related Technologies and Strategies

Introduction

Domain 12 focuses on key strategies for strengthening cloud security. It introduces the Zero Trust model, which enforces strict access controls and continuous verification, no matter where users or devices connect. Artificial Intelligence also plays a role, enhancing threat detection and response automation. By understanding these technologies, professionals can build stronger defenses against cyber threats while staying ahead of emerging risks in cloud environments.

Learning Objectives

Domain 12 focuses on cybersecurity strategies tailored for cloud environments. Participants gain hands-on knowledge to strengthen defenses, manage risks, and apply best practices effectively. This training simplifies complex concepts, making security more approachable and actionable. By understanding threats and implementing smart solutions, professionals enhance protection and reduce vulnerabilities. Stay ahead with practical skills that make a real difference in securing cloud-based systems.

They include:

1. **Understanding Zero Trust**: Participants will learn the technical objectives of the Zero Trust model, which advocates for a security architecture that assumes potential threats both inside and outside the network.

2. **Exploring Zero Trust Pillars**: The course will cover the foundational pillars of Zero Trust and

provide insights into the maturity model, helping learners assess and implement Zero Trust principles effectively.

3. **Integrating Zero Trust with Cloud Security**: Learners will discover how Zero Trust aligns with cloud security practices to enhance data protection and access management.
4. **Characteristics of AI Workloads**: Participants will gain insights into the unique characteristics and security considerations of AI workloads in cloud environments.

Learners gain the skills to apply advanced security frameworks and technologies within their organizations' cloud strategies. They develop a strong understanding of risk management, encryption, and compliance, ensuring data stays protected. With hands-on experience, they confidently implement best practices that strengthen defenses against cyber threats. This knowledge empowers professionals to make informed decisions, keeping systems secure while adapting to new challenges in cloud security.

12.1 Zero Trust

Zero Trust flips traditional security on its head—nobody gets automatic access. Whether inside or outside a network, every user and device must prove they're trustworthy. This approach minimizes risk by continuously verifying identities and enforcing strict access controls. Think of it like airport security—everyone goes through checks, no exceptions. By assuming threats exist everywhere, organizations stay protected while allowing secure access only when necessary. Security isn't about trust—it's about verification.

Here's a simple breakdown:

1. **Trust No One**: Instead of automatically trusting users or devices that are already inside the network (like a company's internal systems), Zero Trust requires verification every time someone tries to access information or systems. This means everyone must prove who they are, even if they seem to be on the "inside."
2. **Only the Essentials**: Access is granted only to the information and resources that someone absolutely needs to do their job. This limits exposure and reduces the chance of a breach. For example, if an employee in marketing only needs access to marketing data, they shouldn't have access to sensitive financial records.

3. **Continuous Monitoring**: Zero Trust emphasizes ongoing assessments of user behavior and device health. If something seems off, such as unusual access patterns, the system might flag or block that access.

4. **Layered Security**: Zero Trust often involves multiple security measures working together, like strong authentication (passwords plus additional verification) and encryption. This creates multiple barriers for anyone trying to get unauthorized access.

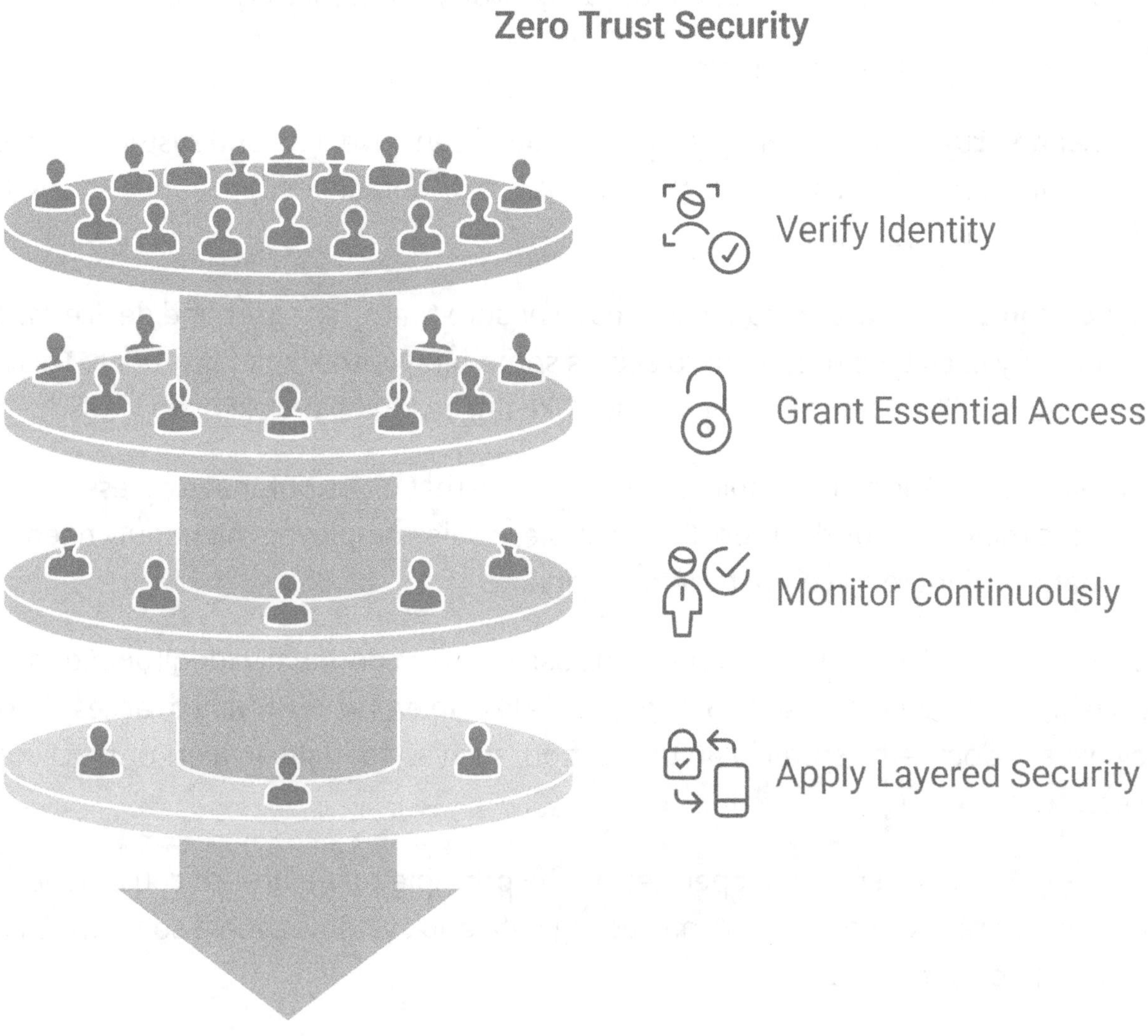

Zero Trust means staying cautious and treating every access request as a potential threat instead of assuming everything inside a network is safe. This approach strengthens security by verifying every user and device, reducing risks in an increasingly complex cyber world. By questioning access at every step, organizations protect sensitive data from threats that often go unnoticed until damage is done. Trust nothing—verify everything.

12.1.1 Technical Objectives of Zero Trust

Zero Trust security aims to protect data by verifying every user and device, no matter where they connect. Organizations set clear goals—limit access, reduce threats, and strengthen defenses. By continuously monitoring activity and enforcing strict authentication, businesses stay ahead of cyber risks. A strong Zero Trust strategy builds trust while keeping sensitive information safe. Security isn't a one-time fix—it's an ongoing commitment to safeguarding what matters most.

Here's an easy-to-understand breakdown:

1. **Enhanced Security**: The primary goal is to protect sensitive data and systems by minimizing the potential for breaches. By not trusting anyone by default, organizations strengthen their defenses against cyberattacks.

2. **Verification Every Time**: Zero Trust aims to ensure that every user and device must prove their identity each time they want to access something, rather than just once. This means using methods like passwords, biometrics (like fingerprints), or tokens to verify identity.

3. **Limited Access**: Another key objective is to ensure that users only have access to the specific resources they need for their job. For example, a sales employee might only need access to sales data and not to all company information.

4. **Monitoring and Response**: Organizations use tools to continually monitor user activity and device health. If something unusual happens—like an employee trying to access information they usually don't—the system can take action, such as sending an alert or blocking that access.

5. **Assuming Breach**: Zero Trust operates on the principle that a breach could happen at any moment. Therefore, it focuses on protecting data and systems even if someone inside the network is compromised.

6. **Secure Connections**: It encourages secure connections between users and applications, regardless of where they are located. This means that accessing company data from a home office or a mobile device should be just as secure as if they were at the office.

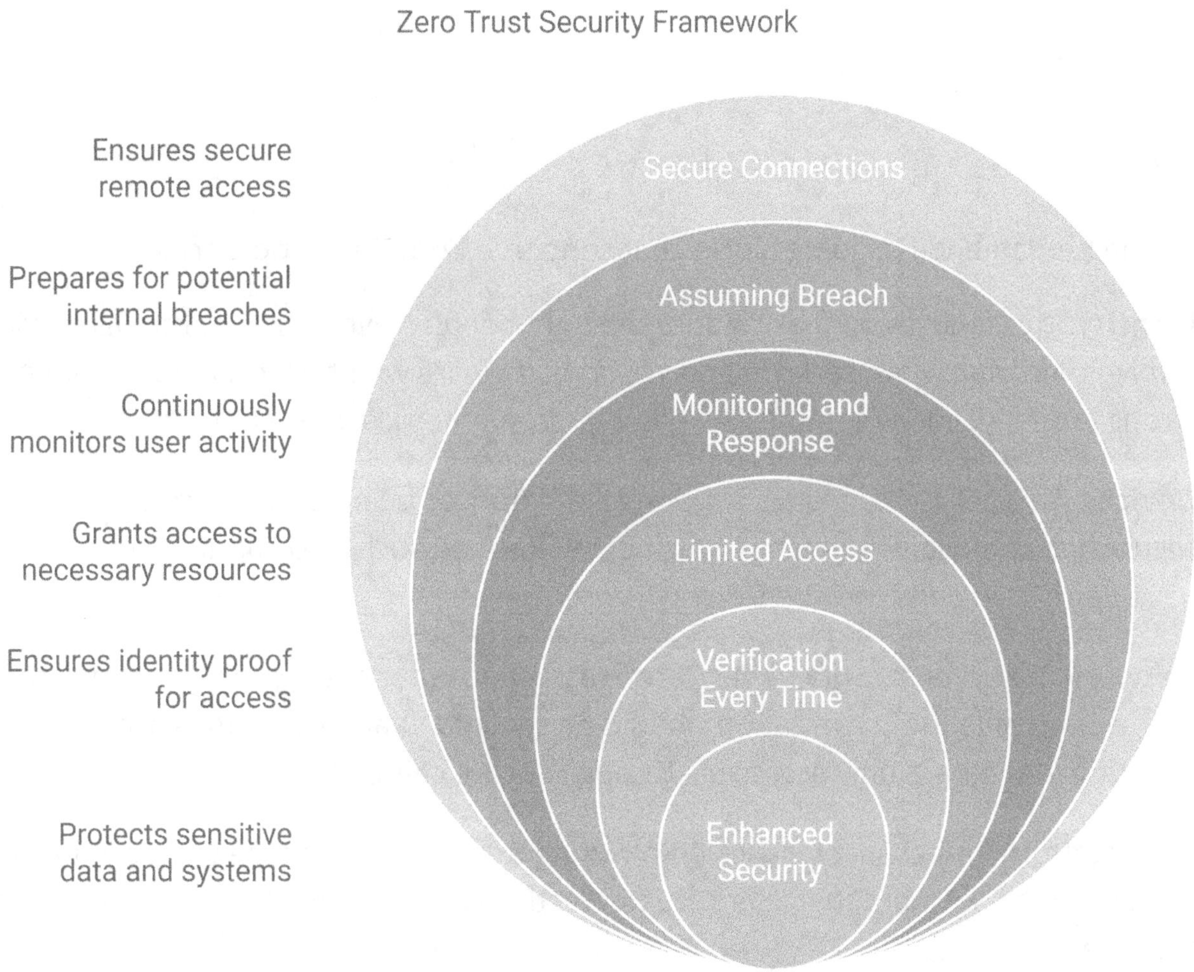

Zero Trust strengthens security by verifying users every time they access information, restricting entry to only what's needed, and continuously monitoring for threats. Security stays a priority at all levels, ensuring protection without unnecessary exposure. By enforcing strict controls and constant verification, organizations reduce risks and keep sensitive data safe. This proactive approach builds trust while keeping systems secure from potential threats.

12.1.2 Zero Trust Pillars & Maturity Model

A Zero Trust security strategy demands a shift from traditional defenses to continuous verification. The 12.1.2 Zero Trust Pillars & Maturity Model breaks down core principles and adoption stages, helping organizations strengthen protection. Instead of assuming trust, every access request gets verified, reducing risks. As threats grow more sophisticated, businesses must stay proactive, ensuring only authorized users and devices gain entry. Adopting this approach builds stronger security and resilience against cyberattacks.

Here's a simple explanation:

Zero Trust Pillars

These are the fundamental building blocks that support a Zero Trust approach:

1. **Identity**: This focuses on making sure the right people have access to the right resources. It involves verifying who users are and ensuring they are who they claim to be, often through strong authentication methods like passwords, biometrics, or security tokens.

2. **Devices**: This pillar emphasizes checking if the devices being used to access the network are secure and compliant. It means ensuring that devices, such as computers and smartphones, have up-to-date software and security protections.

3. **Network**: Network security under Zero Trust means that every connection, whether it's inside or outside the organization, should be secured. It advocates for encrypting data and ensuring that data is only accessible through secure channels.

4. **Applications**: This aspect focuses on ensuring that applications are secure. It involves protecting the software that users are interacting with to prevent unauthorized access and breaches.

5. **Data**: Protecting data is essential. This means identifying sensitive information and applying strict access controls to it, ensuring that only authorized individuals can access important data.

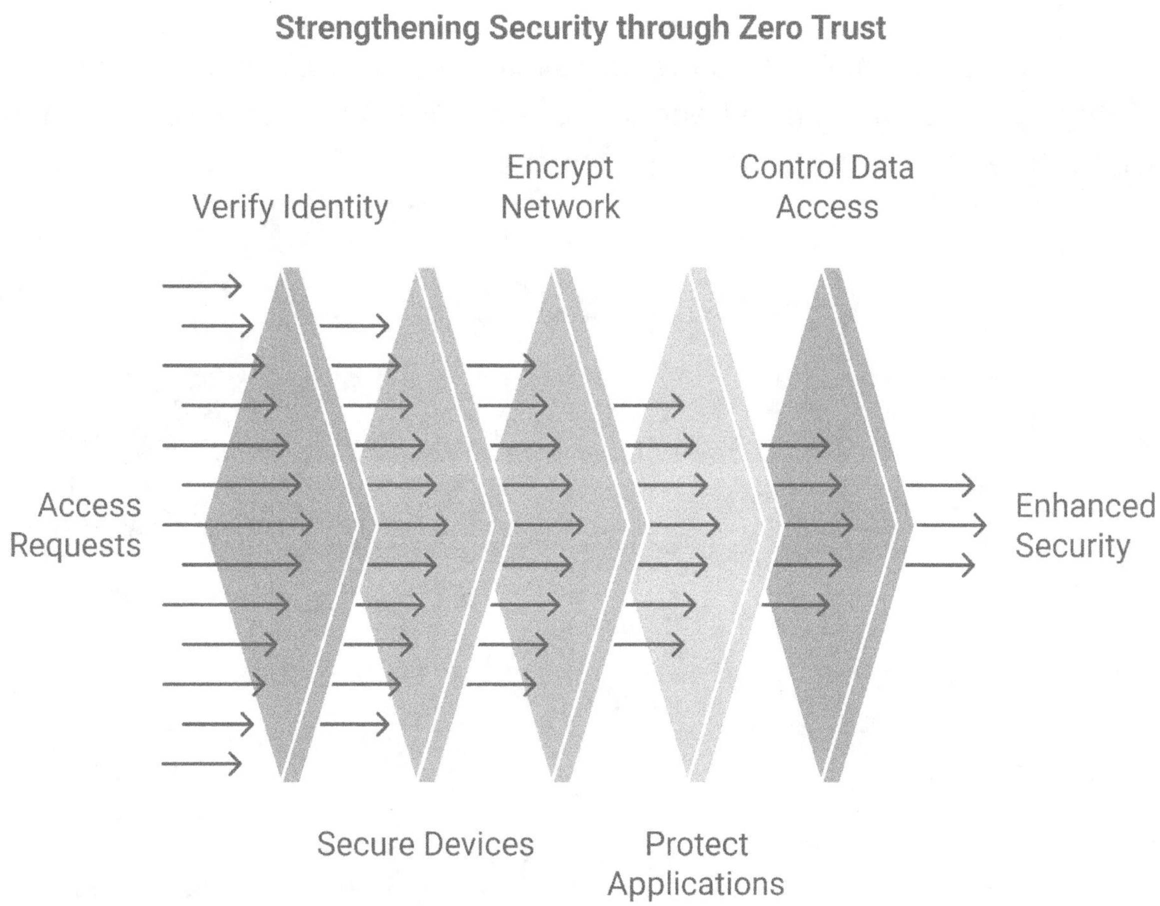

Zero-Trust Maturity Model

The Maturity Model outlines the stages organizations go through as they adopt and improve their Zero Trust strategies:

1. **Initial Stage**: At this point, organizations may have basic security measures but are not fully implementing Zero Trust principles. They might be relying on traditional security methods.

2. **Developing Stage**: Organizations begin to recognize the need for a Zero Trust approach. They start making changes by improving their identity and access management and focusing more on security.

3. **Established Stage**: Here, organizations have implemented many Zero Trust practices and are actively monitoring and managing risks. They have set clearer policies and controls.

4. **Advanced Stage**: At this stage, organizations are fully integrated with Zero Trust principles.

They continuously assess and adapt their security measures based on evolving threats and technologies.

5. **Optimized Stage**: Organizations now have a mature Zero Trust implementation, where security practices are automated, and they continually improve based on lessons learned, emerging threats, and technology advancements.

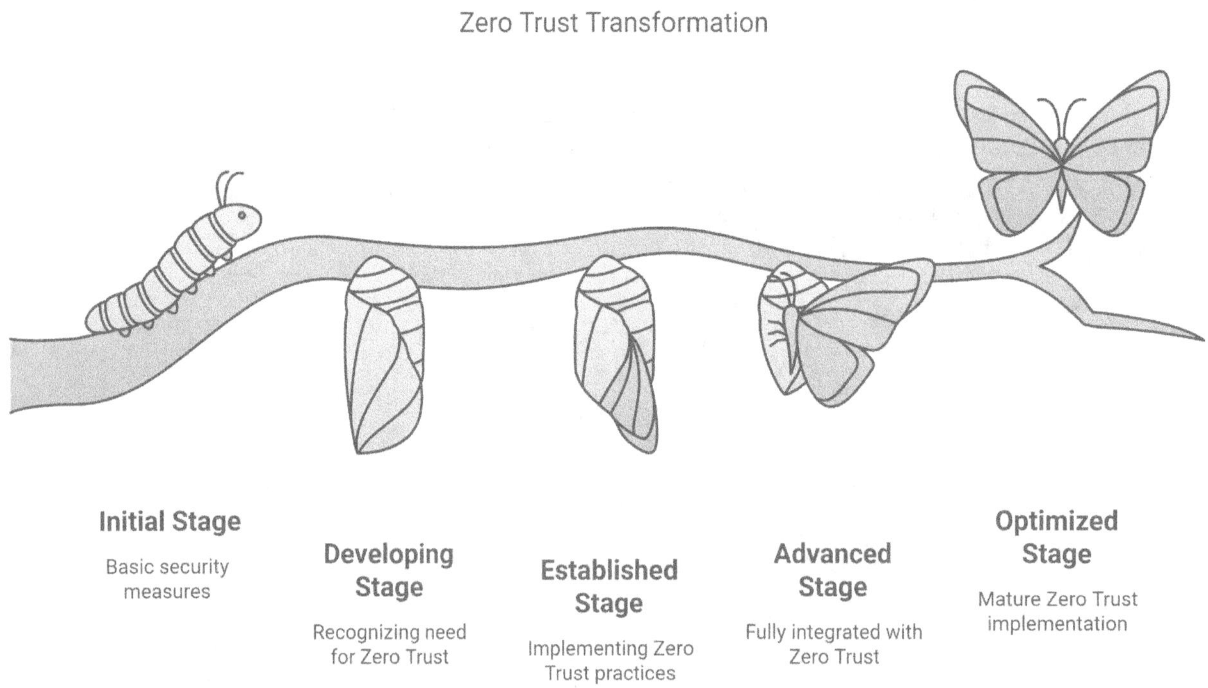

Zero Trust Pillars define key security components, while the Maturity Model maps how organizations strengthen defenses and adopt a Zero Trust approach. Instead of a one-time fix, it's a continuous process that enhances protection step by step. Businesses move from basic safeguards to advanced strategies, ensuring stronger security at every stage. Understanding both helps create a resilient system that keeps threats in check and data secure.

12.1.3 Zero Trust & Cloud Security

Zero Trust reshapes cloud security by assuming no user or device should be trusted by default. Every access request gets verified, reducing risks from breaches. Strong authentication, continuous monitoring, and strict access controls keep data safe. Businesses gain stronger defenses without sacrificing efficiency. By applying Zero Trust principles, organizations protect sensitive information while ensuring only authorized users get in. Security isn't about trust—it's about verification at every step.

Here's a simplified breakdown:

Understanding Zero Trust in Cloud Security

1. **What is Zero Trust?**: At its core, Zero Trust means never automatically trusting anyone or anything inside or outside the network. Every user, device, and application must be verified before being granted access to resources.

2. **Cloud Environment**: Cloud computing involves storing and managing data and applications on remote servers accessed over the internet, rather than on local servers. This flexibility is great, but it also introduces new security challenges.

Why Zero Trust Matters in the Cloud

1. **Increased Risks**: In cloud computing, things like remote work and third-party services are common. This makes it harder to control who accesses your data and from where. Zero Trust helps manage these risks by enforcing strict access controls.

2. **Secure Access from Anywhere**: With Zero Trust, it doesn't matter if you're accessing company resources from your office, a café, or your home. Every access request is verified, ensuring that the connection is secure no matter where you are.

3. **Protecting Sensitive Data**: Many businesses store sensitive information in the cloud. Zero Trust helps safeguard this data by ensuring that only authorized people and secure devices can access it.

4. **Granular Permissions**: Zero Trust allows for more precise control over who can access what. For example, a marketing employee might only need access to marketing data, while a finance team member might need access to financial records. This limits exposure and reduces the risk of breaches.

5. **Continuous Monitoring**: Unlike traditional security measures that might check credentials once, Zero Trust continuously monitors user activities and device health. If anything suspicious happens, like unusual access attempts, the system can respond instantly—potentially blocking access or alerting security teams.

6. **Adapting to Threats**: Zero Trust isn't a one-time setup; it's about being proactive and

adaptable. As threats evolve, organizations can update their security protocols to keep data safe.

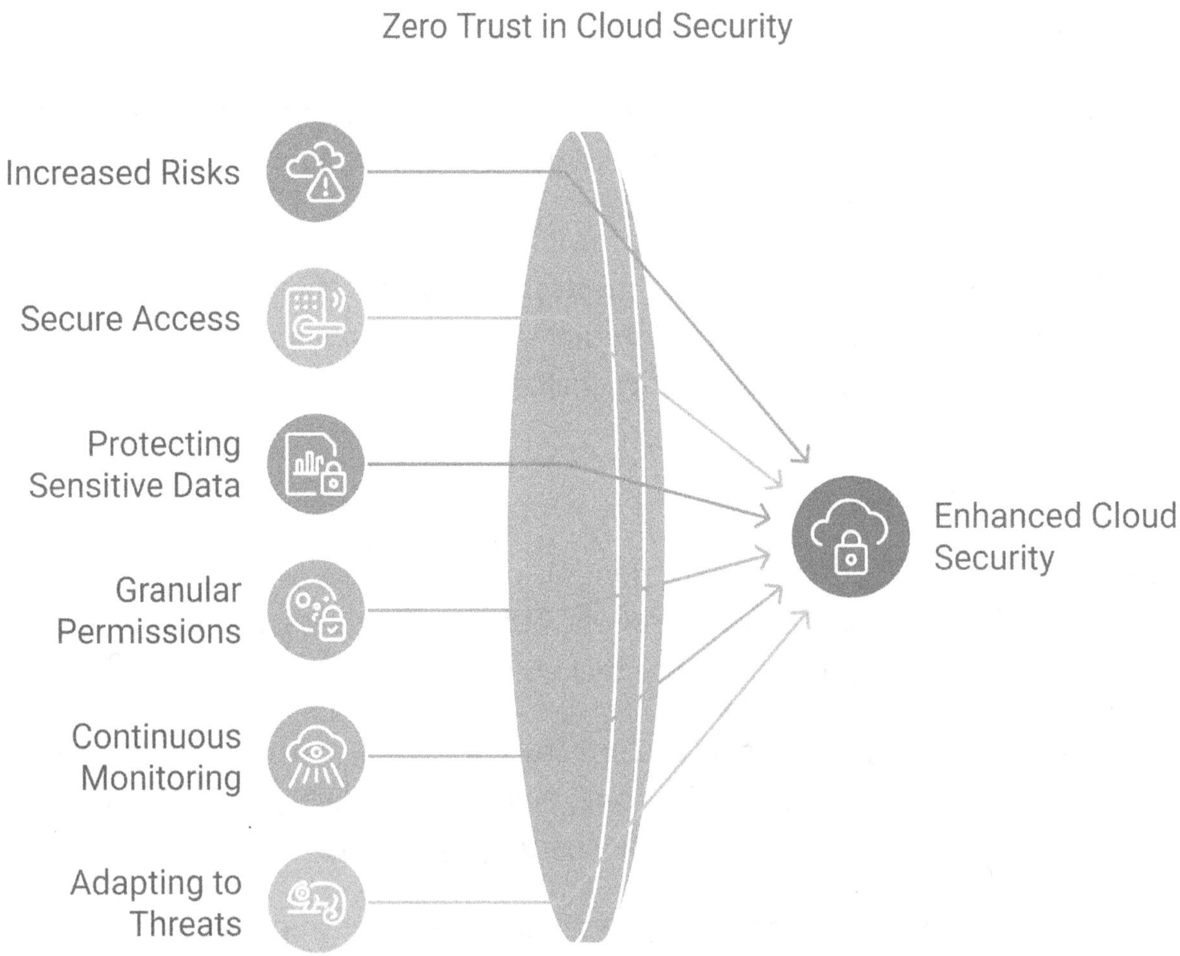

Zero Trust in cloud security means never assuming trust. Every user and device must prove legitimacy before accessing sensitive data. Strict permissions, continuous monitoring, and real-time threat response keep risks low. No matter where users connect from, security stays strong.

By enforcing these principles, organizations protect valuable information while adapting to new threats. Stay proactive—control access, monitor activity, and safeguard critical assets at all times.

12.2 Artificial Intelligence

Artificial intelligence changes how cloud computing works, making processes smarter and more efficient. Businesses gain faster insights, automate tasks, and improve security with AI-driven solutions. This shift reduces costs while boosting performance. Companies using these tools stay competitive by adapting quickly to new challenges. As AI grows within cloud services, organizations must embrace innovation to stay ahead. The future belongs to those who make technology work for them.

Here's a simple breakdown:

What is Artificial Intelligence (AI)?

Artificial Intelligence refers to computer systems that can perform tasks usually requiring human intelligence. This includes things like learning from experience, recognizing patterns, solving problems, understanding language, and even making decisions.

AI in Cloud Computing

1. **Powerful Processing**: The cloud provides vast amounts of computing power and storage, which are essential for AI. Organizations can use cloud resources to analyze large data sets and run complex algorithms without needing their own expensive hardware.

2. **Access to Advanced Tools**: Many cloud platforms offer ready-made AI tools and services, making it easier for businesses to develop AI applications without needing extensive technical knowledge. This means even smaller companies can leverage AI technology.

3. **Scalability**: Cloud computing allows businesses to quickly scale their AI solutions. If a business starts small but sees success, it can easily increase its computing resources as it needs them.

Benefits of Using AI in the Cloud

1. **Automation**: AI can automate repetitive tasks, helping organizations save time and reduce errors. For example, AI can analyze data and generate reports without requiring human intervention.

2. **Better Decision-Making**: By analyzing vast amounts of data, AI can provide insights and predictions, aiding leaders in making informed decisions. For instance, AI can analyze

customer behavior to suggest products people might want to buy.

3. **Enhanced Customer Experiences**: AI can improve interactions with customers through chatbots and personalized recommendations, creating a more tailored experience for users.

Challenges with AI in the Cloud

1. **Data Privacy**: Using AI often means handling large amounts of data, which raises concerns about privacy and security. Organizations must ensure that they are complying with laws and regulations regarding data protection.

2. **Bias and Fairness**: AI systems can unintentionally inherit biases present in the data they are trained on. It's essential for organizations to ensure fairness and prevent discrimination in AI decision-making processes.

3. **Complexity**: Implementing AI can be complex, requiring skilled staff and a good understanding of both AI and cloud technologies. Organizations need to invest in training and resources to effectively utilize AI.

AI in cloud computing boosts efficiency, automates tasks, and sharpens decision-making. Businesses gain speed, intelligence, and a stronger customer focus. While opportunities abound, challenges like data privacy and fairness demand attention. Organizations that embrace AI can streamline operations and stay competitive. Success depends on balancing innovation with responsibility—using AI wisely ensures smarter strategies without compromising trust. Companies ready to adapt will thrive in an increasingly AI-driven world.

12.2.1 Characteristics of AI Workloads

AI workloads come with unique demands, requiring speed, adaptability, and massive data processing. These tasks rely on powerful computing, efficient algorithms, and well-structured models to deliver accurate results. From natural language processing to machine learning, each workload needs specialized hardware and software. Understanding these characteristics helps optimize performance while reducing inefficiencies. As AI grows, businesses must refine strategies to stay competitive and maximize outcomes in an increasingly intelligent world.

Here's a simple breakdown:

What Are AI Workloads?

AI workloads focus on tasks like data processing, pattern recognition, and predictive analysis. These operations help machines learn from information, improving accuracy over time. From chatbots to medical diagnostics, they power applications that enhance daily life. Optimizing performance requires efficient algorithms and strong computing power. As AI advances, so does its ability to handle complex challenges, making everyday interactions smarter and more intuitive.

Key Characteristics of AI Workloads

1. **Data-Intensive**:
    - AI workloads usually deal with large volumes of data. To train AI models, these systems need lots of information to learn from—think hundreds or thousands of images for a facial recognition system or millions of transactions for a fraud detection model.
2. **Complex Processing**:
    - The calculations and algorithms involved in AI can be very complex. This means AI workloads often require powerful computing resources to process the data quickly and effectively. Tasks might include training neural networks, which can take a lot of time doing calculations.
3. **Real-Time Processing**:
    - Many AI applications need to analyze data and provide results immediately or in real-time. For example, a self-driving car must process information from its surroundings instantly to make driving decisions on the spot.
4. **Iterative Learning**:
    - AI systems improve over time through a process called machine learning. They learn from new data and experiences, so AI workloads are often designed to run repeatedly, adjusting and improving with each cycle. This means they continuously gather and analyze data to refine their predictions or decisions.
5. **Variety of Data Types**:
    - AI workloads may handle different types of data, such as text, images, sound, or videos. For example, a speech recognition system interacts with audio data, while an image classifier

deals with visual data.

6. **Scalability**:
    - As the demand for AI services grows, AI workloads need to scale or grow accordingly. For example, if a company suddenly gets a lot more users, its AI system should be able to handle the increased workload without slowing down.

7. **Training vs. Inference**:
    - AI workloads often have two main phases: training and inference.
        - **Training** involves teaching the AI model using a large dataset (which can take a lot of time and resources).
        - **Inference** is when the trained model is used to make predictions or decisions based on new data (this process usually happens quickly).

AI workloads stand out due to their heavy data demands, complex calculations, and need for real-time processing. They handle diverse data types, scale as needed, and continuously improve through training and inference. Understanding these traits helps teams choose the right tools for successful deployment. By preparing properly, organizations can harness AI's full potential while ensuring efficiency and accuracy in every task.

Chapter Sixteen

The Future of Cloud Security

The Unexpected Story Data Reveals

In the spring of 2023, a small software firm in Austin, Texas, faced an existential crisis. Their cloud storage, housing sensitive client data, was breached—not through brute force, but through an AI-assisted social engineering attack. A simple phishing email, tailored perfectly using machine learning, tricked an employee into granting access.

What's surprising isn't that a company got hacked—breaches happen daily. It's the method. Search data tells us that, while terms like "cloud security firewall" and "encryption best practices" have remained steady in search interest, one phrase has skyrocketed: **"AI-powered cyber threats"**.

This defies conventional wisdom. We assume that as cloud security improves, so do our defenses. But search data suggests a different reality—attackers are evolving at an even faster pace, weaponizing AI to exploit human behavior rather than technical vulnerabilities. The future of cloud security isn't just about stronger defenses. It's about outthinking an adversary that's learning, adapting, and improving—just like the very AI systems meant to protect us.

Key Trends Shaping Cloud Security's Future

If you chart the trajectory of cloud security concerns over the past five years, one thing stands out: the rise of insider threats. Search queries for **"insider threat cloud security"** have grown by 150% since 2021. Why? Because as companies move to decentralized, cloud-based operations, employees—whether malicious or just careless—become the weakest link.

But the biggest shift isn't just in threats. It's in our response. Search interest in **"zero trust architecture"** has surged by 200% since 2020. A once-niche concept, Zero Trust flips traditional security on its head. Instead of assuming internal users are trustworthy, it operates on the principle that **no one** is inherently safe—not even the CEO.

And then there's quantum computing. While still years from mainstream deployment, searches for **"quantum computing cloud security risks"** have jumped 300% in just two years. The reason? The looming threat of quantum decryption, which could render today's encryption obsolete overnight.

These small shifts—insider threats, Zero Trust, and quantum risks—are reshaping the future of cloud security. Each trend started as a whisper in niche tech circles. Now, they're at the forefront of cybersecurity strategy.

Explaining The Future of Cloud Security

Imagine a medieval castle. For centuries, security meant building taller walls and deeper moats—just as cloud security once relied on firewalls and perimeter defenses. But today's threats don't come battering at the gates. They slip inside disguised as trusted couriers.

Cloud security in 2024 is no longer about fortifying the perimeter. It's about **constant verification, AI-driven anomaly detection, and decentralized trust models**.

Take **Confidential Computing**, a term that has seen a 400% spike in searches over the past year. It encrypts data even while it's being processed, making it unreadable even to cloud providers themselves. Or **homomorphic encryption**, which allows computations on encrypted data without ever decrypting it—a concept once theoretical, now commercially viable.

And then there's **AI-driven security analytics**, a field exploding in search interest. These systems don't just react to threats; they **predict them**, analyzing millions of data points to detect patterns human analysts would never notice.

The future of cloud security isn't a single technology or strategy. It's a **mindset shift**—from static defenses to dynamic, AI-driven vigilance.

A Sign of Things to Come

The Austin breach wasn't an anomaly. It was a sign of things to come. And search data, often dismissed as mere digital noise, provides a roadmap to our future.

By tracking what people search for—what worries them, what excites them—we gain a deeper, more nuanced understanding of emerging threats. Trends that seem minor today—like AI-powered phishing or post-quantum cryptography—may define the next decade of cybersecurity.

The future of cloud security isn't just about technology. It's about human behavior. And search data, in its raw, unfiltered form, tells a story of shifting fears, evolving threats, and the relentless race to stay one step ahead.

Chapter Seventeen

Case Studies in Cloud Security

Analyzing Successful Cloud Security Implementations

Many organizations have strengthened cloud security with smart strategies. A global retailer safeguarded customer data by layering advanced threat detection with real-time monitoring. Meanwhile, a healthcare provider protected patient records using strong encryption and strict access controls. Regular penetration testing helped them catch vulnerabilities early. These success stories prove that tailored security measures can keep sensitive information safe while allowing businesses to grow confidently in an increasingly connected world.

Strong cloud security starts with proactive risk management. Companies must assess vulnerabilities, update protocols, and train employees to spot threats. Automation also plays a key role—efficient log management and real-time alerts help teams focus on critical issues. Cloud-native tools that apply updates automatically strengthen defenses. Integrating security early in development builds a stronger foundation, reducing risks and improving response times when threats arise. Stay prepared, stay secure.

Building a security-first culture starts with teamwork. Encourage open conversations where everyone shares insights and challenges. Security isn't one person's job—it's a shared responsibility. When teams collaborate, defenses strengthen, and awareness grows. Learn from both successes and setbacks to improve continuously. A proactive approach keeps threats in check while creating an environment where security stays top of mind for everyone involved.

Lessons Learned from Cloud Security Failures

Cloud security breaches happen too often, leaving companies and consumers vulnerable. A well-known case is the 2017 Equifax breach, which exposed sensitive data from 147 million people. The cause? A missed software update. That small oversight led to massive financial penalties and a loss of trust. Keeping systems updated isn't optional—it's necessary to protect both businesses and the people who rely on them.

Learning from failures strengthens cloud security. Every breach reveals weaknesses—whether human error, system missteps, or tech flaws. The 2019 Capital One breach, caused by a misconfigured firewall, proved how small mistakes trigger massive data losses. Constant vigilance and expert management matter. Building strong protocols, conducting regular audits, and staying informed reduce risks. A proactive approach keeps systems secure and prevents costly breaches. Security isn't a one-time fix—it's ongoing protection.

Every cloud security failure offers a chance to learn and improve. Viewing setbacks as lessons helps IT teams build stronger defenses. Regular training, automated monitoring, and open discussions about threats strengthen protection. Staying informed on security trends sharpens response strategies. Cybersecurity isn't a solo effort—working together enhances understanding and safeguards systems more effectively. Turning challenges into opportunities makes all the difference in staying secure.

Key Takeaways from Real-World Scenarios

Studying cloud security cases reveals valuable lessons. A major e-commerce platform suffered a breach due to weak encryption. Protecting data in transit and at rest makes all the difference. Strong encryption protocols help prevent leaks and breaches. Proactive risk management isn't optional—it's necessary. Organizations that prioritize security measures stay ahead of threats, safeguarding sensitive information while building trust with users. Don't wait for a breach to take action.

A healthcare provider fell victim to a ransomware attack, exposing gaps in employee awareness. They quickly realized regular training and simulations could help staff spot phishing attempts and protect sensitive data. This highlights a key lesson—building a security-first culture can prevent breaches. When employees recognize threats early, organizations stay safer, reducing risks and costly disruptions. Investing in education isn't optional; it's a necessity for long-term protection.

Applying these lessons takes ongoing learning and adaptation. Understanding concepts isn't enough—real change happens through daily action. Regular security audits spot vulnerabilities early, while a zero-trust model tightly controls access based on identity and context, reducing risks. Strong collaboration between teams strengthens protection efforts, ensuring everyone contributes to safeguarding assets. Prioritizing security across departments creates a proactive approach that keeps threats in check and operations running smoothly.

Staying updated on cloud security threats keeps you prepared for what's next. Engage in forums, attend webinars, and join industry conferences to gain fresh insights. Security strategies should stay flexible—review and refine them regularly based on real-world challenges. A feedback loop helps strengthen defenses, ensuring continuous improvement. The cloud shifts fast, but with ongoing learning and adaptation, your security approach stays strong and effective.

Chapter Eighteen

Study Materials and Resources

Preparing for IT exams starts with the right study materials. Practice tests help you get familiar with formats and pinpoint weak areas. Look for explanations that clarify answers—they boost understanding. Video tutorials break down complex ideas, making learning easier. A mix of these resources strengthens knowledge and builds confidence for exam day.

Online learning platforms like Coursera, Udemy, and LinkedIn Learning offer courses tailored for IT professionals seeking certifications or skill upgrades. These include videos, quizzes, and hands-on projects to keep lessons engaging. Forums on Reddit and Discord connect learners for study tips and group sessions. Free resources like MIT's open courseware add valuable insights. Engaging with these tools strengthens knowledge while building a supportive network for continued growth.

Find study materials that match your learning style. Whether you like reading, watching videos, or joining interactive sessions, mix different resources to keep things fresh and engaging. This approach strengthens your understanding and makes studying more enjoyable. Create a schedule that balances your time across chosen materials. The right strategy keeps you motivated and prepared for exams while making the learning process smoother and more effective.

Chapter Nineteen

Cloud Security Alliance Tools

To assess security controls in the cloud, the Cloud Security Alliance (CSA) offers tools like the **Cloud Controls Matrix (CCM)** and the **Consensus Assessments Initiative Questionnaire (CAIQ)**. The CSA also provides a repository called the **Security Trust Assurance and Risk (STAR) Registry**, where you can find information on providers' security practices.

Cloud Controls Matrix (CCM)

The latest version of the Cloud Controls Matrix (CCM) is CCM v4.0, which was officially released in January 2021. This version includes 197 control objectives organized into 17 domains, addressing various aspects of cloud security and compliance. The CCM framework is designed to help organizations assess their cloud implementations systematically and provides guidance on security controls that should be implemented by different actors within the cloud supply chain.

In addition, the CCM Implementation Guidelines v2.0 were announced on June 4, 2024, providing best practices for organizations looking to implement the CCM v4.0 control specifications in alignment with the Shared Security Responsibility Model.

You can easily download the cloud controls matrix from the CSA website. It is a valuable resource for understanding and implementing cloud security measures.

Consensus Assessments Initiative Questionnaire (CAIQ)

The Consensus Assessments Initiative Questionnaire (CAIQ), developed by the Cloud Security Alliance (CSA), is an essential tool for organizations assessing cloud service providers' (CSPs) security capabilities. With a standardized set of questions covering various security domains like data governance, identity and access management, and incident response, the CAIQ provides an objective framework for evaluating CSPs' security controls and practices.

By utilizing the CAIQ, organizations gain a detailed understanding of CSPs' security measures. This knowledge enables informed decisions regarding partnerships with trusted providers. The questionnaire identifies potential security risks and eliminates protocol gaps through tailored remediation efforts.

Moreover, the CAIQ spearheads transparency and accountability within the cloud industry. CSPs are encouraged to complete the questionnaire, making their responses available to customers. This level of disclosure fosters trust and confidence among organizations in the cloud service provider ecosystem.

While it is not a certification or compliance framework, the CAIQ is valuable for organizations that gather information and evaluate CSPs' security readiness based on specific requirements and risk tolerance.

In conclusion, organizations can rely on the Consensus Assessments Initiative Questionnaire (CAIQ) to comprehensively evaluate and ensure their chosen cloud service provider's security capabilities meet their needs.

STAR Registry

The Cloud Security Alliance's STAR Registry is a publicly accessible database that provides information about cloud service provider's security and privacy practices. It is a repository of self-assessment reports and certifications that CSPs can voluntarily submit to demonstrate their compliance with industry best practices. The STAR Registry allows organizations to easily compare and evaluate different CSPs based on their security capabilities, increasing transparency and aiding in informed decision-making.

STAR Level 1 - Self Assessment

STAR Level 1 is the base point in the Cloud Security Alliance's STAR Registry. Cloud service providers (CSPs) voluntarily create self-assessment reports demonstrating security and privacy practices. These reports highlight compliance with industry best practices, giving valuable insights for evaluating and comparing CSPs. The aim of STAR Level 1 is to leverage transparency and enable organizations to assess CSPs efficiently based on their security capabilities.

STAR Level 2 - Third-Party Certification

Cloud service providers (CSPs) with a STAR Level 2 certification from the Cloud Security Alliance's STAR Registry go beyond self-assessment. They obtain third-party certifications, validating their security and privacy practices. Independent organizations assess their compliance with industry best practices. The STAR Level 2 certification provides organizations with added assurance and confidence in the security capabilities of CSPs. This makes it easier for businesses to compare and choose a reliable provider.

STAR Level 3 - Continuous Auditing

CSA STAR Level 3, also known as Continuous Auditing, is the highest and most rigorous level of the CSA STAR program, designed for high-risk environments and full-service providers. It emphasizes continuous monitoring of cloud security practices, ensuring organizations consistently meet security, privacy, and compliance requirements. This approach aims to eliminate the gaps between periodic audits, providing up-to-date information on a Cloud Service Provider's (CSP) security compliance.

Chapter Twenty

Tips for Successful Exam Preparation

Effective study strategies can make a huge difference in exam prep. Breaking material into smaller sections helps prevent burnout and improves understanding. Instead of cramming, set specific times for each topic. Engaging with concepts in different ways—like using flashcards or teaching someone—boosts retention. Visual aids work well, especially for complex subjects. A structured schedule keeps everything on track, making learning more manageable and efficient.

Practice exams and mock tests help you get comfortable with the format while identifying areas for improvement. I took one and felt my anxiety fade—I was more prepared than I thought! Repeated practice builds confidence, improves time management, and reduces surprises. Reviewing mistakes reinforces learning, making each session more effective. The more you test yourself, the stronger your grasp of the material becomes.

Reward yourself while studying. Celebrate small wins—finishing a tough chapter or acing a mock test—to stay motivated. Don't ignore self-care amid exam pressure. A short walk, a favorite snack, or a quick chat with a friend can recharge your mind and keep enthusiasm high. Balancing effort with relaxation helps maintain focus and prevents burnout, making the entire process more manageable and enjoyable. Keep going—you've got this!

Preparing for the CCSK exam takes strategy. Since it's open-book, organize reference materials into a single searchable PDF. Keep it on one screen while answering questions on another. When something looks familiar, search keywords to find answers fast. This approach saves time and boosts accuracy. Stay focused, practice with sample questions, and use resources wisely to improve confidence and performance on exam day.

Preparing for the CCSK exam? The Cloud Security Alliance (CSA) offers a CCSK Prep-kit packed with everything needed for success. Designed for focused learners, this resource simplifies complex topics and strengthens understanding. Get access through CSA's website:

https://cloudsecurityalliance.org/education/ccsk/study-guide/. Stay committed, study smart, and boost your confidence for exam day!

The preparation kit includes:

- Sample questions
- A guide to earning your CCSK
- An outline of the topics covered in the exam
- Security Guidance – Simple document
- Cloud Controls Matrix – Excel Spreadsheet
- ENISA's Risk Recommendations – Extensive document

Summary

The CCSK v5 exam allows open-book access, so having all reference materials in one PDF can save valuable seconds. The Cloud Security Alliance offers a Prep Kit with sample questions, study guides, and key documents like Security Guidance, Cloud Controls Matrix, and ENISA's Risk Recommendations. Organizing these efficiently helps with quick searches, but don't rely solely on them—strong understanding matters when you've got a limited amount of time per question.

About the author

John, a seasoned cybersecurity consultant, brings two decades of expertise in banking, finance, and logistics security. A CISSP, PCIP, CCSK, Security+, Network+, and A+ certified professional, he ensures compliance and secure system design. Before cybersecurity, he worked crime scenes alongside law enforcement, specializing in automotive security.

Now a trusted advisor in information security governance, John's hands-on experience makes him a reliable voice in the industry.

Security has always been second nature to John—curiosity, vigilance, and a zero-tolerance stance on cybercrime shape his approach. As a writer for Techopedia and top tech firms across the UK, US, and Canada, he brings expertise with a practical edge. John presents the CCSK v5 with clarity and insight. Passionate about cybersecurity and storytelling, John's work keeps readers engaged and informed.

Also by

CISSP 2025 – Certified Information Systems Security Professional Study Guide

Payment Card Industry Professional (PCIP) v4.0: Your Ultimate Study Guide to Success

Payment Card Industry Professional (PCIP) 3.0: Your Ultimate Study Guide To Success

CCSK v4.0 Cloud Security Knowledge – Focused Exam Revision

www.ingramcontent.com/pod-product-compliance
Lightning Source LLC
LaVergne TN
LVHW080027210926
848481LV00011B/3118